Praise for Michelle Bowden's Persuasion Smart Profile® and Persuasion Blueprint

Michelle Bowden is a legend! We unleashed Michelle and her boundless energy and winning formulas on our top performers and the results have been outstanding. This book is the detail from her winning keynote presentation and it will transform your persuasiveness and change your life for the better.

Tony Bongiorno
Owner and Director,
Bongiorno Financial Services

Michelle is so special. She is incredibly passionate about each and every one of my team winning and she'll stop at nothing to help us achieve our persuasive goals. Her life-changing formulas stay with you for the long term and can be used in all parts of your life. I highly recommend Michelle to you.

Gustav Arianto
CEO, Pierlite ANZ

I loved it! Michelle's workshop on persuasion was very comprehensive and engaging! Lots of great structure and content that will help our people persuade more effectively. Michelle is an awesome facilitator!

Marika Tetere
Medical Director, Boehringer Ingelheim

Michelle helped each pitch member in our large bid team to refine their story, simplify their slide deck, enhance their delivery style and refine their answers to tough questions. Then she helped us in the rehearsal stage to ensure that there was a synergy between the presenters. Our Executive felt that all the presentations went extremely well, and the team did an excellent job. This was in large part due to Michelle's clever formulas, guidance and support.

Felicity Williams-Lovegrove
Regional Head of Bids—APAC

Michelle's pitch coaching sessions had a massive impact and influence on our presenters. I could see they worked hard to prepare and present diligently to their customers using the Persuasion Blueprint process.

Vijayakumar (Vijay) Ekambaram
Sub ISU Head—Banking,
Financial Services and Insurance,
TATA Consultancy Services

Everyone needs Michelle's wonderful models and formulas. My team and I have been working with Michelle for years to shape compelling presentations that achieve excellent results. Her approach is practical, memorable and builds incredible confidence — no matter your current persuasive skill level.

Professor Evonne Miller
QUT Design Lab,
Queensland University of Technology

Learning from Michelle was the first step toward running my own successful business! I have been using the skills Michelle teaches to present a persuasive argument, win business, and present training since I attended her workshop while working in the pharmaceutical industry in 2005 — decades ago! If you are serious about being more persuasive, I recommend How to Persuade. Michelle's insights and teaching will have a huge impact on you, no matter your industry, current skill level or seniority.

Roz Lindsay
Managing Director, Engaging Potential

I worked with Michelle years ago and still use the tips and techniques she taught me to this day. Her clever formulas help me whenever I need to pitch an idea or persuade someone. Her work is highly recommended.

Marisa Laria
Marketing & Communications Manager, Revlon

how to
PERSUADE

how to PERSUADE

The skills you need to get what you want

MICHELLE BOWDEN

Best-selling author of *How to Present*

WILEY

First published in 2022 by John Wiley & Sons Australia, Ltd

42 McDougall St, Milton Qld 4064
Office also in Melbourne

Typeset in Merriweather 9.5pt/14.5pt

© John Wiley & Sons Australia, Ltd 2022

The moral rights of the author have been asserted.

ISBN: 978-1-119-89187-1

A catalogue record for this book is available from the National Library of Australia

Cover design by Wiley
Author photo: Tim Pascoe

Disclaimer
The material in this publication is of the nature of general comment only, and does not represent professional advice. It is not intended to provide specific guidance for particular circumstances and it should not be relied on as the basis for any decision to take action or not take action on any matter which it covers. Readers should obtain professional advice where appropriate, before making any such decision. To the maximum extent permitted by law, the author and publisher disclaim all responsibility and liability to any person, arising directly or indirectly from any person taking or not taking action based on the information in this publication.

I dedicate this book to my best human, Ian Bowden (the very Wise Owl), and to my three beautiful and clever daughters, who inspire me to keep opening my mind to the world and its opportunities.

CONTENTS

ABOUT THE AUTHOR

Michelle Bowden is an authority on persuasive presenting in business. Michelle's name is such a synonym in corporate Australia for presentation skills that people don't say, 'I'm going to persuasive presentation skills training', they say, 'I'm going to Michelle Bowden!'

She is the bestselling, internationally published author of:

- *How to Present: The ultimate guide to presenting your ideas and influencing people using techniques that actually work* (Wiley)

- *Don't Picture Me Naked*

- *Exceptional Presentation Design*

- *STOP! Your PowerPoint is killing me!*

- *Confident Speaking Vocals*

- *How to Present: Presentation Skills Tips from the Masters*

Michelle is also:

- multimillion-dollar pitch and capital-raising coach to executives across industry

- editor of *How to Present* magazine and producer of Michelle Bowden TV

- creator of the Persuasion Smart Profile®, a psychometric assessment that reports on your persuasive strengths and weaknesses in business

- Certified Speaking Professional, the highest designation for speakers in the world; Michelle's keynote presentations educate her audiences on the theory and practice of persuasive communication at work and at home.

Michelle has delivered her two-day Persuasive Presentation Skills Masterclass more than 950 times for over 12 000 people over the past two decades.

Style and approach

Michelle conducts public and in-house Persuasive Presentation Skills Masterclasses for employees from all levels, across all industries. She is renowned for achieving results through learning and laughter. She is an expert, generous and passionate adult educator with the highest standards in relation to behavioural change. Her keynotes, workshops and courses are based on the idea that interaction, high energy and fun, combined with proven theory, create results for your business. Michelle's passion is to see people performing at their best. It's time you worked with Michelle so you can speak up and influence people!

THANK YOU!

In writing this book, I stood on the shoulders of giants. Influence gurus such as Robert Cialdini, Kevin Hogan, Kurt Mortensen, Bob Bodenhamer, Michael Hall and many others have paved the way for me to provide this highly practical, 'how-to' guide to make you an even more persuasive and successful person.

A heartfelt thank you to my wonderful mum (the Friendly Budgie/ Commanding Eagle) and my brilliant and loving daughters Holly (Friendly Budgie/Wise Owl) and Madi (Commanding Eagle/Wise Owl), who diligently read my manuscript and provided countless improvements and insights to make this book better for you. Thank you Brady Dawson (Wise Owl/Commanding Eagle) for your helpful insights and fixes to the various linguistic challenges I faced. A fist-pump to my Annabelle (Commanding Eagle/Wise Owl) for your intelligent and thought-provoking conversations about communication. And a wholehearted thank you to my best human Ian — you are such a Wise Owl/Commanding Eagle, and the wind beneath my wings.

Thank you and hugs to Lucy Raymond (Friendly Budgie/ Commanding Eagle), and Leigh McLennon (Captivating Peacock/ Wise Owl) from Wiley. You have ensured that what's in my head is a helpful resource for others. Charlotte Duff (Commanding Eagle/ Friendly Budgie), you are an editing LEGEND! Thank you Chris Shorten and the whole Wiley team for making this book the best it can be for my precious readers.

And, of course, thank you to all my wonderful, generous, supportive clients who have booked me to run masterclasses, speak for you at your conferences, and coach your bid or pitch teams. You have trusted me (in many cases for over 10 years, and sometimes for more than 20 years) with your most precious asset in your businesses — your people. Together we have learnt, embedded and refined the formulas and systems for persuasive presenting in business so that we won! Together we are most definitely stronger! Our shared experiences have made this book what it is, and you know it (because I say it all the time) — I love you for being an incredibly important part of my life. I love the joyful ring of the word 'yes'! It's thanks to you that we now have a book that will help everyone be more persuasive and hear 'yes' more often too!

WELCOME TO THIS BOOK

Hello and thanks for picking up this book! You know, I have lived a very blessed life. At the ripe age of 50 years, I can confidently say that I am a fortunate person. I have achieved my goals in my personal, work and spiritual life. If you look at me, you might think, *Wow! She is lucky. She has it all—a loving husband, wonderful and successful kids, a beautiful home, a thriving business, a bestselling book, good health, and plenty of life-affirming adventures and notable experiences.* I have clients who love me and describe my impact on them as 'life changing'. I even have two good-looking, well-behaved dogs! (Okay, well-behaved most of the time.)

Yes, I am fortunate, and I am incredibly grateful for this wonderful fortune. But don't for one minute think that any of this came easily to me. I have made my life what it is. I have pitched and persuaded my way to where I am today. I have been studying the art of influence and persuasion since (at the age of eight years old) a mean girl said she didn't want to be my friend anymore because she didn't like my homemade skirt! (Mum, I loved that tiered green and navy skirt you lovingly sewed for me!)

Make no mistake — I'm not lucky. I have coaxed, convinced, motivated, argued, swayed, induced and persuaded my way through life. I have sought out opportunities from primary school through to high school, and through three degrees at university. I have talked my way into jobs that I wasn't perfectly qualified for but knew I could eventually ace. Along every part of my journey, I have studied and applied the actions of powerful persuaders to ensure life goes the way I want. I built my successful national training company off the back of an extraordinarily high sales conversion rate. I have made sure that my friends are people I really want to spend time with. I have crafted a lifestyle where I rest when I want to rest, and work when I want to work. I can afford to buy the things I want for myself and my family. I have grabbed every possible opportunity for growth wholeheartedly and am still always striving and putting my best foot forward to ensure that things turned out the way I want.

I am certain that luck has played no part in any of my fortune! Yes, I was often in the right place at the right time, but only because I made sure I was where I needed to be. I made my own luck by being persuasive.

The same can be true for you too — everything you want and need in life is on the other side of persuasion.

When it comes to genetics or 'natural' ability, I do have an incredibly high predisposition to persuade (or what I call 'P2P'). In persuasion, your P2P is your care factor — your drive to persuade others to your point of view. My P2P score (tested in the Persuasion Smart Profile® I've developed, and which I explain in more detail through this book) is 96 per cent. This is unusually high, and has most definitely served me well. My very high P2P means I am frequently passionate about issues or challenges, and I trust my ability to persuade others, so I am more likely to be driven to persuade. I am unphased by conflict so I frequently feel confident in my ability to persuade others, and I am more likely than most people to attempt it. I am very good at reading the room and can sense when the other person's position is malleable, and I find it a challenge to use what I know about persuasion to change their mind — whether they are fixed in their opinions or not.

Of course, that's not to say you need a naturally high P2P to be persuasive. My husband's P2P is very low and he's one of the most persuasive people I know — when he wants to be! He's just not driven to change people's minds unless he really cares about the matter. This book is all about appreciating what's necessary if you want to persuade others, and then building the skills and approaches you need to get better and more comfortable when persuading others — regardless of how driven you are to change people's minds.

I wrote this book because I am passionate about both the art and science of persuasion. I am driven to make sure that you know what you need to do to make yourself undeniable when you have a great idea, product or solution. Life is too short to hear the word 'no'! I have made it my mission to read and research every nook and cranny of advice, formulas, techniques and tips, and have been teaching what I've learnt to the beautiful learners in my Persuasive Presentation Skills Masterclasses for many decades. Delivering this training every week of my life (for more than half my life) has most definitely helped me refine my thinking on what you need to do if you want to improve your ability to communicate clearly and persuasively at work and at home. I'm just so delighted that I have finally distilled the important parts for you in this book so you can see the results in your life too!

Getting the best from this book

Becoming a persuasive person is not a series of soap box moments where you turn your persuasive skills on and off. While no doubt you will have soap box moments (such as a pitch or an important meeting), becoming persuasive is all about modifying the way that you interact with the world on a minute-by-minute basis. It's about how you are perceived by others 'all the time' not just when the stakes are high.

In this book, I outline the four persuasive approaches (introduced in part I of this book, and outlined in much more detail in part II). These approaches — or persuasive types — each have different strengths and benefits and can be used in different situations and with different types of people. Each has specific behaviours you can develop, build or cement. You will get the most out of this book — and become a more persuasive person — through striving to develop your strength in all four of the persuasive approaches.

I have written this book in a very similar style to the way I speak. You'll probably read my writing style quite quickly. My recommendation is to read part I (chapters 1 to 5) in one go. Once you have the context of persuasion under your belt and you understand the four persuasive types, you can then take your time as you explore the four types in part II (chapters 6 to 9).

Chapters 6 to 9 hold all the tips, techniques, formulas and methods that persuasive people use and follow. And — no pressure — you want to try to be strong in *everything* contained in these chapters. Yes, everything! Thankfully, you'll likely find you're already doing many actions in these chapters (consciously or unconsciously) and you should celebrate this fact — this minute! And then you'll also find you need to learn, develop and cement the rest of the actions that are not yet your current habits.

You might choose to read this book from cover to cover to ensure you're capturing everything contained in these fabulous and rich pages. Or you could read chapters 1 to 5 and then decide you really need to develop one or two persuasive types in particular. Chapters 6 to 9 have been written so you can dip in and out. You can always just jump to the persuasive type that most interests you and go from there. I've also provided lots of case studies and examples throughout, to help illustrate how the actions can be applied.

Wherever your focus leads you, as you are reading:

1. *Take notes:* Find yourself a nice journal to jot things down as you learn to help the ideas stick.

2. *Mark up the book:* Turn this book into your 'go-to' reference guide for persuasion. Use sticky notes or page markers to

highlight the pages you either want to come back to, or that you think will help you better deal with people in your future.

3. *Do the activities:* When you spot areas for growth, you can start implementing a development strategy. As you read a section, complete the included activities. They're a great way to start embedding the learning.

I want you to have the ability to move through your life more persuasively all the time, whether you realise you're in a persuasive moment or not. How do you do this? Through embedding the learning and habits from this book, and aiming to improve your persuasive reach by just 1 per cent every day — starting today!

Embedding best-practice habits

As you read through the book and complete the suggested activities, you might wonder how to go about changing your long-held habits, and lock new ones in place. I suggest a three-step process to help you embed best-practice habits:

1. *Build knowledge:* Understand which habits help and which ones harm your persuasiveness.

2. *Increase awareness:* Simply notice if you accidentally slip up. Once you know you're doing it, stopping it is easier.

3. *Take action:* Make a conscious decision to aim for a 1 per cent improvement every day. Embed the positive habits that make you more persuasive and eliminate any negative habits that are holding you back. If you practise your new skills daily with the people at home who love you, implementing these tips when you must persuade at work will become much easier.

Why only 1 per cent?

Often when we know we need to develop a skill in something, doing so can seem like a massive, insurmountable task. Having so much to learn and implement can mean we either procrastinate or give up altogether. One way to tackle a seemingly insurmountable task is to choose to improve just 1 per cent every day. Aiming for a 1 per cent improvement in your persuasive skills is doable — you'll see instant results and, over time, you'll become a more persuasive person. Excellent!

You may think that 'just a little bit' each day is too slow or ineffective, and the good news is that this is how true personal transformation happens. This is how your new long-term behaviours or habits are formed — over time.

Implementing the 1 per cent

To start working on that 1 per cent improvement, simply pick something little from this book and start doing it. Start today. Then do it tomorrow and the next day, and the next. Keep doing it until that 1 per cent improvement becomes your habit and is easy and innate instead of feeling clunky and laborious.

When you think you've mastered that 1 per cent improvement, pick something else, and so on. These small, seemingly insignificant improvements will add up over the course of a year to create a meaningful improvement for you and build more success in your life.

Don't become someone you are not!

This book is not about turning you into a TV evangelist or anyone else who you think is impressively persuasive. This book is about helping you to be the most persuasive version of *you* that you can be. This book has been designed to give you all the 1 per cents — the small things you can do daily to develop your persuasiveness over time in a way that feels right for you.

I'm pumped for you — so let's get started!

PART I

How persuasive are you?

CHAPTER 1

Why be persuasive?

Fred is a 70-year-old man who lives in Cairns, Far North Queensland. Cairns is on the east coast of Australia and is right up near the top, famous for its access to the Great Barrier Reef, funny-looking giant birds called cassowaries and big, juicy, delicious mangoes. Anyway, back to Fred.

It's a Thursday morning and Fred telephones his son, Josh, who lives in Melbourne, in southern Australia. He says, 'Son, I'm sorry. I've got some bad news for you. Your mother and I are getting divorced — 45 years of misery is enough. We can't stand the sight of each other, and I can't stand talking about the separation. You'll have to telephone your sister and let her know what's happening. I'm sorry'. And Fred disconnects the call.

Josh is distraught! He is standing in his living room holding his mobile phone in his hand in amazement. What is his father saying? What should he do? He telephones his sister, Susie, who lives in Broome, Western Australia, and says, 'Hi Sis, it's Josh. I've just spoken with Dad, and I'm so shaken up. Dad says that he and Mum are getting divorced!'

Susie is furious. She flies into a rage and replies, 'Like heck they're getting divorced! You leave this to me'. And she disconnects the call so abruptly Josh is left once again holding the phone in his hand in disbelief.

Susie phones her father. When Fred answers, Susie cries, 'Dad! 'What are you thinking? You and Mum are *not* getting divorced. You love each other. There is nothing that a good functional conversation around the dinner table with a nice hot cup of tea can't resolve. Now listen here, don't do anything, Josh and I will be there tomorrow'. She pauses to gulp in some air and then continues, 'We will be there very soon. Please don't make any firm decisions. Don't do anything until we get there. Do you hear me?' And she disconnects the call immediately with the intent of booking two flights for herself and Josh to get to Cairns within the day.

Fred also puts down his mobile phone as he sits in his armchair looking out at his beautiful mango trees up in Cairns. He turns to his wife, Bev, and nods his head nice and slowly as he says, 'Okay, Bev, they'll both be here tomorrow for Christmas. Now what will we tell them at Easter?'

Hilarious, right? Or maybe not?!

We all persuade all the time

From the common task of resolving conflict in our families (like with Fred, Josh and Susie), through to negotiating the terms of a deal or a project at work, we all employ a variety of communication strategies aimed at influencing the people around us. Just think about a normal day in your life. Think about all the people you meet, and all the things you need to ask them for to get what you want and need in a day.

Every day we are faced with opportunities to influence those around us. Some occasions, such as a business pitch, formal presentation, business case or sales meeting, are obvious opportunities to persuade. When the stakes are high, or we're pitching in a competitive environment, it's important that our stakeholder listens and takes the action that we require. In these 'soap box' situations, it is essential that we are persuasive. Other opportunities are less obvious, for example, unplanned meetings, impromptu presentations, an informal conversation, a lift ride with a possible referrer, an email, even a friend's BBQ that you decided to attend at the last minute.

Whatever the stakes or the setting, your ability to persuade people throughout your day can be a game-changer.

Our unique persuasion style and personality traits ensure that some people are easier for us to persuade than others. Unfortunately, these same styles and traits can also mean our persuasiveness is limited in some situations, and often we don't take full advantage of the opportunities that present.

There's room for improvement

If you've ever felt unsure of the most effective way to persuade someone, and you want to hear the word 'yes' more often in your life, one thing is for sure: you need to develop your ability to persuade in any situation, not just the easy situations.

Based on a survey I completed with over 800 people:

- 75 per cent of people say they would gain greater respect for their knowledge and expertise if they were better communicators

- only 28 per cent of people say that the most recent meeting they attended moved them to action — meaning 72 per cent went back to what they were doing and did nothing new.

Professor John Croucher AM from Macquarie Graduate School of Management in Sydney, Australia, found similar results in relation to the effectiveness of meetings in persuading people. Croucher reported his study findings that 89 per cent of executives admit to daydreaming during important meetings and conversations — and 33 per cent admit to sleeping during them! Dreadful, right?

These statistics tell us that there's room for improvement when we are persuading our colleagues, clients, employers, and friends and family members.

And the truth is that even if you're not in sales, you still want and need to get things from other people. You want people to trust you. You want people to support you. You want people to endorse your ideas or suggestions. And often this means getting people to do or think something very different to what they were thinking or doing just a minute ago. Indeed, your ability to persuade is the single most important skill you can develop to ensure you are competitive in the knowledge economy.

Persuasive people are made, not born

I know that a lack of confidence in asserting ideas holds many people back from achieving their potential in business. I know that it doesn't matter how good you are at your job, or how compelling your message is, if no-one is listening to you when you speak! And I also know that persuasive people are made, not born. I have seen with my own eyes that anyone can be persuasive — yes, especially you!

As a persuasive presentation skills expert, I have had the opportunity to work with thousands of people, and what I have learnt is that most people are unaware of the many tools and techniques that can transform them into a persuasive communicator. I have observed that once people know what to do to persuade their stakeholder and start doing it, they automatically increase their success at work and at home.

> **TIP**
>
> **Michelle says,**
>
> 'I believe anyone can be persuasive — yes, especially you!'

How persuasive are you?

Here's a question for you. From one day to the next, how persuasive are you? I mean, seriously, how persuasive — are *you*? Do people listen when you speak? Do you often get your own way? What approach would you take to convince your family members to travel across the country for an important family event? For example:

- Would you scheme like Fred in the story?
- Would you demand and behave aggressively like Susie?
- Would you sulk or guilt your family members into travelling?

- Would you delegate like Josh?

- Would you just ask nicely?

What's your natural persuasion style? And, possibly an even more important question to ask yourself, how persistent would you be? If your family member said 'no', would you leave it at that because no means no and trying to force things is pointless. Or would you keep asking them to visit with you? If you did keep asking, would you use the same method over and over until you wore them down? (My husband calls this approach the 'dog at a fence approach'! He means you just keep barking and barking at the fence until the person can't stand it anymore and just gives in and does what you want.) Or would you be more likely to keep trying but use a variety of different methods until the other person was eventually convinced?

What do you think about persuasion?

When you think about the word 'persuasion', what words come into your mind? We've all got a very different perception of what persuasion really is. Do you think of words such as 'charm', 'tempt' and 'cajole'? Or do you think of words such as 'negotiate', 'manipulate' and 'mother-in-law'? These words are all value-laden descriptors that help you decide what you think is functional influence, and what you think is overstepping the mark into dysfunctional manipulation or misuse of your personal or positional power.

Ask yourself:

- Do you think that persuasive people are born persuasive?

- Is there a proven, best-practice approach for persuading?

- Should we all persuade the same way?

- Should we follow a specific model or formula no matter the communication scenario?

- Or does the approach we use to persuade depend on the situation?

- To what extent does your personality affect your approach and your success as a persuader?

These questions are all aimed at helping you reflect on whether you think we can all learn to be persuasive, and whether we should all be trying the same approach. Or should we be doing something different depending on the scenario, the stakeholder, or our own style?

Welcome to *How to Persuade*

Welcome to *How to Persuade*, where I answer all these questions and more. I believe that your ability to persuade — to move hearts and minds — is the single most important skill you can develop to ensure you are competitive in the knowledge economy. You'll learn in this book that we all need to master and demonstrate some simple, practical, and highly effective techniques and approaches on a daily basis if we want to be consistently persuasive. The great news is that anyone can be persuasive, especially you! It's just a matter of knowing what to do and doing it.

TOP TIPS
Why be persuasive?

- We all persuade all the time!
- Some persuasive moments are obvious; others are less so.
- Some people are easier to persuade than others.
- Developing your ability to persuade can help ensure you are competitive in the knowledge economy.
- Persuasive people are made not born.
- Anyone can be persuasive — yes, especially you!

CHAPTER 2

Are you turning people off?

Before we get into the tips for being more persuasive, reflecting for a moment about whether you ever turn people off when you're persuading (without realising it or not) is important. Could you be turning people off? It's a blunt question, isn't it? The fact is, when it comes to persuasion you do plenty of things to attract people. Unfortunately, you also do a whole lot of things to repel your stakeholders and/or turn them off your big, important ideas. Most of us are completely unaware of the hundreds of little things we do daily that are both attracting and repelling people at different times.

If you've ever felt like someone rubbed you up the wrong way, that was you being turned off. Or maybe you've been in a situation where you got a 'vibe' that the other person just wasn't that into *you*. It happens all the time. And when it happens, most of us don't take the time to wonder what it is that we did or said that turned the other person off. We just get on with our life. We might even blame them! Perhaps we tell ourselves, 'Well, that person is just rude!' This means we are highly likely to repeat the turn-off behaviour over and over again without any awareness that we're damaging our persuasiveness.

We're unlikely to give feedback on poor persuasion

I've been teaching persuasion for over two decades. When I'm teaching my persuasive techniques, people are keen to tell me all about their experiences with people who were a 'turn-off' during the persuasion process — including managers, staff, clients, external consultants, and even family and friends. The common element in most people's stories is that they didn't give any feedback to the actual person who behaved poorly, which means the person will never know the impact of their behaviour. In fact, it's my experience that most of us think we're being nice to the persuader by not speaking up or giving feedback about the behaviour that bothered us. In general, we don't want to offend the person who turned us off or cause any unnecessary conflict — particularly if the person who offended us is more senior than we are at work. We definitely don't want to perform a 'career-limiting move' by calling out the boss's bad behaviour! Now, I'm not saying you should go around giving feedback to everyone you meet. I'm reflecting that most people simply won't give feedback when they have been turned off by someone.

So what does this mean when *you* are the persuader?

You may be moving through life turning people off, offending people and missing out on opportunities because no-one has given you feedback that your approach is offensive or ineffective.

The 15 most common persuasion mistakes

To help you avoid insulting, disappointing or upsetting people, let's look at the most important things *not* to do when persuading others. See if you can relate to any of the mistakes in the following list because, if you're doing these things, it's unlikely anyone will be frank enough to tell you — which means you'll never be consistently persuasive.

The 15 most common mistakes people make when attempting to persuade others are:

1. *Displaying pessimism or a lack of enthusiasm and passion:* People generally need your enthusiasm to feel enrolled in your idea. Get appropriately excited about it and you'll be contagious.

2. *Appearing judgemental or untrustworthy:* None of us like to feel judged, and we're also unlikely to be persuaded by someone we don't trust. I recall a powerful activity in a workshop where the facilitator got us to listen to a person in two ways. Firstly, we were asked to listen as though we thought the person was an idiot. Secondly, we listened as though they were a genius. This activity showed us that the frame of mind you take to your persuasive moment informs how you perceive the moment and, more interestingly, also transforms the 'performance' of the person you are listening to. When we were listening as though the speaker was fascinating, the person sensed this and brought their best self to the interaction. On the other hand, listening to them as though they were an idiot affected the person's confidence: their voice, their eye contact, their flow. What does this mean? When you are persuading someone, it's important that they don't ever feel judged by you. Rather, they need to feel accepted if they are going to trust you and listen to your point of view. If you are not sure about the person you are persuading, try hard to remain open-minded and find a way to accept them so you don't turn them off your plan.

3. *Asking too many questions:* Who likes having so many questions thrown at them that it feels like an interrogation? Yes, no-one! Don't over-question your prospect or stakeholder. You have probably heard the saying (attributed to the Greek philosopher Epictetus) that we have two ears and one mouth and should use them in that proportion. Listening more than talking is a good rule to apply when persuading.

4. *Offering one-sided facts:* To ensure people find your message credible, your facts should not be obviously biased or one-sided. Your facts being noticeably skewed is a turn-off. Instead, aim to be thorough, logical, robust and well prepared.

5. *Denying, blaming, or justifying poor decisions:* Denying, blaming and justifying are known as victim behaviours. People who are known to consistently display victim behaviours are not persuasive — they are a turn-off! In general, people prefer that you take personal responsibility for your actions. Acknowledge the role you play in your own life — whether it's good or bad — and, importantly, own up to mistakes. That way, when you have something to persuade about, you'll be more trustworthy and believable.

6. *Using pushy behaviour:* No-one likes a pushy salesperson! When it comes to persuading, be 'others-focused' so you can 'read the room' and best judge how strong to be without turning your prospect or stakeholder off. Commitment, rigour and passion are all fabulous qualities when used in the correct doses.

7. *Offering too many stories to make your point:* Some people just love the sound of their own voice, and they tell way too many personal stories to make their point. Stories are a wonderful way to make your point when they are interesting and memorable, and told brilliantly. Just be careful not to hog the limelight too much.

8. *Seeming desperate:* Desperation has a stink about it that is very easily sensed by your prospect or stakeholder — and it's a real turn-off. Coming across as desperate implies you are unsuccessful. Others infer that no-one else is buying what you're selling! Desperation opens you up to price and value negotiations that will leave you feeling used and unfulfilled. Do what you can to feel confident in yourself and your idea (or offer), and be sure you don't beg or plead!

9. *Forgetting someone's name, or never knowing it in the first place:* Oh, this is one of my pet hates! I was recently involved in a big project where only two women and lots of men were involved. The senior executive called one of the women by the other woman's name. Let me repeat: there were only two women! It was not hard to know which woman was which. Please care enough about your prospect or stakeholder to know their name and get it right every time. And don't get it nearly right. I'm often called Melissa instead of Michelle. To the person getting it wrong, they might seem like similar names; to me, they didn't care enough to get my name right.

10. *Allowing yourself to be distracted by something more 'interesting':* You're talking to someone and they look over your shoulder at something, and you find yourself turning your head to see what they are looking at. Has this ever happened to you? Don't do this! You'll come across as not caring enough to stay connected to the person and their idea.

11. *Not using direct eye contact:* Indirect eye contact makes you appear insincere or uninterested. Direct eye contact is essential for rapport. Look right at the person you're talking to with short breaks. Don't stare intently. Relax your face. Relax your eyes. If possible, even smile with your eyes where appropriate.

12. *Over-stating the facts:* Some people feel they should 'never let the truth get in the way of a good story'! Some of us tend to exaggerate the importance or significance of certain events that are exciting to us. You may not even do this knowingly — rather, it's your way of making the other person sit up and listen. Sometimes, exaggeration can be funny and energising; often, it's just annoying. And exaggeration also comes with a big risk: if you're perceived to be embellishing, over-stating or distorting the facts, you may be seen as lacking in integrity. The point here is to choose your moment.

13. *Forgetting to ask for what you want:* People can't read your mind. If you don't state what you want clearly and specifically, your stakeholder doesn't know what to do next. Always ask for the thing you want. As talk show host and powerhouse Oprah Winfrey wisely said, 'You get in life what you have the courage to ask for'.

14. *Talking about yourself too much:* Only talk about yourself to the extent that it builds rapport and establishes the necessary amount of credibility and connection. Then stop.

15. *Using slick communication:* Slick communication is when you sound rehearsed or scripted and you come across as contrived and insincere. In other words, you are 'too good to be true'. Aim to be as authentic as possible. It's counterintuitive, but you'll be your most authentic and persuasive self when you plan your message thoroughly, rehearse until you can't get it wrong, and then allow yourself to ad-lib and even add some humour in the moment. Thorough rehearsal is the key to being perceived as authentic.

So, there you have it. You want people to trust and respect you instinctively. You want to attract, not repel people. Once you make yourself aware of these common mistakes, the next step is to work out how to better manage your approach so that you don't end up unintentionally turning people off. If you recognise any of these mistakes are things you do, work out what you can do differently to stop right now.

These are just some ideas to help you stop turning people off. The rest of this book delves much more deeply into building trust and making your argument undeniable. I'll show you how to use different approaches for different situations so you can master persuasion. Everything you want in life is found on the other side of persuasion. So you need to do what you can to ensure you are as effective as possible at persuading in every area of your life.

Michelle says,

'Everything you want in life is found on the other side of persuasion.'

TOP TIPS
Are you turning people off?

- You're likely completely unaware of the hundreds of little things you do daily that both attract and repel people at different times.

- You may be moving through life turning people off, offending people, and missing out on opportunities because no-one has given you feedback that your approach is offensive or ineffective.

- The 15 mistakes to avoid when persuading are:

   1. displaying pessimism or lack of enthusiasm and passion

   2. appearing judgemental or untrustworthy

   3. asking too many questions

   4. offering one-sided facts

   5. denying, blaming or justifying poor decisions

   6. using pushy behaviour

   7. offering too many stories to make your point

   8. seeming desperate

   9. forgetting someone's name, or never knowing it in the first place

(continued)

10. allowing yourself to be distracted by something more 'interesting'

11. not using direct eye contact

12. over-stating the facts

13. forgetting to ask for what you want

14. talking about yourself too much

15. using slick communication.

- Be aware if you make these mistakes and plan an alternative.

CHAPTER 3

You cannot *not* influence!

A lot of research highlights the part persuasion plays in influence. Figure 3.1 (overleaf) summarises some of this research, showing the five main ways that people go about influencing others. They range on a continuum from passive, through assertive, to aggressive.

Persuasion's position on the influence continuum

The passive approaches within the influence continuum shown on figure 3.1 are modelling and guiding. The aggressive approaches are forcing and directing. Persuasion is in the middle of the continuum and is the assertive approach to influence.

TIP

Michelle says,

'Persuasion is the assertive approach to influence.'

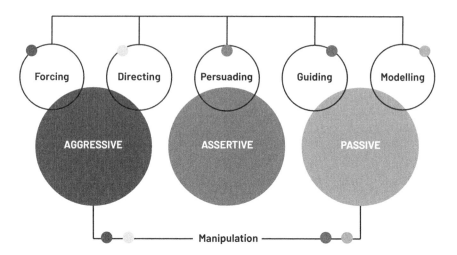

Figure 3.1 Influence continuum

We all oscillate between the points on this influence continuum throughout our days, depending on two main things:

1. time

2. care factor.

For example, imagine you are driving your car. You have a three-year-old child strapped safely in their booster chair in the back seat. As you pull to a stop at a red traffic light, you turn your head toward the back seat of the car to make sure the child is still safe. You realise they are not safe at all. They have unclipped their seatbelt and are jumping around on the back seat of the car having a party. What words would come out of your mouth in this moment? Probably something quite firm like, 'Put your seatbelt on now!'

In this example, you have limited time because you only have a few moments before the traffic light turns green, and you care a lot about the outcome. You want the child to be safely restrained and you don't want a fine from the police for driving with an unrestrained child in your car. This example shows that if you're in a hurry and the stakes are high, you're likely to make a different choice from the one you'd make if time allowed. Rather than modelling or guiding, you're likely to engage in forcing or directing.

The aggressive approach to persuasion

Forcing and directing behaviours can be both overt and covert, and can be demonstrated both knowingly and unknowingly. In other words, people don't always realise when they're being aggressive in their communication style. Regardless of intention, forcing and directing behaviours are often harmful to everyone involved.

We've all had that boss who's a mega micromanager — they have a 'my way or the highway!' kind of vibe. If you've had this kind of boss, no doubt they used forcing actions (telling you exactly how to do things). At the time, you likely did what they said with a huge smile on your face. You might have nodded your head and enthusiastically told them, 'I'm on it!' And they thought they'd won. I'm sure you would agree that this approach is not sustainable. In fact, behind this aggressor's back, you likely spent a lot of time on seek.com looking for another job! Taking an aggressive approach to influence doesn't result in a win–win.

The passive approach to persuasion

Guiding and modelling are the passive approaches to influence from figure 3.1. Just like the aggressive behaviours of forcing and directing, the passive approaches of guiding and modelling can be both overt and covert. You can guide and model knowingly and unknowingly. In other words, people don't always realise when they are being passive in their communication style. And sometimes passive influence isn't a bad thing.

Ian's story: an example of modelling and guiding

At the time of writing, I've been married for 25 years. For much of our marriage my husband, Ian, has been a stay-at-home dad. When my third daughter, Annabelle, was born, we decided that Ian would be the primary carer and I would be the breadwinner. This means that

(continued)

19

my three daughters have been raised in a home where the mum goes to work, and the dad takes care of the family and the home.

When Annabelle was about three years old, Ian used to play a lovely game with her. At the end of every day, Ian would ask Annabelle, 'What did you do today, Annabelle?' Hands often on hips, she would announce very proudly, 'Well, Daddy, today I went to kindy. What did you do?'

And from one day to the next, Ian would make up all sorts of nonsense. One day he said, 'Well, Annabelle, today I was a wizard'. And her little eyes would pop open, and she'd think that he was an amazing daddy. Another day he said, 'Today I flew to the moon in a rocket ship!' Again her little eyes popped. She just loved that her daddy was such an adventurer. Another day, being Australian and having The Wiggles as one of her all-time favourite children's celebrity groups, Ian said, 'Well, Annabelle, today I was a brown Wiggle!' (I came home from work and asked Ian, 'Of all the colours in the rainbow, why would you choose a poo-coloured Wiggle?' Oh dear!)

At the end of one week Annabelle again arrived home from kindy. After telling Ian about her day, she again asked him what he did all day. This time, Ian said, 'Well, Annabelle, today I went to work'. At that moment, Annabelle paused for a moment, then she screwed up her little face, furrowed her little eyebrows, shook her head from side to side and eventually exclaimed, 'No you didn't. Boys don't go to work!'

Annabelle loved that her daddy was a wizard, that he'd flown to the moon and even that he was a brown Wiggle. She simply could not believe that he went to work – he must be tricking her.

Of course, the point here is that we are always influencing, even when we don't mean to influence. Ian and I didn't set out to role-model for our three daughters that girls can choose to go to work, and boys can choose to run the home. Like most people, we were just doing our best effort at living our best life in a way that worked for our family. The fact is that even when we don't mean to, from one moment to the next, we are always influencing – from the outfit you decided to wear today, through to the criticism you bark at a colleague when you're cross.

Remembering that you cannot *not* influence is so important. You are constantly influencing — perhaps aggressively, perhaps passively. This means putting some attention, mindfulness and care into your influence — and perhaps being more assertive with your influence — is also so important. Let's always communicate with empathy and consideration for our stakeholders.

TIP

Michelle says,

'You cannot *not* influence.'

If you can develop your persuasive skills and sit more in the assertive area on the influence continuum, you can get what you want, and everyone wins. As the American economist and writer Mark Skousen says, 'The triumph of persuasion over force is the sign of a civilized society'. In other words, when you want something, you don't need to be rude or sarcastic. You don't need to be aggressive. If you can develop your persuasive skills, you can get what you want with everyone winning. Yet we often don't develop our persuasive skills.

Why don't we develop our persuasive skills?

Well, it's not because we don't want to. Failing to get people to give us what we want — to win that new job or pay rise, to receive support for our ideas — is painful and can feel like failure. It's not that we don't want to develop our persuasive skills. It's simply that we're not taught how to.

In school, we're not taught how to make our facts sexy, or how to establish our personal credibility in a way that doesn't feel like boasting or showing off. We're not taught how to have people really 'connect' with us, and we're definitely not taught how to unleash our personal charm and charisma. We are simply not taught how to persuade. So, what does that mean we do when we want something from someone? We use the techniques that worked for us last time. In other words, we often wing it and hope for the best. Sometimes that means that we win and sometimes, very disappointingly, we lose.

Let's just talk about losing for a minute!

The opposite of persuasion is not simply failing to persuade. A lack of persuasive ability often doesn't result in a neutral outcome — where you speak, the other person listens or doesn't, and then everyone walks away and just gets on with it.

When the conversation happens and we don't persuade, often the other person walks away from the interaction feeling the opposite of neutral. In fact, in the absence of persuasion, the other person may well feel disappointed, unimpressed or annoyed. They may even lose respect for you because you didn't do a good job of the persuasion.

Mucking up the persuasive moment also often means more annoying meetings, and more backwards and forwards with ineffective decision-making. This frustrating waste of time can feel like you're banging your head against a brick wall.

Using persuasion effectively

Using persuasion effectively is important because if you don't put your best foot forward when you communicate with your stakeholders, you're not serving anyone. You're not serving them and you're not serving you.

As Swiss psychiatrist and founder of analytical psychology Carl Jung noted, 'Unless you choose to make the unconscious conscious, it will direct your life and you will call it fate'.

Reading this book sets you up with all the skills and abilities to demonstrate your message credibility, assert your personal authority, establish goodwill, and arouse enthusiasm and passion. Doing all these things will ensure you're as persuasive as possible all the time — and you're not leaving your success to fate.

TOP TIPS
You cannot *not* influence!

- We move from aggressive to assertive or passive influence and back again all day, depending on how much time we have, and how much we care about the matter at hand.

- The aggressive approaches to persuasion are forcing and directing.

- The passive approaches to persuasion are guiding and modelling.

- Persuasion is the assertive approach to influence.

- If you can develop your persuasive skills, you can get what you want, and everyone wins.

- We are not taught how to persuade and so often we just wing it and hope for the best.

- The opposite of persuasion is often not neutral — it can be disappointment, confusion, long-term loss of respect and a frustrating waste of time.

- Let's not leave our persuasive success to fate.

CHAPTER 4

Persuasion versus manipulation

No book on persuasion can get away with avoiding a discussion about the difference between persuasion and manipulation. I've been refining my thinking on this matter for decades. While some will say I'm just getting hung up on semantics, I believe understanding the difference between persuasion and manipulation is important. You should be clear about your intentions when attempting to persuade others — no-one wants to lie in bed at night feeling guilty or sorry about the way they treated their fellow humans that day. In fact, when you engage in persuasive versus manipulative communication and achieve what you want (while the other person also achieves what they want), it's a gratifying experience for everyone involved.

In chapter 3 I introduced the influence continuum, and noted that we all oscillate on this continuum from one moment to the next. We can move from passive to aggressive and back again all day.

So where does manipulation fit in all of this?

Let's look at the definitions of some related words:

- *Manipulate:* To influence or manage shrewdly or deviously.

- *Cajole:* To persuade someone to do something by sustained coaxing or flattery.

- *Hustle:* To pressure or urge someone into an action.

- *Entice:* To attract by arousing hope or desire; lure.

- *Snare:* To catch or trap, or as if in a snare; capture by trickery.

How do you feel about those words and their definitions? None of them is particularly attractive to me! You might achieve what you want using these tactics, but at what cost?

What is manipulation?

Manipulation is the exercise of harmful influence. It's a set of behaviours that derive from either a passive or an aggressive approach to influence. Some people even define manipulation as passive-aggressive behaviour. You cannot be simultaneously persuasive and manipulative.

TIP

Michelle says,

'You cannot be simultaneously persuasive and manipulative.'

People who manipulate others get what they want by assaulting their stakeholders' mental and emotional needs. Sometimes even without realising it, the manipulator uses a variety of strategies to gain control of the other person. This control is never for the good of the other person; it's all about the manipulator exercising power.

Manipulation can happen in all types of relationships at work and at home, and even with people you don't know. Manipulators use guilt, lies, comparisons, whingeing, blame and mind games to get what they want.

Let's be clear: manipulation is not persuasion. It is a form of passive or aggressive influence, and it's not recommended. It's not what this book is about!

Here are the definitions of some different, but still related, words:

- *Convince:* To bring (by the use of argument or evidence) a firm belief or a course of action.

- *Persuade:* To induce to undertake a course of action or embrace a point of view by means of argument, reasoning or entreaty, and where there is a measure of freedom in the decision-making process of the stakeholder.

So convincing or persuading people is about everyone winning! No matter the persuasion scenario, you want everyone to feel like they are on the winning team and that they have freedom over their choices. The other person shouldn't feel that they have been coerced into doing something they didn't want to do.

From the point of view of the persuader, you shouldn't need to do something underhanded in the heat of the moment that, in hindsight, has you feeling guilty or sorry for your behaviour, or something you are not proud of. You shouldn't feel like a 'pushy' person. No-one feels good about themselves or can feel truly happy by making someone else unhappy. You want to be able to lie straight in your bed at night and feel good about the day's communication events. In the following chapters, I cover all sorts of actions that you can take so you feel proud of your persuasive approach.

TIP

Michelle says,

'A basic law of human nature is that no human feels good about themselves or can feel truly happy by making someone else unhappy.'

Are you persuasive or just a common hustler?

When deciding whether you're being persuasive or manipulative, it's important to think about your focus or intent. If you're solely focused on achieving your own needs without any reference or care for your stakeholders' needs, then your approach to influence may well be manipulative.

When you're convinced that you must change the other person's mind at any cost, you'll often employ any means — including deceit or trickery — to get what you want. Whereas, if you are completely focused on the needs and wants of your stakeholder, you will appreciate the need for your stakeholder to feel they have a measure of freedom in their decision-making process. You're therefore unlikely to trick or deceive anyone.

Who cares if you're manipulative or not?

Your prospects or stakeholders care if you're manipulative rather than persuasive. That's why this is such an important question. If your prospect or stakeholder feels they were lured, tricked or pressured into buying your product or service or approving your big idea, they will likely experience 'buyer's remorse' once the deal is done — and you'll have a very unhappy customer on your hands. You could have someone asking for their money back, or 'spreading the word' that you are not to be trusted on project teams or committees, and possibly damaging your reputation.

You can check yourself

The point here is that you can check yourself. Be sure to get into your stakeholder's or prospect's shoes prior to your persuasive moment. Ask yourself some questions so you're sure you are approaching this scenario in the most effective way.

To be sure you're in your stakeholder's shoes, ask yourself the following:

1. What are they thinking, feeling and doing prior to the conversation?

2. What's important to them?

3. What are they hoping to achieve from this discussion?

4. How do they want to feel when we are finished?

5. What's in their best interest here?

6. What's a win–win for us both?

You can then use similar questions to check yourself throughout the persuasion scenario and make sure you haven't crossed the boundary from persuasion into hustling, so that you're still on safe ground.

It's not just semantics. Making sure everyone wins is important.

Reflect on your influence approach. Are you passive, assertive or aggressive in your daily dealings?

What do you need to fix or change so you are trusted, impressive and inspiring, and so you achieve success in all your communication moments?

Mia's story

Mia is in sales. She loves her company, her colleagues and her products. She deeply believes that everyone needs what she sells. Mia came to me for coaching because she was accused of over-selling. Some of her clients had complained about her overzealous explanation of both the benefits and the features of her product, and she wanted to learn how to be passionate without overdoing things.

Often when persuading we fall into the habit of telling our client or colleague absolutely *all* the benefits of our products or services, or our great idea. It's a natural result of being passionate about our offering and being pumped and wanting to help people.

The problem with overloading your stakeholder with all the information you've got is that your audience has their own motivation

(continued)

for buying, or not. They will only buy if you address *their* needs. They don't need to know everything, just the parts that help them to buy. The more you overload them, the more likely they are to switch off.

When Mia came to me, I introduced her to the three phases in a persuasive presentation in business. In summary, the three phases you need to go through are:

1. *Analysis:* Work out who your stakeholder is, what their current state is and where you want to shift them to. What do you have to offer? In other words, what is your unique selling proposition? What's your desired state after this email, meeting or conversation? This is the phase where you get mentally ready. You step into your stakeholder's shoes and work out what approaches will be the most useful and effective in your persuasion moment.

2. *Design:* Craft your message cleverly so that it meets the needs of your stakeholder and achieves what you want. How will you pitch your offer or idea to your various stakeholders for the best results?

3. *Delivery:* Rehearse sufficiently, focus on your audience and then deliver in a way that captivates them.

Mia now uses these phases to get into her prospect's shoes when structuring and delivering her message. She listens more carefully, and she doesn't oversell. She ensures that she does not bury her stakeholder in either benefits or details. The great news is that the feedback on Mia's new approach is overwhelmingly positive from all her stakeholders — including her manager! No-one would think Mia was a manipulator these days.

I cover possible persuasive approaches, including my Persuasion Blueprint, in much more detail through the rest of this book. For more on persuasive presenting in business, see my earlier book *How to Present: The ultimate guide to presenting your ideas and influencing people using techniques that actually work*, also published by Wiley.

TOP TIPS
Persuasion versus manipulation

- It's important to understand the difference between persuasion and manipulation and be clear about our intentions when we are attempting to influence others.

- Manipulation is the exercise of harmful influence, using either passive or aggressive approaches.

- You cannot be persuasive and manipulative at the same time.

- The persuasive approach is about everyone winning, and helps ensure we never do something underhanded in the heat of the moment that, in hindsight, has us feeling guilty or sorry for our behaviour.

- If you are solely focused on achieving your own needs without any reference or care for your stakeholder's needs, your approach to influence may well be manipulative.

- If your prospect or stakeholder feels they were lured, tricked or pressured into buying your product or service or approving your big idea, they will likely experience 'buyer's remorse' and you'll have a very unhappy customer on your hands.

- You can check yourself. Be sure to get into your stakeholder's or prospect's shoes prior to your persuasive moment.

CHAPTER 5

The four persuasive types

In my capacity as a pitch coach, I meet lots of clients who need to be persuasive at work and at home. At the extreme end, I regularly help bid teams to win deals worth $500 to $700 million. I help companies that are up for sale through the acquisition process. I help executives pitch strategy to their board for approval, and analysts pitch solutions to their businesses. I help scientists and academics pitch for funding. I help leaders persuade their team members and team members persuade their leaders! I even help people speak up with courage and confidence in team meetings. My aim is always to ensure these people are as persuasive and successful as possible.

Over the years, what became increasingly obvious to me in my work is that most people have no awareness of their current persuasive strengths and weaknesses. Even in sales, people tend to wing it a lot of the time. So I set out to find a way to give people an insight into where they were already good at persuasion, and where they might need to develop some capability so that they could be more persuasive more of the time.

After many years of research and development, I've identified four sets of 'key persuasion indicators', or KPIs. Based on these four sets, I've also developed four persuasive approaches or types. Without even realising it, you lean towards one or more of my persuasion types, and use these same approaches in every situation where you're hoping to influence someone else. By being more aware of your more natural persuasion type/s, you can get a better idea of your current persuasive strengths and weaknesses. You can also start to build your ability to use other persuasive approaches, depending on the person and situation.

Understanding the key persuasion indicators

We are all persuaded in different ways, and this affects our approach when persuading others.

The body of research on persuasion highlights that the degree to which we are persuaded by someone depends on whether or not they adequately address our 'key persuasion indicators' or KPIs.

These KPIs can be broken into four sets, based on the different focuses people have when being persuaded. These sets, and the KPIs within them, are shown in table 5.1.

Whether by rational thought or feeling, we all tend to place a different level of importance on each set of KPIs. For instance, some people won't be persuaded by you unless your argument is rational and logical, and backed by verifiable facts and research. Other people really care about the credibility of the messenger. They need to know that you have the runs on the board and the vibe that you really know what you're talking about. They need to know you are someone they can trust because you are an authority in your field. Then there are people who need to know you care about them. They need to feel a strong emotional connection to you before they are open to being persuaded by you. And, finally, some people need to sense your passion and enthusiasm before they will be persuaded by you. They need to be swept up in your excitement.

You may find that more than one of the sets of KPIs are important to you. This means you may have a primary type, a secondary type and a least preferred type.

Table 5.1 Key persuasion indicators broken into four sets

	Key persuasion indicator
KPI set 1	Is there wisdom in this argument?
	Does this argument seem logical and rational?
	Does this perspective make good sense to me?
	Is this message irrefutable?
KPI set 2	Is this person an authority in their field?
	Are they believable and trustworthy?
	Do I respect them?
KPI set 3	Is this person kind and accepting?
	Do they care about me and my needs?
	Am I feeling warm towards them?
	Do I feel goodwill towards them?
KPI set 4	Is this person captivating?
	Is their presence magnetic?
	Am I inspired by their confidence?
	Is their enthusiasm and passion contagious?

TIP

Michelle says,

'Whether by rational thought or feeling, we all tend to place a different level of importance on each set of KPIs.'

Introducing the four persuasion types

As mentioned, I used the four sets of KPIs to develop the four different persuasion types.

The four persuasive types, along with the KPI set they're based on, their descriptor and the method they're driven to persuade by, are shown in table 5.2 (overleaf).

Table 5.2 The four persuasion types

Type	KPI set number	Descriptor	Driven to persuade by
Owl	KPI set 1	Wise	Establishing message credibility
Eagle	KPI set 2	Commanding	Conveying personal authority
Budgie	KPI set 3	Friendly	Building goodwill
Peacock	KPI set 4	Captivating	Arousing enthusiasm and passion

Even though I've separated out the four persuasion types, only a rare individual would be strong in one type and not in any of the others.

Similar to your alignment with one or two of the KPIs sets, you'll find you naturally lean towards being strong in two (or even three) of the persuasion types. While you will always be inclined towards these types, being more aware of your approaches, and the other approaches and behaviours available, means you can work on your relative strengths and weaknesses. You can also work towards demonstrating the behaviours of other persuasion types as the situation or stakeholders require it.

TIP

Michelle says,

'Only a rare individual would be strong in one type and not in any of the others.'

Why birds?

Several psychological assessment tools are administered in businesses to help people uncover their strengths and weaknesses. Common options include the Myers–Briggs Type Indicator (MBTI) and DiSC assessment. Perhaps you've used these tools in the past.

In the heat of the persuasive moment, I've discovered that if the model that explains your persuasive approach is too academic or theoretical, you're unlikely to remember the characteristics of each type. If you can't remember the characteristics, you're also unlikely to have the ability to flex or adapt your approach in a way that's going to achieve persuasive success for you and your stakeholders.

I've chosen four birds for my model because their characteristics perfectly match the characteristics of the four persuasive types. Linking a bird to each type makes it much quicker, easier and more fun for you to identify people's persuasive preferences out in the bigger world and then adapt your approach so you can increase your persuasive reach and achieve the outcomes you are seeking.

The following sections introduce each of the types. The chapters in part II explore these types, and how you might develop, build or cement skills in each of them, in much more detail.

Type 1: The Wise Owl

Owls are thought of as wise because of their very large eyes that give the sense they are taking in everything around them. In fact, they can't move their eyes and have to turn their whole head to look in a new direction, which gives the impression of complete concentration and undivided attention — as though they are always listening! The owl is also associated with enigmatic silence, because they rarely vocalise in the presence of humans.

You may relate to the introvert's supposition that the wisest of people are also frequently silent. Indeed, psychologist Professor Leon F Seltzer argues, 'Wise people talk less, are silent more, and listen more than those lacking wisdom'. In other words, if you don't have something wise to say, then be like the Wise Owl and perhaps choose to say nothing at all!

Owls are also considered wise because of their heightened senses and stealth ability to come and go without detection. In ancient times, it was believed that a magical inner light gave owls superior night vision and allowed them to do things that most creatures could not. In the workplace, Wise Owls often similarly move with stealth and go unnoticed. They move through the workplace and the home getting things done without fuss and drama, and are less likely to speak up in meetings. Any opinion they do offer is backed by thorough research, logic and reason.

The ancient Greeks associated the owl with the Goddess of Wisdom, Athena. Athena is described in literature as 'owl-eyed' or 'owl-faced', and is often portrayed holding an owl that, it was said, revealed truths to her. According to the mythology of ancient Greece, Athena was so impressed by the enormous eyes and solemn appearance of the owl that she made it her favourite bird and had it protected. Because of the connection between Athena, wisdom and owls, by association owls were also assumed to be wise. In fact, it is said that if an owl flew over Greek soldiers before a battle, they took it as a sign of victory because they had Athena's blessing. Athena's owl was also portrayed on the reverse side of their coins, keeping a watchful eye on Athenian trade and commerce.

The owl also features as a symbol of wisdom in Roman mythology, where Minerva was the Goddess of Wisdom. Minerva also claimed the owl as one of her symbols. In early Roman times, the deaths of Julius Caesar, Augustus, Commodus Aurelius and Agrippa were all said to have been predicted by a Wise Owl. In Virgil's Latin epic poem from between 29–19BC, the *Aeneid*, owls also have prophetic abilities, further adding to their wise character.

In English folklore a screeching owl forecast inclement weather. If the call of the owl was heard during bad weather, it was believed a change in the weather was imminent.

Wisdom and owls have gone hand in hand throughout history.

How does the Wise Owl persuade?

The Wise Owl has an innate drive to persuade by establishing the credibility of their message. They are thought of as wise because they are discerning, and able to judge what is true or right.

The following traits are typical of the Wise Owl:

- *Analytical:* The careful, systematic study of something.
- *Critical:* Exercising careful judgement or evaluation.

- *Discerning:* Displaying good judgement and understanding.

- *Dispassionate:* Unaffected by personal feeling or bias.

- *Intelligent:* Having high mental capacity.

- *Judgemental:* Skilled in offering an opinion or giving advice based on careful thought.

- *Logical:* Based on sound judgement, reasonable.

- *Methodical:* Using a systematic approach.

- *Prepared:* Organised and ready.

- *Rational:* Exercising reason, sound judgement or good sense.

- *Researched:* Has studied a subject in detail.

- *Scholarly:* Good at learning by studying.

- *Sober:* Having a serious, sensible and solemn attitude.

- *Thoughtful:* Contemplative, reflective, mindful.

The following behaviours are consistent with the Wise Owl:

- analyses the data before drawing conclusions

- assumes that everyone will be as interested in the analysis as they are

- conducts thorough research

- demonstrates composure and calmness in the face of antagonism

- demonstrates good judgement through deep understanding of the argument

- provides sound arguments based on evidence and thorough analysis

- uses a rational, well-structured flow for outlining their argument.

Their catchphrases are:

- 'I like to present sound arguments based on facts and analysis.'
- 'The facts speak for themselves.'
- 'Any logical, rational person won't be able to disagree with me.'

Possible weaknesses for the Wise Owl are:

- may rely too heavily on complex data
- often gets bogged down in the detail
- pedantic tendencies may cause them to lose people in the detail or miss the overall point
- objectivity may be perceived as detached and inflexible
- may care more about showing how knowledgeable they are than winning hearts and minds.

Depending on which type/s you're also dominant in, if you are a Wise Owl you may need to develop in the following areas:

- establishing personal authority
- building goodwill
- arousing enthusiasm and passion.

Type 2: The Commanding Eagle

Eagles are large, powerful birds of prey. They have been a symbol of power for centuries — as far back as Bible times, the imagery of an eagle was used to portray God's power. Eagles are often found on state flags. The bald eagle is a majestic species that is a sign of great strength and power and is the symbol of the United States. As the philosopher Matchona Dhliwayo says, 'An eagle earns its honour from the storms it endures'. In other words, Commanding Eagles have done this before, they are the most experienced, and you can trust that they know the best way forward.

Eagles balance certainty and self-assurance with gracefulness, and they are both honourable and proud. When they choose a partner, it's 'till death do us part'. Commanding Eagles have personal authority and can be relied upon to get the task done. When their 'nest' is damaged or destroyed, the Commanding Eagle gets a sense of urgency and will work around the clock to exceed expectations. Eagles don't let their need for food overrule their tactical thinking and cunning abilities, and Commanding Eagles in the workplace and in other situations can behave with similar focus. At work, they lead by example and will do what it takes to excel.

When eagles are courting, they don't just soar around on the thermals (the upward currents of warm air). Instead, they perform a spectacular, plummeting courtship ritual where they tumble and free fall — they own the sky!

How does the Commanding Eagle persuade?

The Commanding Eagle has an innate drive to persuade by conveying personal authority. They are thought of as commanding because they are assertive and imposing, and inspire confidence.

The following traits are typical of the Commanding Eagle:

- *Articulate:* Expressing beliefs and feelings easily and clearly.

- *Assertive:* Speaking up for beliefs or wants.

- *Authoritative:* Confident and deserving of respect as a source of information, advice and expertise.

- *Believable:* Perceived as real or true.

- *Commanding:* Has authority and demands attention.

- *Composed:* Calm and in control of emotions.

- *Confident:* Being sure of oneself.

- *Credible:* Believed and trusted.

- *Experienced:* Having knowledge and skill through having done something many times.

- *Expert:* A high level of knowledge and skill in a discipline.

- *Forceful:* Expressing opinions strongly and demanding attention or action.

- *Honourable:* Having high principles and doing what's right.

- *Imposing:* Appearing important, stately or grandiose.

- *Respected:* Being admired for one's qualities or achievements.

- *Trustworthy:* Seen as reliable, honest, believable and credible.

The following behaviours are consistent with the Commanding Eagle:

- argues that action should be taken because it is right or wrong based on value or principle

- does not shy away from difficult issues

- draws on examples, analogies and stories to prove expertise

- expresses views forcefully

- is calm under pressure

- self-promotes naturally

- strives to be seen as a subject-matter expert

- uses an authoritative, confident, commanding tone of voice.

Their catchphrases are:

- 'I've done this before and you should just believe me.'

- 'I know more about this than you do.'

- 'You can trust me. Just go with me on this.'

Possible weaknesses for the Commanding Eagle are:

- may care more about doing things their way than building rapport

- tends to be dominant and take over

- can be critical of less experienced people's ideas

- may be thought of as arrogant

- may be described as didactic, impatient and condescending.

Depending on which type/s you're also dominant in, if you are a Commanding Eagle you may need to develop in the following areas:

- establishing the credibility of the message

- building goodwill

- arousing enthusiasm and passion.

Type 3: The Friendly Budgie

'Budgie' is the nickname for a budgerigar — a small, long-tailed, seed-eating parrot and very common household pet. (The same bird is also known in some parts of the world as a parakeet.)

Scientists study some obscure and fascinating things! Prior to 2015, scientists believed that three species (other than humans) experienced that thing called contagious yawning. You know where you see your friend yawning and you yawn too? The three other species were chimpanzees, dogs and lab rats. Then in 2015 an article in the *Animal Cognition* scientific journal reported that budgies also experience contagious yawning. And, importantly, scientists believe that the budgies are not just matching and mirroring or mimicking the physical act of opening the mouth in a yawn. In fact, they are experiencing a deep emotional connection and empathetic feelings towards the other budgie that causes them to yawn, even when not together in the same cage. Budgies like to live in groups and need the company of other budgies. They prefer to live in large flocks in the wild. In some areas after it rains, you're likely to see very large flocks, numbering occasionally in the tens of thousands, socialising and chatting away with each other! Budgies are the heavy hitters of rapport building.

In the workplace and in other social situations, you'll notice the Friendly Budgies going out for lunch, standing around laughing with people in the corridor and generally participating with others. As behavioural scientist Steve Maraboli argues, 'Don't wait for other people to be loving, giving, compassionate, grateful, forgiving, generous, or friendly ... lead the way!' Friendly Budgies have definitely taken this advice to heart.

How does the Friendly Budgie persuade?

The Friendly Budgie has an innate drive to persuade by building goodwill. They are thought of as friendly because they are warm and caring, and naturally build rapport with others.

The following traits are typical of the Friendly Budgie:

- *Candid:* Expressing opinions and feelings in an open and honest way.

- *Caring:* Showing compassion and giving emotional support.

- *Conciliatory:* Attempting to gain goodwill, reduce hostility or end a disagreement.

- *Connected:* In a close relationship with someone.

- *Diplomatic:* Using tact to respect others' position and not cause offence.

- *Disarming:* Naturally and convincingly builds rapport with someone who does not expect it.

- *Empathetic:* Able to imagine how someone else feels.

- *Generous:* Liberal in giving or sharing.

- *Genuine:* Sincere and honest, free from pretence.

- *Goodwill:* A kind, friendly and helpful feeling or attitude, approval and support.

- *Interested:* Being engaged by someone or something and wanting to give them special attention.

- *Likeable:* Pleasant, agreeable, pleasing.

- *Open:* Not decided, certain or closed-minded.

- *Respectful:* Showing admiration, politeness, deference.

- *Warm:* Feeling of affection, gratitude and empathy.

The following behaviours are consistent with the Friendly Budgie:

- actively tries to get to know people

- finds ways to help people

- genuinely compliments others

- is non-judgemental and accepting of other people

- quickly builds rapport with most people

- remembers key facts about others

- uses active listening.

Their catchphrases are:

- 'People need to know that I care before they will care about my ideas.'

- 'The more you give, the more you get.'

- 'We're in this together.'

Possible weaknesses for the Friendly Budgie are:

- may be seen as lacking authority

- can be conflict-avoiders

- may lose sight of own goals or needs

- can be seen as a pushover

- may be thought of by others as so friendly they are too good to be true, or insincere.

Depending on which type/s you're also dominant in, if you are a Friendly Budgie you may need to develop in the following areas:

- establishing the credibility of the message

- establishing your personal authority

- arousing enthusiasm and passion.

Type 4: The Captivating Peacock

Peacocks are driven to be captivating. It's their strength. When peacocks are courting, they do everything they can to be persuasive. Some people think the male does the choosing when, in fact, the peahen or female makes the mating decision. So, the peacock must do everything he can to convince the peahen. Scientists have found that when peacocks are in their mating season, they are prone to find any reflective surface they can — including mirrors and even hub caps — where they can check themselves out to make sure that they are looking as sharp as possible! They're certainly keen to put their best talon forward.

And have you seen a peacock in the act of persuading a mate? They don't just fan open their fabulous feathers in a fantastic fashion. They put everything into it. They shimmy, strut and even dance. They are going for it! They're saying, 'I've got to persuade! I've got to persuade! Look at me! Look at me! Pick me! Pick me!' (Their namesake, the Australian native peacock spider, performs an equally energetic dance to persuade its mate.)

Hilariously, peacocks also make a terrible noise when mating. Scientists have worked out that the smart peacocks go around making the same noise all the time, giving the impression they're in high demand! This is a classic example of the influence strategy called *social proof* — where everyone else is doing something and so you do it too. (For example, everyone in your neighbourhood is buying an electric car, you get one too.) In the case of the peacock, the peahen hears the peacock causing this terrible din and making all this commotion and, scientists believe, likely thinks to herself, *He must be a stud. This guy is constantly doing it!* So, the most persuasive peacock gets the prize — and gets to reproduce.

In the workplace and other social situations, Captivating Peacocks display just as much charm and charisma, often putting on a 'show' to build passion and entertain and inspire. The Scottish philosopher David Hume probably put it best for all Captivating Peacocks when he said, 'Eloquence, at its highest pitch, leaves little room for reason or reflection, but addresses itself entirely to the desires and affections, captivating the willing hearers, and subduing their understanding'.

How does the Captivating Peacock persuade?

The Captivating Peacock has an innate drive to persuade by arousing enthusiasm and passion. They are thought of as captivating because they command attention, exude charm, and excite.

The Captivating Peacock has the following distinguishing qualities:

- *Attractive:* Providing pleasure or delight in appearance and manner.

- *Captivating:* Holding attention by being extremely interesting, exciting, pleasant or attractive.

- *Charismatic:* A special quality, appeal or charm that attracts attention and admiration.

- *Charming:* Delights and fascinates others.

- *Confident:* Being sure of oneself.

- *Emphatic:* Communicating in a strong, clear way.

- *Enthusiastic:* Having an energetic interest in something.

- *Expressive:* Full of expression in a way that conveys meaning or feeling.

- *Infectious:* Causing others to take on one's positive emotion and join in.

- *Inspiring:* To arouse positive thoughts and feelings.

- *Interesting:* Holding attention by being unusual, exciting or informative.

- *Magnetic:* Extraordinary power or ability to attract.

- *Optimistic:* Taking a favourable or hopeful view.

- *Outgoing:* Openly friendly, energetic and responsive to others.

The following behaviours are consistent with the Captivating Peacock:

- communicates confidently, dynamically and often dramatically

- derives pleasure from being the centre of attention

- dresses smartly or in a unique way

- overtly expresses emotions such as passion, excitement and joy

- socialises easily in gatherings

- tells memorable stories to entertain and inspire

- uses an expressive, animated communication style.

Their catchphrases are:

- 'All the world's a stage.'

- 'I'm passionate about this. You should be too.'

- 'Go BIG or go home!'

Possible weaknesses for the Charming Peacock are:

- may be seen as melodramatic

- may be seen as superficial

- can be thought of as 'over the top'

- can take too long to get to the point

- may overstate the facts in favour of entertainment.

Depending on which type/s you're also dominant in, if you are a Captivating Peacock you may need to develop in the following areas:

- establishing the credibility of your message

- establishing personal authority

- building goodwill.

How the four types combine credibility and charisma

I've used the four persuasive birds to create my Four Persuasive Types model, shown in figure 5.1 (overleaf). This model highlights three persuasive preferences to explain the similarities and differences between the four persuasive types. These three preferences are:

1. credibility

2. charismatic

3. dominance.

Remember — in the real-world application of the four persuasive types, your approach to persuasion is highly likely to be a blend of your top two or even three types. Rarely can someone score very high on only one of the types. Despite this 'blended' reality, identifying the four types, and where you sit within them, helps you work out your relative strengths and weaknesses, and improve your overall persuasive power.

TIP

Michelle says,

'In the real-world application of the four persuasion types, your approach to persuasion is highly likely to be a blend of your top two or even three types.'

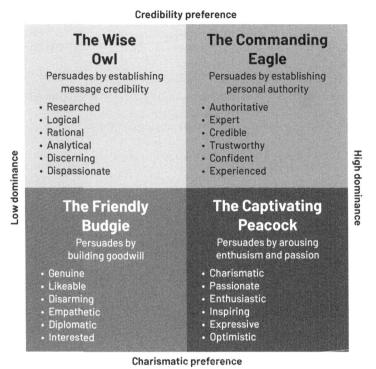

Figure 5.1 The impact of credibility, charisma and dominance within the four persuasive types

Let's consider this combination of credibility, charisma and dominance within the four types. In essence, the Wise Owl and the Commanding Eagle both have a credibility preference, while the Friendly Budgie and the Captivating Peacock have a charismatic preference. The Commanding Eagle and the Captivating Peacock display high dominance, while the Wise Owl and the Friendly Budgie do not rely on dominance.

Here's how the three factors play out within each of the four types in more detail:

- *Credibility preference:* The Wise Owl and the Commanding Eagle prefer to persuade others by establishing strong credibility. For these two types, credibility is critical to persuasiveness. Being credible refers to being trusted, believed and convincing. The Wise Owl is most driven to establish the credibility of their message, while the Commanding Eagle is most driven to establish their personal authority. The Friendly Budgie and the Captivating Peacock do not rely on credibility to persuade others.

- *Charismatic preference:* The Friendly Budgie and the Captivating Peacock are the charismatic types. They are more likely to be extroverted and 'people's people'. For these two types, charisma is critical to persuasiveness. Charisma is the ability to attract the attention and admiration of others and to arouse loyalty and enthusiasm. The Friendly Budgie is most driven to establish a strong connection with others, while the Captivating Peacock is most driven to use their charm. The Wise Owl and the Commanding Eagle do not rely on charisma when attempting to persuade others.

- *Dominance:* A measure of dominance is an excellent way to appreciate the differences between the four types. The Commanding Eagle and the Captivating Peacock both display a high level of dominance in the way they attempt to persuade others, by actively trying to assert control over others. The Commanding Eagle pursues dominance by establishing their personal authority over others, while the Captivating Peacock pursues dominance by being more noticeable and by actively displaying excitement, passion, and enthusiasm. The Wise Owl and the Friendly Budgie are driven to persuade in ways that do not rely on dominating others; in fact, they are inclined to remove the focus from themselves.

Using your strengths and weaknesses

Many of us want to be able to improve the way we communicate with the people around us so that our relationships become easier. Discovering your persuasive strengths, and committing to adapting your persuasion style where necessary, will help improve results in many aspects of your life.

For example, you will see improvements in the way you:

- *Understand yourself:* You will gain an awareness of how you prefer to persuade others as well as how you are most likely persuaded yourself.

- *Sell with greater confidence:* You will be better able to recognise your prospects' preferences. You'll also appreciate the importance of adapting your approach to suit your prospects' persuasion type, to give you the best chance of winning business.

- *Inspire and lead your team:* You will better appreciate the different preferences of your team members. You'll appreciate the importance of adapting your approach to suit your team members' individual needs, and in doing so inspire productivity and commitment to your cause.

- *Improve customer relationships:* You will recognise the persuasive preferences of your customers. You'll appreciate the importance of adapting your approach to suit your customers' needs with the goal of providing excellent customer experiences.

You're not trying to persuade yourself!

Many of us attempt to persuade others in the way that we prefer to be persuaded. This is what feels natural. Remember, though, that people are persuaded in different ways, so you will become more persuasive and improve your 'persuasive reach' when your approach to persuasion is as multi-dimensional as possible.

You'll improve your persuasive skills when you:

- *Know yourself:* You have taken time to learn about your persuasive strengths and weaknesses and the way you like to be persuaded yourself, as well as how you typically try to persuade others.

- *Know others:* We are all persuaded differently. You endeavour to elicit the preferences of your stakeholders. You remember you're not trying to persuade yourself!

- *Become as strong as possible in all four persuasive types:* The most persuasive people are those who are strong in all four types, all the time! You strive to build your strength across all persuasive approaches (not just your current preferences) so you are consistently persuasive all the time, no matter who you are persuading. That way you will be more persuasive with more people.

- *Adapt your approach to meet the needs of your stakeholder:* You know how to extend your persuasive reach and appeal to all four persuasive types through a variety of formulas, actions and techniques. If you elect to just 'wing it' the next time you have what I call a 'soap box' moment — where you must consciously persuade someone — you'll tend to adopt the approach that would work on you or that feels natural to you, not the actual approach you should be using to get the outcomes you are seeking.

TIP

Michelle says,

'People are persuaded in different ways, so you will become more persuasive and improve your 'persuasive reach' when your approach to persuasion is as multi-dimensional as possible.'

When you understand and master all of these considerations, you will become what I call Persuasion Smart. For more information on being Persuasion Smart, head to my website. While you're there, you can also check out the Persuasion Smart Profile — the psychological assessment tool I developed to assess and then report on your current persuasive strengths and weaknesses. Just go to shop.michellebowden.com.au/products/persuasion-smart-profile.

Dan's story

Dan is a technical expert in his field and is a highly logical and rational thinker. He is less competent in building relationships, connecting with others and motivating people to feel compelled to support his cause. Dan mistakenly thinks that his colleagues will all be persuaded by being presented with the relative data and facts — in other words, in the same way as he is. The truth is that they may or may not be persuaded in the same way as Dan. Should Dan decide to develop his ability to use means other than his preferred approach, he'll likely find he is more consistently persuasive with more people and in more and varied situations.

Becoming aware of your persuasion strengths and weaknesses will place you in a better position to maximise your persuasiveness. You will be more persuasive overall if you can appeal to all four persuasive types by incorporating all four approaches in your persuasive efforts.

Reflect for a moment on which of the types represent your strengths and which represent your weaknesses.

Decide if you'd like to strengthen your strengths or tackle your weaknesses.

Once you have made that decision, go straight to the relevant chapter in part II and begin your journey of growth.

TOP TIPS
The four persuasive types

- For someone to be persuaded, they must be given answers based on their own 'key persuasion indicators' or KPIs. These KPIs can be broken into four sets.

- The four sets of KPIs led to the development of the four persuasive types: the Wise Owl, the Commanding Eagle, the Friendly Budgie and the Captivating Peacock.

- Most of us give preference to one, two or maybe even three of these persuasive types when we are being persuaded, and tend to persuade others in the way that we ourselves would be persuaded.

- Remember – you are not trying to persuade yourself!

- If you want to be more persuasive with more people, you need to appeal to all four persuasive types, not just the ones you favour. You need to work out the other person's preferences and adapt your approach to deliver your message in the way they need to hear it.

PART II

Understanding the types and working out which one to use when

CHAPTER 6

Type 1: The Wise Owl

So, you'd like to build more of the Wise Owl into your persuasive approach. Maybe this is because the Wise Owl type isn't your strength. Maybe someone you have to persuade often — such as a manager, team member or even family member — is predominantly a Wise Owl and you want to persuade in the way that best works for them. Or maybe the Wise Owl is your strength, but you'd like to enhance your persuasiveness by establishing undeniable message credibility. Maybe you're following the wise words of peace campaigner and Nobel Peace Prize recipient Desmond Tutu: 'Don't raise your voice; improve your argument'.

The Wise Owl is one of the credibility types and they are thought of as wise because they are logical and analytical, and they communicate robust, well-founded arguments. This chapter is devoted to helping you learn, develop or cement how to do this. Firstly, let's look at why message credibility is so important.

The importance of message credibility

Message credibility means your stakeholder approves of your content and believes that what you are saying is true. This is an essential part of the persuasive process. Without it, the other person won't trust you or take the action you require.

Message credibility is the level of veracity and accuracy of your content, and it relies on a well-structured and logical argument. Someone with message credibility covers all angles and issues, delivers a dispassionate portrayal of the facts, and communicates their thorough analysis and logic clearly. Their message is undeniable. A Wise Owl who has message credibility backs up their arguments with facts and research and uses technical terms and jargon. Wise Owls are calm and measured in their delivery and they generally care more about showing how undeniable the argument is than about winning hearts and minds.

TIP

Michelle says,

'Without message credibility, the other person may not trust you or take the action you require.'

Ensuring message credibility

You can take several actions to ensure that you bring out your inner Wise Owl and convey the credibility of your message. They are:

- Structure your message so it resonates and sticks.
- Use external proof to support and strengthen your message.
- Use rhetorical questions to signpost your content.
- Don't use fluffy language that is ambiguous and distracting.
- Add power words to liven up your argument.
- Limit your options.
- Use numbered lists.
- Use your visual aids brilliantly to captivate and convince.
- Package your numbers.
- Rehearse until you can't get it wrong.

The following sections in this chapter take you through the detail of each of these actions so you can make these your new (or stronger) habits.

Structure your message so it resonates and sticks

Wouldn't it be amazing to be able to pitch any idea so that it sticks in the other person's mind, and they feel compelled to take the action you require? The good news is that in 1979 Dr Bernice McCarthy, an award-winning teacher, invented the 4MAT System, which you can use to structure your argument when persuading (in person or in writing) so that you do just that — compel people to action.

Understanding the 4MAT System

We know that when we are persuading other people they take in information differently, learn differently and form opinions quite differently to each other, and often differently to us. The 4MAT learning styles model that McCarthy invented takes all the different learning styles into account and ensures that you present your information in a logical, well-structured way. Following this model makes it easier for your stakeholder or prospect to absorb your argument piece by piece until they are ultimately convinced. This model also ensures that you address all the elements of an important argument, not just the parts of the argument that are interesting to you!

Remember — you're not trying to persuade yourself. You are aiming to persuade your stakeholder. Therefore, it's important that you cover all the issues and angles in a way that makes sense to them, not necessarily in the way that would make sense to you.

The 4MAT System recognises that if people are to sit up and listen and then take the action you require, you need to answer four key questions.

These questions are:

1. *Why?* The person needs to clarify the context and rationale.

2. *What?* The person needs to identify the detail of the message.

3. *How?* The person needs to explore how to use and apply the information.

4. *What if?* and *What else?* The person needs to know the alternatives for the new information so they can modify, adapt and create new contexts. They also need to know what will happen if they don't take the action you are suggesting.

The 4MAT System is a commonsense approach that is incredibly effective for structuring a persuasive message. If you are keen to know more, I cover this model more thoroughly in my first book *How to Present: The ultimate guide to presenting your ideas and influencing people using techniques that actually work* (also published by Wiley).

Applying the 4MAT System using the Persuasion Blueprint

I've been teaching people how to best structure their communication for over three decades, and everyone I work with loves the logic of the four questions in the 4MAT System. Unfortunately, often a bit of confusion still creeps in! People can still sometimes be unclear about when to say the things they need to say. So, in 2006 I came up with another model that sits over the top of the 4MAT System to help you use this best-practice model more effectively. I call my model the Persuasion Blueprint.

The Persuasion Blueprint combines all the key elements of a persuasive communication and helps you know exactly what to say, with precision, accuracy and linguistic mastery, in the right spots and at the right time.

The following sections outline the steps in my Persuasion Blueprint so you can truly enhance your message credibility.

STEP 0: THE ICEBREAKER

Hook the person's attention with an icebreaker. Icebreakers are delivered in the first 30 seconds of the conversation. The objective of the icebreaker is to wake the person up, so they are sitting up in their chair (literally or figuratively) and excited to hear more from you. Why is it listed as step 0? Because this step is not always necessary. It's an option for you if needed.

STEP 1: BUILD RAPPORT

People need to know how much you care about their needs before you tell them all about yourself and explain your key points. Use statements that are inclusive in nature and reflect to your audience what they already know to be true. Use the words you say at this step to show empathy for your stakeholder's situation. For example, 'We know that...', 'You'd agree that...' or 'You have mentioned that you're interested in...'

The important thing about this step is that you must reflect what the other person already knows to be true, not what you want them to know. The role of this step is to get them nodding because you are saying something that they know and agree with.

STEP 2: LEAD THE AUDIENCE

A leading statement is your key message, or the main thing you are persuading about in this meeting, email or conversation. Leading statements often have contentious words in them such as, 'It is essential that you...', 'We must...' or 'You need to...'

STEP 3: MOTIVATE

Persuasive people know that their stakeholder isn't always intrinsically motivated to listen. It's your job to motivate your stakeholders to lean in and listen. This step is where you explain what's in it for them to listen to and apply your argument or ideas. Remember also that some people are motivated by the metaphorical stick (or risk), whereas others are motivated by the metaphorical carrot (the reward). This means it's a clever idea to tell your stakeholder what they will reduce, maintain and improve. In this way, you'll motivate the person whether they are motivated by a stick or a carrot.

STEP 4: MANAGE OBJECTIONS

In this step, you address all the key objections that the person has about you, your content or the timing of this message. You deal with them now so that people can relax and listen to the rest of your message.

A clever way to do this is follow the following five-step objection-handling technique:

1. *State the objection that the person is thinking or expressing:* For example, 'I know you are concerned about...'

2. *Say 'and' or 'so' or pause:* Don't say 'but' or 'however'. These words activate the limbic system — your stakeholder's fight or flight response. Instead, use an inoffensive, unemotive joining word such as 'and' or 'so', or pause and say nothing.

3. *Use the words 'actually' or 'in fact' to make the idea seem more convincing:* For example, 'You may be concerned about cost and, in fact...'

4. *Offer your solution:* Where possible, make sure that your solution is the opposite of the problem. And make sure the solution is an actual solution to the problem.

5. *Use the word 'because':* 'Because' is the most powerfully persuasive word in the world! Why is this? Because it's human nature to need explanations. (See what I did there?!) People like to have reasons for what they do. We need to know why. When we ask for something, we will be more successful if use the word 'because' and provide a reason. According to research from Dr Robert Cialdini (the self-styled 'Godfather of Influence'), people are 34 per cent more likely to be persuaded if we include the 'because' and the reason in our argument rather than leave it out.

The word 'because' has transformed every facet of my life — from my client relationships to my personal relationships, to my ability to close deals, and my overall persuasiveness as a passionate educator. I recommend you start trying it too. Use 'because' to link your idea, your pitch or your argument to the action you want your customer, colleague or prospect to take, and they will be more compelled to take the action you require.

TRY THIS

Think about an upcoming objection you need to handle. It might be via email, or within a proposal, phone call, virtual meeting or pitch.

Aim to use the five-step objection handling technique to resolve the matter. Be sure to say 'because' and then give the best reason you can think of to manage the objection and persuade your stakeholder to your way of thinking.

Using 'because' allows you to show why something works, or what your customer or prospect will get out of your idea. And it gets results.

Remember — people who don't know why, don't buy. So give them a why, dissolve their objections and watch them buy — whether that's your product, your service or your next big idea!

TIP

Michelle says,

'Without knowing 'why?', people don't buy. So give them the why and watch them buy!'

STEP 5: SET THE GROUND RULES

Here you set out all the rules and boundaries for the meeting, so everything runs as smoothly as possible. For example, you can explain what's happening in the meeting, who is speaking, who else is there, when to ask questions and anything else people need to know to relax and pay attention.

The first time you establish the ground rules this late in your opening comments, it will feel a bit late in the process. I promise that if you do this a few times, it will eventually seem natural, and your stakeholders will thank you for it. This is a much better point at which to set the rules, rather than at the start of a meeting or proposal. Use steps 0 to 4 to build rapport, and then set the rules once everyone is listening.

Note: Steps 0 to 5 form the *Why?* of the 4MAT System.

STEP 6: THE WHAT?

Now it's time to deliver your actual content. Start with the big picture, and then narrow down your explanation and give the detail. Include the facts and statistics and any research findings that back up your proposal.

Handy tip: *Don't start your sentences with, 'There is' or 'There are'. Weak sentences start in this way. Instead, get to the point, use the real subject, and start there.*

For example, compare the following two sentences, and notice how much stronger the second sentence is through not starting with 'there are':

- 'There are a number of people in both teams who strongly disagree with the proposed implementation timeline.'

- 'Operations and Marketing strongly disagree with the proposed implementation timeline.'

STEP 7: THE HOW?

In this step, you explain the steps and application. When you are in the *How?* section of your Persuasion Blueprint, it's important to note that some people need you to number your suggested actions or steps, while others don't care one way or the other. (For more help in this area, see the section 'Use numbered lists', later in this chapter.)

Handy tip: Use short sentences. In this busy life we lead, no-one has the time or the interest to read or listen to long cumbersome sentences. Aim to use short, clear sentences. As a rule, I suggest writing the sentence, then re-reading and editing to reduce waffle.

STEP 8: OTHER INFORMATION

This is the place to add any of those extra little bits of content that might add to your persuasiveness and that don't fit anywhere else! Include those important things you want to say that would distract the person from your key points if you mentioned them any earlier. This section often starts with something like, 'By the way...' You can also add here that it's been your pleasure to speak with these people today and give your contact details if you want.

STEP 9: THE SUMMARY

Sadly, most people have often forgotten your key messages by the time you get to the end of your conversation or meeting. You can use this step to remind the person of the three key messages from your meeting or proposal. Information is best remembered and then repeated to people who were not in attendance at your meetings and conversations when you deliver it in the rhythm of three. I suggest you add one point from the *Why?*, one point from the *What?* and one point from the *How?* sections of your Persuasion Blueprint.

> **TIP**
>
> **Michelle says,**
>
> 'Information is best remembered and then repeated to people who were not in attendance at your meetings and conversations when you deliver it in the rhythm of three.'

STEP 10: CALL TO ACTION

The whole reason you are persuading is to achieve an outcome — that is, to shift the other person from where they are to where you want them to be. This step is where you ask for what you want. Your call to action should be clear, direct and explicit, and encourages a yes/no response. Examples include, 'I respectfully request that you endorse this recommendation' and 'Please endorse the proposed solution and recommendations by 30 November'.

STEP 11: Q&A

If you are an interactive communicator and like people to ask questions throughout your meeting or conversation, then by all means allow that. If you prefer to have a more formal slot for your Q&A in your meetings, I recommend you insert the Q&A at step 11 of the Persuasion Blueprint. Be sure not to finish with a Q&A session because doing so often means people may not leave with your key messages in their minds. Do the Q&A here and then make sure that — whichever way the Q&A goes — you, the persuader, can ensure that the final word is driving towards the outcome.

STEP 12: NEGATIVE AND POSITIVE CONSEQUENCES

In this step, you remind the other person what happens if they don't do what you've asked, and then what happens when they do. Use the words 'if' and 'when' so you are as persuasive as possible. For example, 'If you don't approve the funding then ... and when you do ...'

STEP 13: CLOSING STATEMENT

You're nearly there! The final thing to do is ensure you end with a 'sizzle'! A closing statement is short, punchy and sells the sizzle of your message. It doesn't call your stakeholder to action (because most people don't love the hard sell and you don't want them to describe you as 'pushy'). A closing statement is an exciting statement that indicates you are at the end and makes the other person feel great. For example, 'This is an exciting opportunity for us to ...'

Handy tip: *Your closing statement should always link to your opening.*

Note: Steps 8 to 13 form the *What if?* and *What else?* part of the 4MAT System.

The following case study provides an example of a full Persuasion Blueprint in the business world.

Alice's story

Alice is a combination Wise Owl/Commanding Eagle client of mine who works in data intelligence and analytics. Alice needed to persuade her colleagues to perform root cause analysis more often because, in her Wise Owl opinion, it was not something they were doing enough. Alice organised a virtual meeting to discuss the matter and persuade her colleagues. And the good news? This message was so well structured, interactive and compelling that her colleagues agreed with her during the meeting. They now perform more regular root cause analyses in the course of their daily work — a win–win for Alice, her colleagues and their business.

The following outlines how Alice used the Persuasion Blueprint to structure her message.

Step number	Step name	Statement
Step 0	Icebreaker	During the 1990s, the US government discovered that several of their large national monuments were falling apart. In May 1990, a 50-pound block of marble fell many metres from one of the Jefferson memorial columns and hit the ground, shattering upon impact. Thankfully, no-one was injured. After some investigation, it was found long-term monument deterioration could be reduced simply by turning the memorial lights on 30 minutes later each day!
		Today we're going to explore how this unlikely solution to save these historic buildings demonstrates the importance of understanding a problem's root cause here in our business. Let's discover how we can apply some simple patterns to quickly arrive at a root cause and leave today with an understanding of how determining root causes can make your work more efficient.

(continued)

Step number	Step name	Statement
Step 1	Build rapport: Inclusive statement	Most of us realise that we can't solve problems permanently without understanding their cause.
Step 1	Build rapport: Inclusive statement	Working solely on the symptoms usually won't fix the problem.
Step 1	Build rapport: Inclusive statement	We'd love to reduce the amount of duplication in our work.
Step 2	Leading statement	Every problem has a root cause, and it's our job to find it if we want to be more productive.
Step 3	Motivate: Reduce, maintain and improve	Let's work out a solution to minimise duplicate issues, maintain a stable environment and improve our efficiency.
Step 4	Manage objections: 'I'm too busy'	I understand you have tight SLAs [service-level agreements] that make you too busy – *pause* – and, in fact, finding a root cause will actually allow you to save more time overall, because fixing the problem will mean you won't have to deal with the symptoms again.
Step 5	Set ground rules	• Cameras on • Microphones unmuted Agenda: • Today's presentation will cover two patterns of root cause analysis you can use every day. • We will have an opportunity to apply the patterns to some example problems and for you to ask questions. Expectations • You will be expected to display a level of competency going forward, so ask questions today if needed.

Step number	Step name	Statement
Step 6	What?	• [Alice would delve into the detail of the following points here.]
		• What is a root cause?
		• What is root cause analysis?
		• What is a problem?
Step 7	How?	• [Alice would delve into the detail of the following points here.]
		• The 5 Whys method of root cause analysis (works well with single causes).
		• The Fishbone Diagram method of root cause analysis (works well with branched causes).
		• Practical application examples.
		• Applying these methods to the national monument problem in the icebreaker.
Step 8	Other information	By the way, other methods are available, and we could talk through some of them at a later stage.
Step 8	My pleasure	It's been my pleasure to present this session today. We've had some valuable insights into how root cause analysis can help our team reduce duplication, save time and fix problems permanently.
Step 8	Contact details	Please reach out to me after this session if you need any further help or information.
Step 9	Summary: Why?	Root causes help us avoid only dealing with symptoms, and instead allow us to fix problems permanently and minimise duplication.
Step 9	Summary: What?	Every problem has a root cause.

(continued)

Step number	Step name	Statement
Step 9	Summary: How?	We've been 'armed' with two methods to find root causes for ourselves.
Step 10	Call to action	When you return to work, it is essential that you use what you've learnt today to find root causes for every problem you encounter.
Step 11	Q&A	I'm interested in your questions; for example, you may have a question about problems with multiple root causes or other aspects of what we've covered today. Or your question may even be about what to do if the root cause is outside your control.
		Who would like to start?
		What questions do you have?
Step 12	Negative consequence ('if')	If we don't determine root causes, we're bound to continue treating the symptoms of problems day after day without ever actually fixing the underlying problem.
		How annoying!
Step 12	Positive consequence ('when')	When we determine root causes, we have a real opportunity to make meaningful changes that stop problems from occurring, permanently!
Step 13	Closing statement	You now have an exciting opportunity to apply the root cause analysis methods you've learnt today to every problem you come across. From saving national monuments to fixing broken servers, applying these skills will set you apart as a person who can get to the root of a problem quickly and fix it permanently.

Can you alter the order of the steps?

Yes, of course! If you've completed a thorough stakeholder analysis and you know that your prospect needs to hear the points in a different order, then follow your instincts. I present them in this order because this is the way most stakeholders need to hear an argument.

I am very proud of this model, and I recommend you use it in all your communication moments, particularly when you need to persuade.

Use external proof to strengthen your message

Facts, statistics, quotes and subject matter experts strengthen your message through adding external proof that your argument is justified and to be believed. Any opinions that you offer will always be seen as more believable if you use external proof. External proof verifies that you've done your research, you thoroughly understand the topic, and your points of view or assertions are based on logic and facts rather than emotion or subjective opinions. As US sales trainer and coach Jack Malcolm highlights, 'When everyone else is relying on vague, unsupported emotional appeals, those who state their case calmly, but with airtight confidence based on a tenacious grasp of the evidence, can stand out because hardly anyone does it anymore'.

Let's look at how you can use external proof.

Facts

A fact is a piece of information that is known to be true. Wikipedia explains that 'facts are independent of belief and of knowledge and opinion'. Facts include data, trends and forecasts, research and points of interest that can be proved to be accurate.

You — like the Wise Owl — can use facts to back up your point at any part of your message. Be sure to only use facts from appropriate and reliable sources to strengthen your message credibility.

Brian's story

Brian works as a data analyst in a large corporation. He needed to persuade some people in his company to change a process. Of course, the actual meeting went for around 30 minutes. Nevertheless, here's a quick example of one of the ways Brian used facts to help his stakeholders believe his argument.

At the very start of his meeting, Brian said,

> *Did you know that our data analysts have been spending an average of three days every month just validating the financials? This is three days that could have been better spent on proper insight analysis, or even critical data modelling tasks. It's good to see you today. I am Brian. Today let's go through a workable solution to solve this waste of time.*

No sensible person could argue with the logic of this argument! Irrefutable facts helped Brian get his approval for the process change.

What facts can you add to your next conversation?

Statistics

The Wise Owl uses statistics to make their argument undeniable. Statistics are numbers or patterns that are used as external proof to give your message credibility. They help your prospect or stakeholder believe what you are saying. They are also used to prove that you know what you are talking about and can be trusted.

Statistics can go anywhere in your message — the start, middle or finish. Be sure to only use statistics from appropriate and reliable sources to strengthen your message credibility.

Niina's story

Niina is a gorgeous client of mine who had to deliver an important presentation to all the staff in her business about the importance of participating in RUOK day. RUOK is a suicide prevention charity in Australia that encourages all of us to notice the signs of mental health struggle in friends, family and colleagues. RUOK have created a day every year where they ask people to check in with their colleagues and friends with a simple question: 'RUOK?'

Niina needed to persuade everyone in her business to sign up for the day and participate wholeheartedly. This was a cause very close to Niina's heart, but she realised that not everyone was as naturally emotionally connected to it. To be honest, some people didn't want to participate at all. Niina realised that she needed some emotionally evocative statistics to bring her message to life and enhance her message credibility.

Here's what Niina said,

> In the last four weeks the daily call volumes at Lifeline [Australia's main crisis line] hit record highs due to stress and anxiety in our population. Over this time, 96 273 calls were taken, which is an increase of 33.1 per cent from the same period in 2019. We can see that people are struggling.

No sensible person could argue with Niina's statistics. The number of people reporting feelings of anxiety has increased significantly in recent times, and we all should check in with our colleagues to make sure they are indeed okay. Niina's use of statistics helped make her argument undeniable – and, yes, people threw themselves wholeheartedly into RUOK day in Niina's company. Win–win!

TRY THIS

What statistics can you add to your next conversation?

Quotes

Quotes are an excellent way to bring your content to life, to elicit an emotional response and to reinforce that you know what you are taking about. They are used by the Wise Owl as part of 'social proof' — which is where someone clever thinks *xyz*, so you should think it too! Quotes prove your message is backed by other people's opinions too.

Handy tip: *Always remember to attribute the quote.*

Quotes can go anywhere in your message — the start, middle or finish. Be sure to only use quotes from appropriate and impressive sources to strengthen your message credibility. If you're keen to find relevant quotes for your subject area, try searching for the subject matter you are persuading about with the word 'quote' after it in your preferred search engine.

For example, if you search for 'quotes about quotes' you may find the following from author Joseph Geran III: 'The beauty of quotes is that they allow us to glimpse into other minds and understand how they think and look at the world'.

Alasdair's story

Alasdair is a wonderful client of mine who works in the IT industry. He regularly pitches for huge deals. In one of his many pitches, he said the following to add credibility to his message:

> There's a saying from a 1902 edition of *Puck* magazine that goes, 'People who say it cannot be done should not interrupt those who are doing it'.

This quote was used to give credibility to the fact that Alasdair's company is very experienced at the work they were pitching for. The implication was that Alasdair's client should award his company the work because they already have the runs on the board, so to speak. They are the undeniable choice for this opportunity because they have done this before with great success. Yes, they won the pitch!

TRY THIS

What quote can you add to your next conversation? Type a keyword followed by the word 'quote' in your preferred search engine to help you search for relevant quotes.

Subject matter experts

Subject matter experts or SMEs are people considered thought leaders in their industry. They are the 'go-to' person for the subject at hand. Mentioning the name of these people in your persuasive moment gives your message credibility by association. Quoting other experts also shows that you are prepared and reinforces your claims because someone else shares the same sentiment.

Quoting a subject matter expert can go anywhere in your message — the start, middle or finish. I most commonly see this used successfully in the *What?* and *How?* sections of my Persuasion Blueprint (covered earlier in this chapter). Be sure to only use quotes from appropriate and impressive SMEs to strengthen your message credibility.

Michael's story

Michael McQueen is a multi-award-winning speaker and trend forecaster. Professional speakers are generally very good at using quotes and referring to other subject matter experts in their field to give weight to their claims and inspire their audiences — and Michael is no exception. In one of his persuasive articles, he refers to a Professor of Business from a prestigious university to back up his own assertions about innovation.

(continued)

Michael writes,

> When it comes to innovation, I recall a quote by former business professor at the University of San Francisco Oren Harari, 'The electric light did not come from the continuous improvement of candles' ... Companies cannot reach the innovations of tomorrow while holding onto the assumptions of yesterday.

You can see here that the fact that Professor Harari believes this to be true implies that Michael is also to be believed in his assertions. This quote by a respected thought leader adds value and credibility to Michael's personal assertions.

TRY THIS

Which subject matter expert can you reference or quote in your next conversation to give your message credibility?

Use rhetorical questions to guide people

We know that people attend our meetings, conversations and business pitches with their heads full of their own thoughts and feelings about the matter being discussed. Getting people to focus on what's important can be difficult. One way to bring them into the room is to signpost your thoughts using rhetorical questions.

A rhetorical question is a question that you ask and then answer straightaway. Using rhetorical questions is a clever engagement tool because as long as the other person is listening when you ask the question, no other thought can coincide in their mind. They can only wonder about the answer to your question.

Let me show you. I say to you, 'Why is this important?' If you are listening when I ask you that, chances are high that the only thing you are wondering right now is, 'Yes, why is this important?' You can see that the rhetorical question directs the thinking of your stakeholder and forces them to only think about the thing you are talking about right now.

How do you use rhetorical questions in persuasion?

A simple way to include rhetorical questions is to use variations of the 4MAT System questions from earlier in this chapter. For example, you could ask any or all of the following:

- Why is this important?
- Why should we do this?
- What's in it for you to approve this idea?
- What is the challenge?
- What is the issue on the table?
- How might we solve this?
- How will we fix this?
- What are the next steps?
- What do we need to do now?
- What if we don't act now?
- What happens once you agree with the proposal to proceed?

David's story

David works in a prestige lighting company. I heard him speak up in a meeting about a fabulous range of lighting called Platek. When he got to the *What?* section of his Persuasion Blueprint, David said, 'What is the Platek range?' And then he answered the question. He asked the question to open his listeners' minds, and then he answered it.

An added bonus of using rhetorical questions is that it also signposts where you're up to in your own mind, so it stops you going off track, or waffling too much. Your stakeholder will thank you for making your message clear and easy to follow.

Handy tip: *Try bolding and/or underlining your rhetorical questions in your written communication. This helps to further signpost your data and improves the flow of information. It makes it easier for your stakeholder to work out what your key points are in your writing, and it ultimately makes you more persuasive.*

Eliminate fluffy language

Have you ever put a great deal of thought into the 'best' way to say something, only to have the conversation completely backfire on you? Perhaps you even created a dispute that you did not foresee? In this situation, you likely found yourself reeling. You might have thought something like, *How did that happen when I had such good intentions?* We know that unless we are super clear when we speak, it's very possible that the other person can derive a completely different meaning from our words than we intended. Even when we try to speak as clearly as possible, people can very easily misunderstand our meaning and intentions. One of the biggest contributors to misunderstandings in persuasion is the use of what I call 'fluffy language'.

Our different life experiences determine how we read the meaning of someone's communication. Fluffy language occurs when you use a noun, verb, generalisation, rule and/or comparator in a way that could be misunderstood by your stakeholder. For example, you may say, 'Five of those are resting on the shelf'. The questions here might be, 'five of what?' and, 'on which shelf are they resting?' In practice, most of us don't inquire further when someone uses fluffy language — we just guess what we think the person means, which can lead to all sorts of misunderstandings and confusion.

Let me share a story of my own here. Many years ago, I was annoyed at my husband. I visited a relationship counsellor to vent. (Read:

tell her all about how frustrating he was!) The counsellor was very patient. She listened to me rant and rave for some time. I said, 'I just need more help' and 'I need more support'. You get the drift. And when I ran out of steam, she was very brief and clear with her words. She said to me, 'I have one thing to say to you. Just one thing. Men can't read your mind. If you want help with the garbage, you need to ask specifically for it. Don't just say, "I need more help". Explain clearly — more help with what, when and how? Your requests haven't been clear. If you want backup and support from your husband when you set a rule for your children to follow, you need to ask clearly and specifically for Ian to both support your decision, and to articulate his support to the children, so they know both parents agree with the rule. This means Ian will be very clear about what you need, and he can make an informed choice about whether to help or support at that time. Your husband needs to understand your specific request, or he won't know what action to take'.

The counsellor's message was simple and powerful, and the very good news is that I've been married for another 18 happy years since then. She was right, of course. Men can't read your mind — and it's not just men. No-one can read your mind! For this reason, ambiguity in communication can be troublesome. The clearer you can be when you speak and write, the more persuasive you'll be.

Avoiding fluffy language

To avoid using fluffy language, train yourself to be as clear and specific as possible when you speak or write. Read over emails before you send them. Ensure you remove or qualify any words that may be misconstrued. If you do this with your written communication, it will eventually become your habit when you speak.

Here are some extra tips for avoiding fluffy language:

- *Nouns:* If you spot a fluffy noun, ask yourself, 'which [noun] specifically? For example, 'Are you going to eat that?' might become, 'Are you going to eat the last piece of pizza in this box?

- *Verbs:* If you notice yourself writing or saying a fluffy verb, replace it with a stronger or clearer verb. For example, say you said, 'Let's get the February monthly board report done by the weekend'. Ask yourself, 'What do I mean by "done"?' This sentence also has a fluffy noun: 'weekend'. You could ask yourself, 'Which weekend?' In this case, you'd change the sentence to, 'Can you please finalise the February monthly board report by 5 pm Friday this week?' Here's another example. Say you write in an email, 'Just checking in to see if we will proceed?' You can see that this question assumes the reader knows what you're talking about. How many emails do you receive in a day? And is it possible that you get busy and forget things? In many cases, the reader of this email would know broadly what you're talking about, but they'd have to look up the specifics about what you were doing together and when you were doing it. The clearer you can make your emails, the more likely you'll encourage your reader to respond rather than leave your email half read. So, instead, you should say something like, 'I'm emailing you to check whether you are ready to confirm our Persuasive Masterclass on 2–3 June at your training venue in Sydney?'

- *Generalisations:* If you spot a fluffy generalisation such as 'never', 'always', 'everyone', 'all', 'they', it's wise to double-check that the generalisation you are using is correct. For example, if you noticed you had written, 'Everyone has asked for the performance appraisal template to change', you could ask yourself, 'Everyone?' After more consideration, you might change the sentence to 'Eight out of 10 of the executives in our business have asked for the performance appraisal template to include an opening paragraph explaining the purpose of the document'.

- *Rules:* If you spot a fluffy rule such as 'should', 'shouldn't', 'must', 'have to', or 'can't', it's a good idea to work out if the rule is legitimate before saying it or writing it. One way to challenge yourself on fluffy rules is to ask yourself, 'What would happen if we did?' and 'What would happen if we didn't?' For example, say you used the rule 'We shouldn't go across the NSW–Victorian border in December'. What would happen if you did? If you still want to say this sentence in this way, you might need to also provide a justification so you retain your message credibility. As another example, say you write in an email, 'We have to postpone this project for now'. To challenge yourself on this fluffy rule, you could ask, 'What would happen if we didn't postpone?', 'What would happen if we did postpone?' and 'What other evidence will I need to prove this is the right way forward at this time?

- *Comparators:* A fluffy comparator is a word without a specific antecedent — for example, 'It's going to be easier for everyone if...' In this example of a fluffy comparator, check that you have used the correct word by asking yourself, 'Easier than what?' Once you notice it's a fluffy comparator, you could change the sentence to be, 'Fred will be able to focus his full effort on his integration project if we hire someone with five years coding experience and the new hire can start in the job without needing Fred's training'. You can see this is much clearer than the previous sentence.

TRY THIS

Can you bust the fluff in the language presented here?

- We should make that decision soon.
- Our sales are up.
- I know you think that.
- They say you can't trust her.
- We need to get that done ASAP.
- We can't do that.
- That candidate is the best one for the job.

You can see that holding yourself accountable for the words you choose to say takes a bit of effort. If you plan to focus on removing fluffy language for 63 days (yes, it takes 63 days to form a new habit) you'll notice that your communication is clearer than before you read this book. Clear communication is an essential element of message credibility and crucial when persuading a Wise Owl.

TIP

Michelle says,

'Clear communication is an essential element of message credibility and crucial when persuading a Wise Owl.'

Add power words to liven up your argument

Power words are persuasive and descriptive words that trigger an emotional response in the other person. They help make your statements stronger and they cause people to feel something that prompts them to act now. Try to use relevant power words in your communication to increase the strength of your message and your overall persuasiveness.

Table 6.1 shows some examples of power words.

Table 6.1 Power words

Abated	Addressed	Coordinated
Abbreviated	Awarded	Corrected
Abolished	Balanced	Counselled
Abridged	Bargained	Created
Absolved	Benchmarked	Critiqued
Absorbed	Benefited	Cultivated
Accelerated	Budgeted	Customised
Acclimated	Built	Dealt
Accompanied	Calculated	Debated
Accomplished	Canvassed	Debugged
Achieved	Captured	Decentralised
Acquired	Categorised	Decreased
Acted	Challenged	Deferred
Activated	Changed	Defined
Actuated	Commissioned	Delivered
Adapted	Committed	Demonstrated
Added	Convinced	Depreciated

Encouraged	Minimised	Registered
Endorsed	Motivated	Regulated
Enforced	Multiplied	Rehabilitated
Engaged	Negotiated	Reinforced
Exchanged	Nurtured	Safeguarded
Executed	Observed	Salvaged
Exempted	Obtained	Saved
Expanded	Offered	Screened
Expedited	Opened	Secured
Explored	Orchestrated	Segmented
Exposed	Ordered	Selected
Extended	Organised	Separated
Extracted	Oriented	Served
Fabricated	Originated	Signed
Facilitated	Overhauled	Simplified
Fashioned	Participated	Simulated
Gained	Performed	Supplied
Gathered	Persuaded	Supported
Gauged	Pioneered	Surpassed
Generated	Placed	Systematised
Hosted	Planned	Tightened
Identified	Purchased	Trained
Illuminated	Pursued	Transacted
Illustrated	Qualified	Transferred
Implemented	Quantified	Transformed
Improved	Quoted	Uncovered
Improvised	Raised	Underlined
Incorporated	Ranked	Undertook
Increased	Rated	Unearthed
Incurred	Received	Unified
Individualised	Recommended	United
Judged	Reconciled	Updated
Lightened	Recorded	Upgraded
Liquidated	Recovered	Urged
Litigated	Recruited	Utilised
Lobbied	Rectified	Validated
Maintained	Redesigned	Valued
Managed	Reduced	Won
Mapped	Refined	Worked
Maximised	Regained	Worthy

Uplifting your message credibility using power words

The simplest way to intensify your sentences with power words is write the sentence out first, and then add the power words where you can. Some theorists suggest that you can look to add adverbs (words that make an adjective or verb more exciting) before the verb — for example, powerfully persuade. You can also look to add adjectives (words that describe a noun) before the noun — for example, 'a power persuader'!

An example of this can be seen in former British prime minister Winston Churchill's famous 1940 'Blood, toil, tears and sweat' speech. Churchill said,

> You ask, what is our policy? I can say: It is to wage war, by sea, land and air, with all our might and with all the strength that God can give us; to wage war against a monstrous tyranny, never surpassed in the dark, lamentable catalogue of human crime.

You can see that power words make your sentences more intense.

Handy tip: *Adding power words won't save weak or fluffy language, so ensure your verbs and nouns are already strong before you look to add power words to them. For example, 'completely done' is just as fluffy as 'done', and the change to 'finalised and signed-off by Nick' is stronger.*

Power words will ensure that your important communication is more dynamic and vibrant, which will positively affect your persuasiveness.

The next time you plan a presentation or write an email, aim to include some power words to intensify your message.

Limit your options

Have you ever found yourself perusing a long menu in a restaurant — with a plethora of fabulous choices — and found yourself incapable of choosing something to eat? In fact, after looking at all these fabulous choices you might not even be hungry anymore. It's not you, it's them!

The body of research on persuasion talks a lot about the need to carefully balance the number of choices or options you offer your prospect or stakeholder. Offering one choice seems more like a demand, with the prospect given no freedom to make an actual decision. Two choices still feels pushy, while too many choices puts us into overload and renders us incapable of making a choice at all for the fear of getting it wrong.

In 2004 Sheena Iyengar, Professor of Business in the Management Department at Columbia Business School and widely known as an expert on choice, researched company-sponsored retirement programs for nearly 800 000 workers. She and her team looked at the impact of choice or options on participation rates and, yes, they found that the more choices that were offered, the less likely people were to enrol in the program. When only two funds were offered, the rate of participation was around 75 per cent and, interestingly, when 59 funds were offered, the rate dropped to around 60 per cent. A drop of 15 per cent is significant when you're dealing with 800 000 people!

The same researchers did a similar experiment with jam flavours. When they displayed six flavours at a tasting stall in a fancy supermarket, 30 per cent of passers-by tasted the jam. When they displayed all 24 flavours, only 3 per cent of passers-by tasted the jam. I've seen this myself when my butcher offers a taste of too many sausage flavours sizzling on a hot plate out the front of the butcher shop. After trying them all, I don't want to buy sausages at all!

When too many choices are available, and with too many chances to get the choice 'wrong', the decision-making process becomes more risky. When we go into overwhelm, our mind shuts down and we simply can't make any decision.

Sometimes offering lots of options works!

Sometimes you want to offer lots of options. This could be because you want the publicity that comes with offering wild and crazy options, or perhaps you want to offer every possibility so that people can always find something they want with you and they never have to visit your competitor. In this case, you need to give out lots of free samples or offer a rigorous try-before-you-buy scheme in order to reduce the inherent risk in making the wrong choice or decision.

This approach was proven by the ice-cream wonderland known as La Casa Gelato in Vancouver, Canada, which offers 238 wild and crazy ice-cream flavours — ranging from aged balsamic vinegar to garlic flavour. In November 2019, they claimed their title as the Guinness World Record Holder for 'Most commercially available flavours'. They do this to capture people's imagination and, in the process, get lots of cool publicity in the style of zebra marketing. (This is where you really stand out, like a spotty as opposed to stripy zebra.) Or, to use author Seth Godin's analogy, this ice-cream shop is like a 'purple cow'. It really stands out!

The way La Casa Gelato gets around the overwhelm of over 200 flavours is they have a generous sampling process where a visit to the store is about experiencing the full ritual — from tasting and sampling, to deciding on your flavour of choice. It's not meant to be a shop where you make a quick choice and off you go. It's a process and the journey is the destination.

Knowing when to limit the options

The point is that unless you want to engage in the rigorous and possibly costly exercise of zebra marketing, less is more. Here's the three-step process for you:

1. The next time you must persuade, think through all the choices that might be exciting to your prospect or

stakeholder. Remember — it's not persuasion if the choices you are offering are not appealing to your prospect; that's manipulation or coercion (refer to chapter 4).

2. Narrow your appealing options down to three or four choices.

3. Pitch them in the most enticing way you can with the word 'or' as your link. For example, 'Would you prefer to implement the persuasion module in December without the links and help information, or in January with just the links, or in February with the links and help information?'

In this way, you eliminate the chance of either a 'no' from your stakeholder, or of overwhelm (which is a form of 'no'). Neither of these is any good as an outcome because it's a lose–lose outcome where no-one gets what they want. Offering three or four attractive options increases the chance of 'yes' (one of these options will work), which, ultimately, is our intention when we enter into a persuasive communication situation. You can even do this yourself in that restaurant with the busy menu. Narrow down the choices to your top three or four options that will be wonderful for you in this moment. That way, whatever you choose will be delicious and much enjoyed.

Use numbered lists

Lists are used in persuasion for two main reasons: to appeal to a wide variety of people (if the person doesn't like one item in the list, they may like another), and to allow the person to scan the list quickly to find the most important points.

When using lists, most people use either bullet points — otherwise referred to as dot points — or they use numbers. If you want to be as persuasive as possible, I recommend you replace the bullet points with numbers where possible, especially if the order matters, or if you are going to refer to specific points by their assigned number in the list.

Some people really need a number next to each item on your list. It helps them organise your information in their head. They simply won't listen or remember anything about your message unless you allocate a number to each item on the list.

If you have options or key points, or if you refer to the number of items in your list, make sure that you place a number next to each point.

Katherine's story

Katherine is an architect. She was keen to persuade her colleagues to specify dimensions in their lighting designs for their architectural projects to speed up ordering and construction time. At a certain point in her conversation with her colleagues, she said the following:

> By using this simple calculation based on dimensions specific to the room you can easily determine:

1. set-back from wall

2. spacing between fittings

3. quantity required.

Katherine used the numbers to imply the logical order of decision-making. She showed with the '1, 2, 3' that the steps had a sequence that her client should follow.

Handy tip: In your presentations and meetings you can similarly emphasise numbered lists with a gesture. That means, as you say each number out loud, you hold up the same number of fingers. This will help people who need the numbers to concentrate.

Tom's story

Tom is the head of business development in a large corporation. He was pitching to a client and, when he reached the *How?* section of his Persuasion Blueprint in his pitch (refer to earlier in this chapter) he asked a rhetorical question. He said, 'How can we fix this?' And then (because it was a rhetorical question) he immediately answered his own question with the following words. As he spoke, he used his fingers to count off the steps.

Tom said,

We should implement three steps:

One. [Tom raised one finger in the air.] *We should analyse productive and unproductive time on a weekly basis through planning and analysis of variance to previous plans.*

Two. [Tom raised two fingers in the air.] *We must employ calendar management strategies to minimise the opportunity for disruption and to enable more opportunities for prolonged focus time.*

And three. [Tom raised three fingers in the air.] *We will note and escalate senior management interruptions to the executive.*

If this were a written document rather than a conversation or meeting/pitch, Tom would simply include the number next to each point. Again, these steps have a sequence that should be followed and, to help people realise this, they are numbered '1, 2, 3'.

You can see from both Katherine and Tom's examples that using numbers makes it easier for your stakeholder or prospect to listen and remember your numbered points.

The next time you write an email, aim to include some numbers rather than bullet points next to your ideas where appropriate.

Use visual aids to captivate and convince

We've all been there! The presenter puts up a slide with 500 words and eight-point font and they say the infamous words, 'I know you can't read this, but I'm going to show you anyway!' Don't do this! So many people overdo the number of words, diagrams and data sets on their slides that the phrase 'death by PowerPoint' was coined. If it wasn't so funny, I'd be crying right now at the number of awful slide decks business presenters use. Now let's not kid ourselves here. If your aim is to be persuasive, these busy slides are not the best way to present your data. You know this! So, what are you doing? You have *no excuse* for awful slides that bamboozle your audience and cause cognitive overload.

The good news is that using visual aids *is* effective. Assistant Professor of MIS University of Arizona Douglas R Vogel reported that people who use excellent slides are 43 per cent more likely to persuade than those with no visual aids. Visual perception is the most powerful and common way people take in information and remember key points. When you use slides well, you're making yourself memorable for all the right reasons.

Slides serve two purposes:

1. To help your stakeholders understand your message more effectively than they would without visual aids.

2. To help your stakeholders remember what you've said for longer.

Used well, your slides will contribute greatly to your message credibility.

Avoiding death by PowerPoint

To avoid overloading people with your slides, and to help people get your point quickly, ask yourself the following essential question: *Is this the best way to visually reinforce this point?*

This question is so important, and I suggest you ask this of every single slide in your slide deck. If the answer is 'yes' to a particular slide, keep that slide as is. If your answer is 'no', change or delete the slide and find a better way. Please don't ever apologise for something on your slides. If you believe something will be hard to read or understand, don't use it — instead, remove it, change it, improve it.

TIP

Michelle says,

'When considering each slide in your presentation, ask yourself: Is this the best way to visually reinforce this point?'

USE HANDOUTS

Say you're a Wise Owl with a lot of technical information to impart (or you want to persuade the Wise Owls in the room) and you know this level of technical information is not best presented on a slide. In this situation, using a handout instead may be the better option.

When it comes to busy slides, I teach, 'If they can't read it, don't show it!' Replace busy slides with handouts. Handouts are great if your audience is a size you can manage — I even use handouts with an audience in the thousands. In meetings and presentations, handouts are perfect for complex patterns, graphs and models. They can also be very helpful as a tool for interaction and engagement if you leave blanks for people to fill things in as they go if appropriate.

Handy tip: If your handout is busy, you will need to explain how and when to look at it. You may even prefer to provide the handout after the meeting or persuasive moment is over as a reference.

TIP

Michelle says,

'If they can't read it, don't show it on your slide!'

REMEMBER A PICTURE SPEAKS A THOUSAND WORDS

Use photos and images where possible on your slides, rather than bullet points or lists. Remember that a picture is worth a thousand words. Your message will be much clearer if you reinforce certain elements with an image rather than with a whole lot of bullet points that overwhelm people. You might like to check out free photo libraries for stunning, evocative images that reinforce your emotional objective.

Handy tip: *I like to advise my clients to take slides with three bullet points and turn them into three slides. Each of the three bullet points becomes the heading in 30-point font across the top and a captivating image takes up the rest of your screen.*

Using images in this way is much more memorable and persuasive than simply having three bullet points on a slide. And while I'm talking fonts…Keep your font size nice and big. Aim to stick with large, clear fonts.

DON'T PUT YOUR REPORT FORMAT ON YOUR SLIDES!

A report is a standalone document that usually has lots of information — including facts, statistics, data and graphs. A report is intended to be read like a book or a brochure. And, yes, even though reports are often created in PowerPoint, that doesn't mean they should be shown on your presentation screen. If you show your report on your presentation screen, your audience will be confused by the small text and lack of focus, which will distract them while you are speaking. They can't read your busy slide and listen to you speak at the same time (attempting to do so creates what's called 'cognitive overload'). Instead, make sure your slides only reinforce your key messages and ensure you provide a pre-read document, handout or leave-behind that they can refer to for the detail.

USE GRAPHS, CHARTS AND DATA SETS CREATIVELY

Use graphs, charts and data sets as creatively as possible and be sure to only include the points you want to reinforce on your slides. Don't just cut and paste busy graphs from Excel into PowerPoint. That means that if you generated the graph in Excel, either make sure the source graph in Excel is simple and only highlighting your point, or recreate the graph in PowerPoint and leave every single thing that's not completely essential off the new version of the graph. For example, if the graph shows growth in net profit versus growth in gross profit versus growth in wages but you only want to focus on gross profit, take everything else off the graph.

Remember to use big fonts on graphs and colour-code key areas on graphs to make them clear and memorable. Additionally, unless you are using the contrast principle (in which case, two graphs side by side might be powerful) you'll better persuade if you put one image or one graph per slide.

DELIVER SKILFULLY

It's a fact that we can't hear, listen and process two different conversations at once. When we try to, it causes cognitive overload. Have you ever been at a cocktail party where you are part of a bigger group in conversation? Suddenly you hear your own name mentioned in a nearby conversation and your attention is diverted to that conversation — to the exclusion of the first conversation. In fact, you can't hear the first conversation at all. This is called the 'cocktail party phenomenon' and it's worth remembering this when you communicate. Only ask for one thing at a time, and let the other person hear your first request and act on it before you ask for anything else.

I bet you've been to a meeting where the presenter overloaded you with incessant talking while their slides were up on the screen. Often the slides don't reinforce what is being said and you have no idea what the key message is, or what action to take. It's just like being at that cocktail party with too many things going on. Wise Owls are logical and analytical, and they communicate (and want to hear) robust, well-founded arguments. They don't overload their audience with information so that no-one remembers what was said or agreed.

AVOIDING COGNITIVE OVERLOAD THROUGHOUT YOUR MEETING

Let's look a little deeper at this concept of cognitive overload in connection to your slides in meetings. The concept has been further proved by Australian research lead Professor John Sweller from the University of NSW. Sweller's development of and research into cognitive load theory suggests that the human brain processes and retains more information if it is digested in either verbal or written formats, not both. In a 2007 interview, Sweller argued, 'The use of the PowerPoint presentation has been a disaster. It should be ditched'.

Further, he suggests that while diagrams can be useful, saying the same words that are written on the diagrams isn't effective because this puts too much load on the mind and decreases the audience's ability to fully comprehend what is being presented. If you want to use graphs, diagrams, bullet points or words on your slides to persuade, understanding Sweller's theory of cognitive load is important.

To avoid 'cognitive overload', ensure the audience is clear about when they should be looking at you. You can do this by speaking with them from the middle of the meeting space, with the screen image blanked out, or just a picture behind you. Similarly, you also make it clear when the audience can look at the screen — as you stand out of the way and allow them time to read the slide, for example, or put your arm up and gesture towards the screen.

Handy tip: If you press the 'b' key on your computer keyboard, you will blank your screen. Then press 'b' again and your slides will reappear. This only works when you have your slides on presentation view. (It doesn't work if you are showing a pdf, for example, or a different file on the screen.) You can also blank your screen by pressing the 'blank' button on your portable clicker or remote. Press it again and the slides reappear. Perhaps experiment with the best way for you.

Slides and other visual aids can dramatically improve the credibility of your message. Always think through what you can do with your visuals to make sure they make your message clearer rather than more confusing or distracting.

TRY THIS

Next time you use slides in a meeting to persuade, think about applying the ideas listed in this section. Make your slides stunning, clean and succinct. Use large fonts and evocative images. Only reproduce the important parts of graphs and colour-code key areas on graphs to make them memorable.

Remember — when persuading your stakeholder, it's not about the slides; it's about you, the power persuader, connecting with your audience through the words you say, and the way you say them. Beautiful, clean, crisp visuals will reinforce your key messages and compel your audience to action.

Package your numbers

Even Wise Owls (who typically love facts and research) need your information to be clear and persuasive if they are to believe it and take the action you require. It's a fact that when confronted with irrefutable numbers that back up your assertions, it's close to impossible for your stakeholder to disagree. They must let go of their initial perspective. When your numbers are undeniable, they cause your stakeholder or prospect to sense strongly that they agree with you.

'Packaging your numbers' means presenting the numbers in a way that sells your main idea.

How do you package your numbers?

Wise Owls (and those aiming to convince Wise Owls) know how to sell their numbers in a way that works. Here are a few tips to help you do this too:

- Pitch your number persuasively.
- Give your number a meaningful value.
- Use contrast.

PITCH THE NUMBER PERSUASIVELY

This is where you think about the best number to quote in a statistic.

Let's say you work for a wine distribution company and 78 per cent of your customers buy premium wine. You could either say, '78 per cent of our customers buy our premium wine'. Or, you could say, 'More than three quarters of our customers buy our premium wine offerings'. In this example, if you wanted to be as persuasive as possible, you'd need to think about who your stakeholder is, and which number would work best for them.

Let's look at another example. Say you planned to say the following:

> We have a financial year target of 13 endorsed blueprints, of which four have been completed and three are in progress. That leaves six of our blueprints to action. This is excellent news.

The numbers of seven out of 13 or six remaining aren't that exciting, so how might you pitch this one so it sounds persuasive? Do you think the following example is a better way to say this?

> We have a financial year target of 13 endorsed blueprints, and more than half are either completed or in progress. That leaves less than half of our blueprints to action. This is excellent news.

In another example, let's say you're selling a product that is $15 000 for 10 people. The overall number is quite large, so the most attractive way to pitch this is to divide the number and quote the per head investment.

You could say, 'The investment is $15 000'. Or you could say, 'The investment is $15 000, which is only $1500 per person'.

It's always best to try to work out the most attractive way to sell the numbers.

GIVE YOUR NUMBERS A MEANINGFUL VALUE

This is where you use a metaphor or analogy to bring the number to life, so the other person gets a clear picture of the significance of the fact. For example, 'That's 52 Olympic swimming pools full of re-work!'

Let's look at an example where you are trying to persuade a senior manager to approve a fix to the bugs in your company computer system. You could say, 'Did you know that re-work and re-runs due to bugs in our code is costing our team one to two days each month?' Or you could say, 'Did you know that re-work and re-runs due to bugs in our code is costing our team one to two days each month? That's five people, each working up to 16 hours or a total of 80 full-time salary hours wasted'.

You can see that by pitching your numbers in this way, you're making your argument undeniable.

USE CONTRAST

When two numbers are placed next to each other on a slide, in a document or even in the spoken word, we perceive each number as more obviously different, which makes it easier to work out which number appeals to us the most.

This 'contrast frame' can be used as a before and after situation. For example, say you're deciding whether to sign up to a diet plan. The example used in the advertisement for this diet plan shows you a photo of 'Mary' weighing in at 78 kilos at the start of the program. (And the number '78 kilos' is placed strategically near the before photo of Mary.) After completing the 12-week diet plan, the advertisements tell you, Mary now weighs 65 kilos — and a convincing photo is included right next to her 'before' photo with the number '65 kilos' placed right near her 'after' photo. You can appreciate that, in this example, Mary's diet plan seems to have worked very well based on her before and after weight. The example works to convince you by the contrast of both the before and after number, and the before and after photographs. This argument is undeniable.

You can also reduce the argument to the 'ridiculous' contrast. This is where you use two numbers to convince your stakeholder to agree with you through the benefit or saving being so extreme that they must be persuaded. For example, 'This is costing us four days and $4000 a month, which is a total of $48 000 a year. Contracting someone to fix this will only cost $5000 in total, which saves us a whopping $43 000 this year alone!' By contrasting the numbers, you are making your argument undeniable. Who wouldn't want to save $43 000?

Another option is to use the 'no chance' contrast — where you ask for a lofty request that the person is likely to refuse because it's too expensive, too time-consuming or just not possible. Then you follow your lofty request with a smaller request that, by contrast, seems reasonable and doable.

Let's say you're applying for a role, and you know the salary options are between $100 000 and $150 000 per annum. You've received all the right signals that you're the top candidate for the role and the new employer is very keen to hire you. The 'no chance' compliance contrast approach suggests that you request a salary of $160 000 ($10 000 more than the top of the possible range) and then negotiate down to $150 000 once you are sure you want the role. This approach helps you maximise the chance that you're offered the top of the salary offer, not the bottom.

Another example applies to consulting. For example, say your client has indicated that they will need between 50 and 75 consultants onsite to manage their huge information technology requirements. You pitch your solution with a requirement of 85 employees, knowing that they will never agree to pay the salaries for this many consultants. Once you know you are on the short list you pull back to an offer of 73 people, saving them the salaries of two full-time team members (that is, two fewer than their top expectation, which was 75, and 12 fewer than your initial quote of 85) while still achieving their needs. You're giving them less than what they said was the top of their possible outlay — how could they say no?

To look at another contrasting option, let's say you're a business coach. You have two programs and a book. Your book is $25, your public group training course is $1995 per person, and your personal coaching program is $15 000. In other words, each of these resources is more expensive than the last and a huge difference exists between the cheapest and the most expensive. The law of contrast suggests that you should always pitch the most expensive option first and your best option (the one that you want to persuade your stakeholder to buy) last. The reason is that people will be compelled to buy something from you, and they are more likely to choose the last option. This is where the contrast kicks in. In this example you would explain all about the $15 000 coaching, and then you'd talk about the book for $25. Finally, you'd persuade them to buy a place in the public group training course. The good news is that a small percentage of people are driven to buy the best and you might just sell some $15 000 programs as well!

And, interestingly, in the world of persuasion you'll likely also sell the $25 book. This is because when the cheapest option is so cheap, often people will choose to buy that as well as one of the other options.

Lastly, you can use the 'adding value' contrast approach. For example, at the time of writing, I sell places in my Persuasive Presentation Skills Masterclass at $1995 (+ GST) per person. In addition, I give each participant extra resources to the value of $500 per person to ensure that they don't forget what they learnt from me. When someone is deciding whether to work with me or not, even if they feel that everything else is equal (such as my content, delivery, experience and skill) compared to other trainers out there, the added value is so extraordinary they realise they'd be silly to work with anyone other than me.

TRY THIS

The next time you need to pitch an idea, find some numbers you can package to help you sell your idea more persuasively. Remember — the key is to establish message credibility and packaging your numbers will do this for you.

Rehearse until you can't get it wrong

Another characteristic of message credibility — and a Wise Owl behaviour trait — is your ability to speak about anything without notes or prompts. You can achieve this using only one method, and it's to rehearse. And the good news is you don't need to rote learn (this is where you practise every word in the perfect order). Unless you have three to four weeks to focus on rote learning (or you are an accomplished actor who knows how to learn their lines) rote learning is a recipe for going blank. Good rehearsal is all about practising your points and saying them in different ways each time. You're aiming for the gist of the point to be clear and persuasive.

It's frightening what people can say when they speak without rehearsing — including those in powerful positions. When George W Bush was the US President (from 2001 to 2009), he was known for regularly saying 'Bushisms'. Bushisms were linguistic blunders characterised by unclear communication, incorrect sentence structure, and words he made up on the spot. Let's look at some of my favourite 'Bushisms':

> I want to thank the dozens of welfare-to-work stories, the actual examples of people who made the firm and solemn commitment to work hard to embitter themselves.
>
> **April 2002 at the White House**

While 'embitter' is a word, it means to make bitter or more bitter — it is surely not what Bush meant! The whole sentence is confusing and characterised by incorrect grammar, and is also an example of using words you don't understand and then sounding silly instead of clever. Doing this negatively affects the credibility of your message.

Bush also said,

> Our enemies are innovative and resourceful, and so are we. They never stop thinking about new ways to harm our country and our people, and neither do we.
>
> **August 2004 in Washington**

Bush is implying that the US Government never stops thinking about ways to harm their country and citizens. Oh dear! And George W Bush is not the only one who must lament their own unstructured, confusing communication. Many people regret that they are not good at presenting a clear, well-structured argument. When I quiz these people in my capacity as a presentation skills trainer, they often admit to throwing together their argument at the last minute and rarely rehearsing. The fact is that persuasive communicators rehearse. And then they rehearse and rehearse and rehearse. And then they rehearse some more — you get the point! They rehearse until they can't get it wrong.

TIP

Michelle says,

'Persuasive communicators rehearse until they can't get it wrong.'

What is rehearsing?

Rehearsing is where you run through your key messages repeatedly, so that you embed the general 'gist' of your message. (Sometimes you will also end up, almost accidentally, committing some of the parts of your message to memory.) While you may inadvertently memorise some of your content, you'll find with rehearsal that you will say most of your message in a different way each time, with the result being you will sound more natural. You're likely too busy in your life to try to completely rote learn what you want to say prior to the meeting, so embedding the gist is enough and the best way to do it.

How should you rehearse?

Find a variety of places to practise saying your key points. The greater number of locations you rehearse in, the more comfortable you will feel in the actual location of your persuasive moment — no matter where it is. Book a variety of meeting rooms at work over the course of a week to rehearse in; have a few turns in front of your bathroom mirror at home; go out into the garden for a practice if you can; and then try delivering your message in a variety of other rooms in your home. I know, it sounds a bit crazy, doesn't it? Well, it works to make you comfortable in any location!

Liam's story

I have a client named Liam. He is very senior in his company and highly respected. He's very good at his job but his CEO was not always sure that Liam's message was credible — because Liam tended to stumble over his words from time to time, especially when he was nervous, which was often. For Liam, rehearsal is a must, or he falls to pieces with nervousness.

After some coaching with me, we realised that Liam has a deep-down concern that he's going to go blank in important meetings. I explained to Liam that he needs to do several run-throughs of his content before he leads meetings if he wants to be sure that he is thoroughly prepared. He now rehearses to camera (on his mobile), and with his supportive family. He even rehearses while power walking around his local area. Liam rehearses a lot. Would you like to know the good news? Liam's CEO contacted me directly after Liam's most recent meeting to confirm how impressed he was with Liam's newfound ability to express himself clearly and persuasively.

For some of us, rehearsal is more important than for others. If you are someone who needs to run through your key points many times, accept this fact and, as Nike says, 'Just do it'. When your message is credible, you are undeniable.

TRY THIS

When will you next need to speak up in a meeting? Make sure you follow either the 4MAT System or the Persuasion Blueprint (both covered in this chapter). Add any of the other actions from this Wise Owl chapter into your presentation script. Then rehearse, rehearse, rehearse. I wish you well. Go for it!

A final word about message credibility

Remember — no-one is just a Wise Owl. We all have a combination of the types in us, just in varying degrees. Regardless of whether message credibility is one of your strengths or not, you can see from this chapter that you can start focusing on so many wonderful things right now, so you build and develop your inner Wise Owl! Some of the tips are small things and very easy to adopt. Others are more of a stretch and will take longer to embed as habits.

Without message credibility, being persuasive will be very difficult for you. In most persuasive situations, a robust argument is something your stakeholder is expecting from you. Plan to tackle one or more of the areas in this chapter each week, and over the coming months you'll see people will believe your argument more and more. You have an exciting opportunity to use message credibility to improve your overall persuasiveness in life.

TOP TIPS
The Wise Owl

- Message credibility is essential for persuasion. When people believe your argument, they are more likely to trust you and take the action you require.

- Wise Owls cover all angles and issues and deliver a dispassionate account of the facts.

- You can do 10 things to establish message credibility:

    1. Structure your message so it resonates and sticks, using either the 4MAT System or my Persuasion Blueprint.

    2. Use facts, statistics, quotes and subject matter experts to strengthen and support your message — these can be used anywhere in your persuasive process.

(continued)

3. Use rhetorical questions to signpost your content and lead your stakeholder logically through your message.

4. Don't use fluffy language that is ambiguous and distracts — for example, a noun, verb, generalisation, rule and/or comparator that could be misunderstood by your stakeholder.

5. Add power words to liven up your argument — these are persuasive and descriptive words that trigger an emotional response and make your argument stronger.

6. Limit your options to help reduce overwhelm or incorrect decision-making.

7. Use numbered lists to help people follow your argument and understand the order of steps or choices.

8. Use your visual aids brilliantly to captivate and convince, and make yourself memorable — and persuasive — for all the right reasons.

9. Package your numbers to back up your assertions and make your argument undeniable.

10. Rehearse until you can't get it wrong, running through the key messages repeatedly, so that you embed the general 'gist' of your message.

• Remember — no-one is just a Wise Owl. We all have a combination of the types in us. In most persuasive situations, a robust argument is something your stakeholder is expecting from you — so use message credibility to improve your overall persuasiveness in life.

CHAPTER 7

Type 2: The Commanding Eagle

So, you'd like to build more of the Commanding Eagle into your persuasive approach? Maybe this is because the Commanding Eagle type isn't your strength. Maybe someone you have to persuade often — such as a manager, team member or even family member — is a Commanding Eagle and you want to demonstrate the behaviours that are most persuasive for them. Or maybe the Commanding Eagle is your strength, but you'd like to be even more proficient in persuading through your personal authority. As US business magnate, investor and philanthropist Warren Buffett argues, 'If you want to soar like an eagle in life, you can't be flocking with the turkeys'.

The Commanding Eagle is one of the credibility types. The Commanding Eagle has an innate drive to persuade by conveying personal authority, and is all about *personal*, rather than *message*, credibility. They are thought of as commanding because they are assertive and imposing, and they inspire confidence in others.

This chapter helps you learn how to build your inner Commanding Eagle or personal authority so you become an impressive person who persuades without trying!

The importance of personal authority

If you look at persuasive people in history — from Martin Luther King or the Dalai Lama, through to the everyday persuasive people in your own life (relatives and friends, or perhaps a remarkable colleague or manager) — you'll note that they all have one thing in common: personal authority. Personal authority is an essential attribute of a persuasive person because it causes people to trust and respect you, which can lead to bigger and better opportunities. If you want to be persuasive, then personal authority is something to master.

In the previous chapter, I talked about the Wise Owl and their focus on message credibility. The Commanding Eagle, on the other hand, is a shining light and someone to follow because they have personal authority in their chosen field. While message credibility is where you use your mastery of the research and facts to support your position, personal authority is all about you and your experience and expertise. Personal authority is where you demonstrate your superior knowledge and proficiency. You have personal authority because you are an expert in your field and have done this before, so you're known as someone people can trust.

TIP

Michelle says,

'You have personal authority not because you have a mastery of the facts and research, but because you are an authority in your field, have done this before, and are known as someone people can trust.'

When you have personal authority, your stakeholder believes in you and respects you. The body of knowledge on authority (and the role authority plays in the process of persuasion) tells us that people who are trustworthy, reliable and experienced, and who have good character, high integrity and a solid reputation based on objective measures, are deemed to have authority and credibility. And this personal credibility is so important — as bestselling author and speaker John C Maxwell highlights, 'Credibility is a leader's currency. With it, he or she is solvent; without it, he or she is bankrupt'.

I've been teaching people how to be perceived as having personal authority and credibility in their workplace for over two decades, and I've got two pieces of very good news for you here:

1. *Anyone can become credible:* Building your credibility is just a matter of putting your attention to developing a variety of micro skills within each of the subcategories of credibility. I'm going to give you many great suggestions in this chapter to get you started.

2. *You don't need to actually 'be credible', to be persuasive:* All you need to be is perceived as credible. In the short term, that's great news if you don't yet feel you are as credible as you would like to be — which accounts for most of us mere mortals! In other words, you can fake it while you're on the journey to making it.

Becoming credible

People usually build their personal authority and credibility over time. You can build your personal credibility and bring out your inner Commanding Eagle in the following ways:

- Become an expert in your niche.
- Communicate your competence.
- Raise your profile.
- Be trustworthy.
- Refine your elevator pitch.
- Calm your farm.
- Speak with elegance.
- Back yourself.

- Tell stories that impress.
- Always exceed expectations.

The following sections cover each of these actions in more detail so you can make these your new (or stronger) habits.

Become an expert in your niche

The ability to do something efficiently and successfully, with expertise and competence, is an essential characteristic of the Commanding Eagle. When someone is an expert, you have a strong sense that they know what they are doing, they have the runs on the board, and they know the best way forward. The best way to build your expertise is to develop your proven skills and your proven knowledge.

Commanding Eagles specialise in a niche, and they work on becoming an expert in that niche. You don't need to be all things to all people — or, as the saying goes, 'a jack of all trades and a master of none'. Trying to be expert at everything will result in you diluting any gains in perceived expertise that you make. And do you know what's even better than a niche? A niche within a niche! This means it's an excellent idea to specialise within a field and then specialise within your speciality. Greek philosopher Socrates provided some excellent advice here, highlighting, 'The way to gain a good reputation is to endeavour to be what you desire to appear'. Over the course of your professional life, make it your plan to strive to be the expert in your area of choice, your niche within the niche.

My own story is an example of this approach. In 1999, I began specialising in presentation skills development for businesspeople. In 2001, I further specialised into persuasive presenting for businesspeople. I've stuck with this niche ever since and now my name is a synonym for persuasive presentation skills in Australia. People don't say, 'I'm going to a persuasive presentation skills course'. They say, 'I'm going to Michelle Bowden'. That's what it means to specialise in a niche within a niche. I have achieved many wonderful benefits from owning my niche.

TIP

Michelle says,

'The ability to do something efficiently and successfully, with expertise and competence, is an essential characteristic of the Commanding Eagle.'

Aim to build all six of the following actions for expertise into your daily life:

1. Seek opportunities for work experience.

2. Access workplace mentors, or get a teacher or coach in your chosen field.

3. Study and read widely.

4. Get certified.

5. Remember practice makes perfect.

6. Commit to growth.

Let's look at each of these actions in more detail.

Seek opportunities for work experience

Where can you volunteer your time to build your experience? If you've just finished studying, could you apply for a graduate program? Or perhaps you could apply for an internship program, where you are given wonderful, enriching experiences for a reduced salary. Might a not-for-profit organisation value you offering your skills to their clients? No matter your age or stage, someone out there needs your help for free, or a small fee.

Handy tip: *If you are already in the workforce and are aiming to change specialisations, you could offer to help in that new area one day a week. Or you could volunteer to assist with a particular project after hours. Work experience will help you to build your expertise and personal credibility.*

Access workplace mentors

Why make the mistakes that others have made when you can learn from them and avoid the errors in the first place? Ask yourself which Commanding Eagles you need to bring into your circle to elevate yourself and your learning. I have about 20 mentors — and some of them don't even know that they are my mentors. I follow them on social media, read their books and listen to their podcasts. Some of them are people I pay to advise me, and some are friends. I learn a lot from hanging around them. As I learn and grow from spending time with these people, I build my subject matter expertise and personal credibility.

Study and read widely

These days, podcasts, vlogs, blogs and books (to name just a few resources) are sometimes free and often inexpensive to access. Read everything you can get your hands on to increase your expertise in your niche.

> **TRY THIS**
>
> Pick something to learn about today to enhance your expertise in your niche and make yourself more personally credible.

Get certified

Who accredits you in the skills you desire? Many wonderful courses are available to give you the skills you need to feel confident in applying for new or different roles. Maybe you could simply attend a short course or do some personal coaching to achieve the qualifications you need. Reach out to experts in the industry you want to specialise in and ask them which certification is the most valuable from their point of view. Do your research and find the place to study these things so that you gain certification or qualifications that will build your personal credibility and impress others.

Remember practice makes perfect

At all costs, find a way to practise what you are learning. Even if you just help a friend for free.

Jim's story

Jim is a financial counsellor. Finding a job in this area has been tricky of late due a big cut in not-for-profit funding. Jim decided to take a leaf out of US industrialist Henry Ford's book. Ford said, 'You can't build a reputation on what you are going to do'. Jim took action and sought opportunities to develop his skills while helping others.

To keep his skills current and fresh, Jim decided to offer to help a friend with his recent divorce and financial affairs. So while his friend was receiving free and incredibly helpful advice, Jim was practising and refining his craft. Jim mentioned to me that he was learning so much from the experience, and all while contributing and feeling good about helping a friend. This is what you call a win–win situation!

Commit to growth

My family and I are all mad-keen basketball fans. One of the best all-time point guards in the NBA is Stephen Curry—and in our family, Curry is a legend! Curry once said, 'Success is not an accident; success is actually a choice'. What he means is that if you want to be successful at establishing your credibility, you need to commit to a growth mindset. Strive constantly to add to your back story, personal history and experience so you're a well-rounded person. And, importantly, don't just talk about doing it. Actually do it! Take classes, read books, listen to podcasts. Become a whole person who is always learning new things and adding strings to your bow. The more interests you have, the better placed you'll be to add value to other people's conversations and meetings.

Also understand that brains and intellect are not the only things that matter when it comes to a growth mindset. Your dedication and hard work as you learn new things (and become fundamentally interesting in a variety of environments) will make you an expert in the long run. People with a growth mindset put more energy into learning than they do worrying about failure.

Try the following four options to embrace the growth mindset:

1. *Set goals:* Write down your goals and the steps you'll take to achieve them. Research has shown that when you write down your goals, you strengthen the image of that goal in your mind, and this helps you focus on achieving it. This vision creates clarity and direction, which can lead to a change in how you then act. From a neuroscience perspective, we know that writing down a goal improves what's known as the 'encoding' process — or the process where things are stored in your long-term memory. This encoding makes it more likely you will remember and action the goal.

2. *Reflect on your failures:* Take time to acknowledge, reflect on and embrace all your failures. Remember — growth is on the other side of discomfort, and failure is just another word for discomfort! What are you going to learn from the experience? How will you make sure you do better next time?

3. *Use 'yet':* You can add this to the end of so many sentences; for example, 'I'm not there — yet'. 'Yet' becomes the important word in this sentence. It highlights that you will eventually achieve your persuasion goals, you're just not there yet. To take a lesson from the character Dory in *Finding Nemo*, 'Just keep swimming, just keep swimming' and, through hard work, determination and focus, you will ultimately achieve your goals. Integrating the word 'yet' into your vocabulary signals that, despite any struggles, you will eventually develop the skill or ability you are seeking.

4. *Foster grit:* Grit is defined as a toughness and determination. It's about resilience and that drive to keep trying even when

you fail. You have grit when your 'never say die' mentality forces you to persist through adversity. Grit is an important element of the growth mindset.

In the final area of fostering grit Sarah Lewis, Associate Professor at Harvard University (and recipient of the Freedom Scholar Award), offers some advice: 'Grit is not just a simple elbow-grease term for rugged persistence. It is an often-invisible display of endurance that lets you stay in an uncomfortable place, work hard to improve upon a given interest, and do it again and again'.

TIP

Michelle says,

'People with a growth mindset put more energy into learning than they do worrying about failure.'

TRY THIS

Think of something that has you feeling like you're failing. What can you plan to do in the next few days to move yourself forward with this currently dissatisfying endeavour? Determine to work on moving this challenge forward in some way with drive and persistence.

You can see a lot of work is ahead on your journey to becoming a true expert in your field and establishing your personal credibility. Stressing about the huge journey ahead is pointless. Just tackle something that moves you forward one day at a time. Remember the 1 per cent every day I covered in the introduction for this book. Be diligent and consistent in moving yourself forward one tiny bit by another tiny bit. All those tiny moves forward add up to something exciting over time — and eventually you'll look back with pride at your impressive effort and say, 'Wow! I've come a long way!'

Communicate your competence – let everyone know!

We know that people form their impression of you very quickly. If people don't get an immediate sense that you are an expert, how will they trust you? Inspirational writer Israelmore Ayivor highlights, 'Dare to be competent. Competency is what makes everyone remain at peace when things are being handled by you'.

For people to feel comfortable taking the action you require, or to approve your big ideas, they need to feel you are an authority on the matter, you know what you're talking about, and you can be relied upon. I talk in more detail about making a good first impression in chapter 9 (where I cover the Captivating Peacock). For now, the point is that you need to do what you can to always convey your personal credibility.

TIP

Michelle says,

'For people to feel comfortable taking the action you require, or to approve your big ideas, they need to feel you are an authority on the matter, you know what you're talking about, and you can be relied upon.'

Communicating your competence and credibility

Credible people know how to talk about their competence without boasting and in a way that inspires others. The two important considerations when talking about yourself are:

1. *Be confident, not up yourself:* It's important to work out how to talk about yourself in a way that's not arrogant or sarcastic. You don't want to sound like you're boasting about yourself — because that's a real turn-off!

2. *Be assured:* You don't want to appear as though discussing your achievements makes you uncomfortable.

To help you, you can use what I like to call the 'credibility formula' to explain your experience. The key with this formula is to always make sure that you link whatever you mention about yourself with your prospect or stakeholder's pain, challenges, problems, difficulties or frustrations.

The credibility formula works like this:

> In the *x* years I have worked as a specialist in the *x*, what I have learnt is *x* [reflect stakeholder's pain]. What this means for you is *x*.

Note that at the point in the formula where you 'reflect stakeholder's pain', that means you should reflect what is annoying, challenging, frustrating, difficult or painful in the other person's situation at the moment.

Here's a real-life example of how this credibility formula was used by one of my clients:

> Before I joined ACME, I worked as a financial adviser specialising in insurance, so I know how hard it is to convert a lead into a sale and then keep that policy holder engaged. (pause) Today, we'll cover some examples of initiatives that are working to ensure we carry out our legal responsibilities, provide excellent service and, therefore, retain more clients.

The reason this formula works is that the words you are saying are more about reflecting your understanding of your stakeholders' pain (challenges, problems, difficulties or frustrations) and how your experience resolves this pain, than about boasting about your achievements. It allows you to clearly state something about your experience that is relevant to this stakeholder, and that adds to your overall credibility.

A different version of the same script is as follows:

> I was speaking with *x* and they mentioned *x*, and I thought *x* [reflect stakeholder's pain]. So today it's important that we discuss *x*.

Here is an example of how this was used successfully by one of my clients:

> I was speaking with the CEO of a North American generics company and she mentioned that they were battling to meet product launch timelines due to shipping delays. I thought shipping is a big problem when promising deliverables to clients, and maybe that's the same for us. So today it's important that we set up a preferred shipping protocol, so we avoid the same delays.

This approach is clever and, in my experience, you can weave this formula into almost any conversation. The important distinction to make is that you can talk about yourself forever if you ensure that you link what you are saying about yourself to your stakeholder's pain, and then solve it. Otherwise, when you talk about yourself, you'll sound full of yourself and you'll turn people off your ideas. This credibility formula prevents you from appearing boastful.

Knowing what to talk about

The sorts of things you might want to mention when discussing your personal credibility is your qualifications, achievements and awards, testimonials from others, and examples or stories about past positive experiences. You should also aim to use credible words.

Let's look at each of these in more detail.

QUALIFICATIONS

Let people know about the study you have done and the qualifications you have gained as a result. Include your academic qualifications on your email signature and social media profiles with your job title and contact details. Perhaps put your degree up on the wall behind your desk so people see it when they meet with you.

ACHIEVEMENTS AND AWARDS

If you have won awards or achieved professional designations, it's important that people know this about you. Place academic achievements and awards where people can see them — perhaps on your desk, behind you on Zoom, and/or in your social media profiles. For example, I'm a Certified Speaking Professional or CSP, which is the highest designation for speakers in the world. I put the letters 'CSP' after my name on social media and in my email signature, and I have my certificate from 2009 on the wall behind me in many of my Zoom meetings — with the accompanying medal hanging off the frame! Potential clients often ask about this when they see it. People associate speaking competence with this designation, so I use this to my advantage in winning and keeping clients.

TRY THIS

Spend a moment working out what your achievements and awards have been over the past few years.

Once you've determined them, make sure they're listed on your social media profile where relevant. Where else could you mention these achievements without seeming like you're boasting? Do you have any certificates that should be hanging on your office wall?

TESTIMONIALS

Use client testimonials where possible. A testimonial is a comment or statement that reflects a customer's perspective about a positive experience they had with you, and your products or service. They are external proof that you are both dependable and worth the investment.

Using other satisfied customers (who are keen to speak up about the excellent experiences they have had with you) is a powerful persuasion technique that encourages new prospects or stakeholders to make the same choices. Testimonials use the law of social proof (which states that people use the actions of others to decide on proper behaviour) to encourage your prospect or stakeholder to believe that agreeing with your argument is a great idea.

Yes, testimonials put people's minds at ease. Research reported by consulting company Invesp tells us 90 per cent of consumers read online reviews before visiting a business. Research from global research company Mintel (with 2000 respondents) found that nearly 70 per cent of consumers rely on online reviews before making a purchase. Of the respondents who read online reviews, 90 per cent said positive ones affected their buying decisions, while 'excellent' reviews caused customers to spend 31 per cent more. Testimonials are very helpful external proof that you are personally credible.

TIP

Michelle says,

'Testimonials put people's minds at ease and are very helpful external proof that you are personally credible.'

Using testimonials cleverly

I'll be honest with you that many of the testimonials I read are not worth the paper they are written on, because they don't prove either dependability or value. A good testimonial includes:

- the benefits of working with you

- the results or value that was achieved.

In addition, a good testimonial must be motivating, truthful and plausible (not too good to be true), and they should always be from people who are impressive, and from awesome and relevant companies.

For example, here's a testimonial from Carolyn, one of my very important clients. Note that this testimonial has all the things you're looking for when deciding about someone's value:

Michelle Bowden's Persuasive Presentation Skills Masterclass is a solid staple in our annual Management Development Program. Year on year, our managers experience true transformational change — integrating practical models to craft a message that will engage and influence, and to deliver that message more effectively with powerful stagecraft techniques. The feedback is always exceptional with the team truly valuing the skills, tools and expansive resources they add to their leadership arsenal. Our team move forward armed with both the confidence and capability to positively influence and impact every communication opportunity.

Carolyn Shaw, General Manager Talent Development APAC, JELD-WEN

Let's look at some contrasting examples of testimonials that do and don't work here. First, a not-so-great one for Daniel, a time-management trainer who sells his courses online. He includes the following testimonial on his social media and website:

I enjoyed the training. It was just what I expected. Thank you.

Mary, small business owner

Let me ask you, would you sign up for Daniel's services after reading that? Probably not! No-one cares what Mary thinks! Her last name has not been mentioned and her company name is not specific. She's certainly not from a well-known organisation. This testimonial could very well have been made up by Daniel. Her comment is dull, the benefits are not clear and the value is not high. No, you wouldn't sign up to Daniel's time-management course.

Now let's contrast Daniel's example with Grace's. Grace works in a speakers bureau. A testimonial on her social media and website is as follows:

Grace is a true expert when it comes to finding speakers. She took the time to understand my needs and the needs of my stakeholders, and she found the perfect speakers for our event. Our delegates were delighted. She completely exceeded my expectations. Highly recommended. I will certainly work with Grace every time I need speakers for a conference.

Leanne St John, Marketing Executive, Amazon (or equally exciting company!)

Would you book Grace to find your speakers? Probably! Everyone cares what Leanne (the high-profile, high-powered, impressive executive from a well-known corporation) thinks! Leanne's comment is clear and specific. The benefits for both Leanne (as Grace's client) and Leanne's audience are clear. The value was very high. Leanne says she will work with Grace again and that helps you trust that you would have a similar experience if you chose to partner with Grace.

In these examples, you can see that when both the benefit and value are mentioned, and the testimonial provider is also credible, it's a lot more persuasive.

Knowing where and when to use testimonials

Testimonials can be used on your website and social media. They can also be mentioned in conversations, meetings, emails and other communication situations. If you are using testimonials in these situations, you will have to 'name drop'. For example, you may say something like, 'When I was working for Google...' Or 'Bill Gates always said to me...' Or 'I'm so excited that Sarah from Westpac just said "life changing" is not an overstatement about my masterclass. How wonderful!'

As always when talking about yourself, use your 'name dropping' for the right reasons. I had the fortunate opportunity to take a team of medical professionals in the pharmaceutical industry through my Persuasion Smart Profile (the world-first psychological assessment tool that assesses your persuasive strengths and weaknesses at work). This team was managed by a qualified and very experienced psychiatrist.

When I'm talking about the value of the Persuasion Smart Profile with potential new clients, I am quick to mention the psychiatrist's testimonial: 'I loved it!' This adds incredible weight to my overall competence and the validity of my assessment tool — on which this book is based!

TRY THIS

Find some testimonials that you can use to prove your competence. Feature these either in writing on your website and social media, or in conversation with stakeholders or other people you're hoping to persuade at some point.

BACK UP WITH EXAMPLES

Use examples from your past experiences when explaining what people should do, why they should do it or how you think they should proceed. And practise using examples when answering key questions — where the response you give can further cement your competence in the minds of your stakeholders.

Let's look at how using examples might play out. Say you're hoping to persuade stakeholders about the need for the business to implement SAP — an enterprise resource planning software — in modules over six months. In this situation, you need to establish your personal credibility by explaining your experience and your learnings. Your personal examples — your backstory — makes you credible. So you would say something like:

> We should implement SAP in modules. In my last role at XYZ Company, we implemented SAP in modules over the course of a six-month period. We delivered one module at a time and focused our energy on the individual teams who would be using that module alone. This staged rollout made it much easier for the employees to manage the change process.

USE CREDIBLE WORDS

When speaking about yourself, be sure to always imply (and sometimes blatantly use) credible words — for example, qualified, skilled, proficient, authority, experienced, expert, approved, trained, skilful, practiced, professional, certified, licensed, official, authorised or accredited. These words highlight your competence.

Jake's story

Jake is a young friend of mine in his early twenties who received a high-distinction average in his university studies. This young person has only recently joined a large organisation and is still finding his way in the corporate world. When he told me about his incredibly impressive high-distinction average, I immediately exclaimed (because Commanding Eagle is one of my strengths!), 'You must tell your new boss about that!' He was horrified! He said, 'No way! They will think I'm up myself'.

Please always remember that people can't read your mind. The boss of this young man will never know that he is excelling at university. What a shame! Don't you think his boss would love to know that the person they just took a gamble on is scoring high results at university? Don't be shy, or worry about appearing too boastful. Tell people about your achievements — just do it with humility!

If communicating your competence doesn't come naturally, I'm sure you'll be wondering how to begin some of these actions! For some, many of the suggestions so far in this chapter will be terrifying! My advice is to begin by doing some of these suggestions a bit more with the people who love you — your friends and family.

Handy tip: Practise communicating your competence in easier situations first so that eventually you become more comfortable about promoting yourself in a professional capacity.

Raise your profile

If you want to improve your credibility, getting yourself noticed for all the right reasons is important. I suggest that you speak, contribute, volunteer and generally be involved in an impressive way. You want people to notice that you are interested and interesting. You can do a whole lot of things to raise your profile in business. The following sections outline some options.

Join committees

Work committees are a great way to practise your communication skills, demonstrate your value, and build your personal credibility and authority.

Joining a committee offers the following benefits:

- You'll get some excellent experience.

- You'll meet people who need to know you — remember the saying, 'it's not what but who you know in business'!

- You'll build awareness of who you are and what you stand for.

- You'll have the chance to run projects, lead groups and speak out.

- People will see you in action and be more likely to recommend you for future opportunities.

Rose's story

Rose joined her company social club to build her networks. She helped organise lots of social events. People in high places in her company noticed her drive, commitment and expertise at arranging events. Before she knew it, Rose was promoted to Executive Assistant to the CEO.

Speak at conferences and on panels

Being accepted to be a speaker or panellist at an event is a public endorsement of your skills and brand as an expert. You are someone others should hear from. Embrace this opportunity with both hands! Panels are often formed to discuss important industry topics and trigger an exchange of viewpoints. Your job as a panellist is to share your knowledge and expertise. All the usual public speaking rules apply to panel participation. When you do a great job, you'll be thought of as a true industry expert with the confidence and authority of a Commanding Eagle.

Handy tip: If you need help learning how to speak at a conference, I highly recommend my book How to Present: The ultimate guide to presenting your ideas and influencing people using techniques that actually work *(also published by Wiley).*

Attend your company's social events

It's important to be seen to be there! Attend everything at your workplace, support everyone and generally be interested in what's going on at work. Often the most important conversations in business occur at social events because people are relaxed and they have their guard down — so make the most of every opportunity to spread your Commanding Eagle wings! If you don't attend, you'll be out of the loop and may be seen as uninterested. But don't let *your* guard down! Remember — you cannot not influence. You're always influencing, even when you are out socially. Don't drink too much and lose the plot, or you'd have been better off staying home in bed!

Attend networking events in your industry or area of interest

Commanding Eagles network easily. Networking helps you connect with key people and stay up to date — and if an expert speaker is at the event, you will learn something too! Getting to know people in a relaxed environment strengthens relationships and helps remind people you are the go-to person when they need results. I was at a networking event the other day and a leader in industry casually told me over a drink about his strategy for making $5 million in 10 years, booked me to speak at his conference and then introduced me to his friends. What a valuable networking event that was!

Contribute to podcasts, blogs and vlogs

Lots of global organisations operate as connection agencies, connecting guests to podcast, blog and vlog hosts. Many of these organisations allow you to submit your profile for free. Hosts are sent your information, and they can reach out to you if they'd like you as a guest. I've been a guest of hosts based in all sorts of far-reaching locations, from Sydney to Mumbai and the United States. As a result, my profile is known around the globe. No matter your role in business, maybe today is the day to submit your profile to a podcast introduction agency and see what happens?

Join a board

Becoming a board member has many benefits, including learning an incredible amount about how a business works from the inside out. You will also gain a variety of professional skills such as communication, leadership, delegation, problem-solving and decision-making. Joining a board is a public confirmation of your expertise and value as a business professional that raises your profile.

Comment intelligently on people's social media posts

So many people are posting on the various social media platforms around the globe. These people are keen to inspire, educate and even pontificate. When you comment on a post in a sensible way and add value for the reader (in as few words as possible), you'll show people you are an expert and cement your brand as an authority.

TRY THIS

Pick a few subject matter experts that you admire on social media and see if you can add to their posts in a meaningful way.

Seek out PR opportunities

Publicity, or PR, cultivates a positive reputation with the public through various forms, including interviews on traditional media and social media and at in-person events. Seek out ways to be quoted or featured as an expert where possible. One place to start is the industry publication in your field.

TRY THIS

Write an article that helps others in your industry with a key problem or challenge. Find out the name of the editor of the main magazine, ezine or blog for your industry and ask them to publish your article.

Handy tip: Raising your profile is a terrific way to get yourself noticed. Don't be shy about this! Make sure everyone knows about your capabilities, drive and confidence. Commanding Eagles do this naturally and, as a result, they are often the ones who own the room.

Be trustworthy

Trust is something that you earn over time. If you are consistently reliable, honest and authentic, you'll be trustworthy. When you are trustworthy, people know they can count on you, and so they let their guard down and give you the benefit of the doubt. Trustworthy people are more persuasive than those who are not!

If you want to be trustworthy, you need to cultivate the following five qualities:

- authenticity
- consistency
- integrity
- reliability
- availability.

> **TIP**
>
> **Michelle says,**
>
> 'When you are trustworthy, people know they can count on you, and so they let their guard down and give you the benefit of the doubt. Trustworthy people are more persuasive than those who are not!'

Authenticity

Authentic people are true to their personality, values and spirit in the way they think, speak and act. If you want to be known as authentic, it's important to be honest with yourself and others and make sure that your actions mirror your values.

Consistency

People trust consistent, reliable behaviour. Consistency is about repeating the same actions, habits and rituals over and over, and adapting where necessary to improve. Consistency in your actions encourages people to feel safe and secure around you, which will positively affect your persuasiveness.

Integrity

If you have integrity, you are seen as honest with strong moral principles that you always uphold. Integrity compels you to tell the truth no matter the consequences, and admit to doing something wrong (even if you might have gotten away with it). Yes, people of integrity take responsibility for their mistakes. As scholar and novelist C S Lewis noted, 'Integrity is doing the right thing, even when no-one is watching'.

Reliability

Reliability includes doing what you say you'll do. A lot of people are guilty of saying they will do things and never following through.

They say, 'Oh, we must catch up!' and that commitment is never followed up. Or they offer to help you in some way — perhaps provide an introduction or opportunity for you in your career — and then...crickets! You hear nothing. They don't come through for you. When this happens, you're left wondering, 'Is it me? Did I do something wrong?' or 'Perhaps they don't like me?'

People lacking in reliability frequently break rapport and are not persuasive. On the contrary, when you do what you say you will do, it suggests you are reliable and trustworthy.

Handy tip: People respect others who do what they say they will do. Importantly, if you do what you say you'll do, you will also feel good about yourself. Doing what you say you will do opens up your persuasive opportunities.

Availability

If you want to be trustworthy, you need to be there for people. Make sure you are available to support and guide others. Be sure to make time for people, look up from your desk when people walk into your office, answer your phone and reply to your emails. Simply being there creates rapport and makes you more persuasive.

TRY THIS

Reflect for a moment on the five elements of trust: authenticity, consistency, integrity, reliability and availability. Decide which of these to focus on first and do three things this week to improve in that area.

Refine your elevator pitch

You're at a networking event and it comes time for everyone to take turns to stand up and introduce themselves to the interested onlookers. One after the other, the people before you bore everyone with their dreary descriptions of their work. Now it's your turn. You're going to either captivate them with a fascinating pitch that's relatable and compels them to know more, or bomb with another forgettable, nervous or lacklustre response.

When someone asks you, 'What do you do?', how are you going to stand out? One way is with a stunning elevator pitch! An elevator pitch is a short and clear business pitch that can be delivered in the time it takes to catch the elevator from one floor to another. If you want to make the most of opportunities that come your way, you need to be prepared to give an impressive elevator pitch at any time, especially when attending networking events.

Why refine your elevator pitch?

People who don't have a good elevator pitch may struggle to capture people's attention, which could result in missing an opportunity to persuade. Entrepreneurs need a great elevator pitch to persuade potential clients about the brilliant product or service they have to offer the world. Whereas, if you're an intrapreneur (working inside a business), your elevator pitch might mean the difference between meeting the right people and not, or the difference between getting that next perfect role and not.

Plus, in truth, being able to explain what you do quickly is just good practice. It helps you get to the heart of what you do, and why you do it.

Delivering a good elevator pitch

A lot of fuss surrounds elevator pitches. I'm frequently asked for my opinion on how to write a good one! I once attended a seminar on how to craft one and they taught us a nine-step model. Yep — nine steps! This is complete nonsense. An elevator pitch doesn't have to be that complicated. In fact, it shouldn't be complicated or you'll sound self-obsessed.

I'm going to suggest two different styles to you. The first style is very short — I call it the 'one-line elevator pitch'. The other, called the 'five-step elevator pitch', is longer in case you have just a minute of extra time.

ONE-LINE ELEVATOR PITCH

The one-line approach is where you explain how you help people in just one sentence. You can start with, 'I help people' and then say what you achieve. Or you can start with your title and then further explain what that means by outlining how you help people. Here are some examples:

- 'I help people who feel trapped and unfulfilled in their corporate jobs ditch the ladder, escape the nine to five and live a life of purpose, success and abundance through running their own business.'

- 'As an executive strategist, coach and speaker, I bring clarity to complex situations, enabling difficult decisions to be made with confidence.'

- 'I'm a pitch coach, and I help people to communicate their ideas persuasively, so they are undeniable and win more often.'

- 'I'm an accountant with PwC and specialise in corporate tax. I'm working on an interesting project at the moment to help a global client minimise their tax liability.'

You can see that using this approach is memorable. If the other person needed to ditch their boring corporate job, make more important decisions in their executive role, pitch their idea or minimise their tax liability, they would know who to go to.

THE FIVE-STEP ELEVATOR PITCH

If you'd like a longer elevator pitch, the five-step elevator pitch is a simple way to plan out what you'd like to say. What to focus on at each of the five steps is as follows:

1. *Problem:* Briefly introduce the problem first — for example, 'Many people find...'

2. *Solution:* Then outline the solution — 'Imagine if...'

3. *Target audience:* Explain who benefits from your product or service.

4. *Proof:* List one or more clients who have reaped the rewards of your help.

5. *Statement of fact:* Ensure the audience is convinced by finishing with a statement of fact about what you're offering.

An example of the five-step pitch is as follows:

> Have you ever felt like you were banging your head against a brick wall when trying to convince someone to say yes to your ideas? Imagine if you knew the formula that successful business presenters use to persuade people. I specialise in helping businesspeople pitch their ideas so people listen, engage, and say yes more quickly. Last year I helped several corporate clients win multimillion-dollar pitches. The reason we follow formulas is because they work.

Here's a slightly longer example:

> Most people fear speaking in public. In fact, you've probably heard that people fear public speaking more than death. Imagine if you could learn what awesome public speakers do to manage their nerves so that you captivate an audience and never feel fearful when speaking in public again. I specialise in helping businesspeople overcome their public speaking fears so they can communicate with confidence, clarity and influence every time. I've just helped an amazing woman called Amy. When Amy was only 10 years old, she was booed by her teacher and classmates while doing a speech in class. How horrible. Poor Amy! Amy was fearful of public speaking from that moment on. Now 22 years later, when she was 32 years old, Amy contacted me and explained that she had decided to overcome her fear. She had signed up as a keynote speaker at a conference of 120 people. Her brief to me was, 'Cure me'. No pressure! Amy learnt the three phases to a persuasive presentation in business. And the good news is that Amy was told she was the best speaker at the event. She's cured forever. Anyone can be a confident presenter — it's just a matter of knowing what to do and doing it.

TRY THIS

Can you create an elevator pitch using either the one-line elevator pitch or the five-step elevator pitch?

Once you've written your pitch, practise saying it so that the next time you find yourself at a networking event and you're asked what you do, you're ready to go. I'm sure you'll be glad you did.

Calm your farm

Yes! Commanding Eagles are calm under pressure. They don't lose their temper, raise their voice or frighten people. As Latin writer from the first century BCE Publilius Syrus noted, 'Anyone can hold the helm when the sea is calm'. The impressive thing about Commanding Eagles is they demonstrate composure and calmness in the face of antagonism also and, in doing so, they keep everyone around them calm too.

The opposite of calm is stress and anger. These reduce your cognitive performance, increase your chances of obesity and heart disease, and make the workplace generally unpleasant for everyone around you. An organisation called TalentSmart EQ (a leading provider of EQ training) conducted research with more than a million people and found that 90 per cent of top performers are skilled at managing their emotions in times of stress in order to remain calm and in control. If you want to be seen as personally credible you need to demonstrate similar composure — in other words, you need to learn to calm your farm!

TIP

Michelle says,

'If you want to be seen as personally credible you need to manage your emotions in times of stress and remain calm and in control — in other words, you need to learn to calm your farm!'

Maintaining composure

You have many options available to help you maintain composure under pressure, including meditation, planning your responses and working with your breath.

MEDITATION

Meditation is a wonderful way to make calmness your habit. Plenty of studies have proven if you make mediation a regular part of your week, you'll be calmer as you move through life. Even just five minutes of meditation a day makes a substantial difference to your levels of tension and your reactiveness.

PLAN YOUR RESPONSES IN ADVANCE

Think in advance about all the points that your stakeholder could raise that might worry, upset or anger you. Plan how you will respond calmly and functionally if or when they are raised. In chapter 6, I outline a wonderful linguistic pattern for managing objections, as part of my Persuasion Blueprint. Brainstorm all the issues that you need to resolve in your next meeting and refer to the five-step objection handling technique from chapter 6 to plan out your responses.

Poornima's story

I have a terrific client called Poornima who works for a big IT company. Poornima was pitching for some business, and I had the chance to work with her on the pitch. She knew her potential client would want to ask her several contentious questions. Poornima suspected the potential client might even be a bit tired and too busy to phrase the questions politely, and that this might cause her to feel threatened and stressed. We know that when we are threatened and stressed, we can tend to stammer and waffle and mess up our answers, even when we are the subject matter expert!

(continued)

So together we made a plan. Poornima brainstormed all the questions that she might be asked. Then she wrote out some impressive, audience-focused answers that were sincere and convincing using the objection handing technique outlined in chapter 6. Then she practised answering those same questions with a colleague. And, yes, they won the job!

TRY THIS

What are the contentious issues you find yourself needing to discuss with others? Climate change? Economic issues? Leadership matters? Performance issues? Plan your responses in advance. Use the five-step objection handling technique from the Persuasion Blueprint (outlined in chapter 6) to write out a brief argument for your points of view about the pressing key issues you must discuss in your life.

PRACTISE DIAPHRAGMATIC BREATH

You may think that breathing is a natural thing that we just do properly. Unfortunately, most of us shift to unhealthy, shallow chest-breathing when we are faced with a situation of stress or pressure — instead of lovely deep breathing using our diaphragm that improves oxygen circulation and calms us. Your diaphragm is located below the lungs and is the major muscle of respiration. Let's look at how you breathe diaphragmatically:

1. Place one hand on the middle of the upper chest and the other hand on your belly, just beneath the rib cage.

2. Inhale by slowly breathing in through your nose, drawing your breath down toward your belly. Your belly should push upward against your lower hand, while your chest remains still.

3. Exhale and tighten your abdominal muscles, letting your belly fall downward, while your again chest remains still.

A diaphragmatic breath should fully engage your stomach, abdominal muscles and diaphragm.

The trick is to be conscious of breathing diaphragmatically every time you feel stressed or worried. You want to teach yourself to automatically breathe in this way under pressure. You want diaphragmatic breathing to become such a habit that you maintain it always. If you can practise making diaphragmatic breathing a natural response when you're stressed, you'll always appear calm.

Being calm at work helps you think more clearly and make better decisions — which means you'll be perceived as more controlled and reliable, and someone to follow. In other words, you'll be perceived as a Commanding Eagle.

TRY THIS

Pick something from this 'Calm your farm' section that will improve your ability to stay calm under pressure, and implement it today.

Speak with elegance

When credible people speak, they demonstrate fluidity, elegance and smoothness in their speech. And, interestingly, they often speak just a little faster than average, as though they are just that little bit more intelligent and, therefore, able to form their thoughts more quickly than the average person! Credible people give you that impressive sense that they can think on their feet no matter the issue being discussed.

Here's how you build spoken elegance:

- write out your answers in advance

- articulate well

- resonate vocally

- pause for power

- use vocal flexibility

- eliminate annoying linguistic habits.

Let's look at each of these actions in more detail:

Write out your answers in advance

Credible people don't waffle. As scientist, inventor and statesman Benjamin Franklin is said to have wisely noted, 'When you fail to plan, you are planning to fail'. While no substantive evidence exists that Benjamin Franklin employed this adage, the words are powerful. And the opposite is also true: when you plan thoroughly and you know that your words are going to shift your stakeholder from where they are to where you want them to be and then you practise until you can't get it wrong, you'll be undeniable.

To improve your spoken elegance, brainstorm and then write out a list of possible matters you will need to discuss. The writing process helps you refine your thinking and craft your perfect response. I have clients with a special notebook that they use for this purpose. In preparation for upcoming meetings where they might be asked their opinion on a matter, they jot down their thoughts and then refine them so they are brief, insightful and can be delivered smoothly. The writing also acts as another type of rehearsal.

Fun fact: Ronald Reagan was a master at delivering short, impactful messages. The story goes that he kept more than 30 palm cards with him that contained his key points on a wide variety of subjects that he might find himself discussing—everything from the world economy to race relations and the Cold War. Before attending an event he flipped through the cards to find the most appropriate conversation starters and responses.

Articulate

Articulation is the clarity of your words and, as US entrepreneur, author and motivational speaker Jim Rohn highlights, 'Accuracy builds credibility'. It's a fact that if you speak quickly, focusing on emphasising the beginning and ends of your words, so they are clear and crisp, is very important.

To articulate, warm up your lips, teeth, cheeks and tongue so that you can say your words nice and quickly without tripping or choking. Blowing raspberries, stretching your lips into the shape of a kiss (with your lips pouting) and then a grin (with your top and bottom teeth showing), and neighing like a horse all help to warm your articulation. Have some fun with this! The point is that you want to speak with clear, crisp articulation so you further cement your personal credibility.

Handy tip: A whole chapter in my first book is devoted to techniques to warm up your body, your mind and your voice—check out How to Present: The ultimate guide to presenting your ideas and influencing people using techniques that actually work *(Wiley) to find out more.*

TRY THIS

When you wake up tomorrow morning, begin a routine of warming up your lips, teeth, cheeks and tongue by blowing some raspberries and doing some big kisses! Notice how much more clearly you speak throughout the day. Awesome!

Resonate vocally

We associate authority and credibility with people who have a deep, rich vocal tone (male or female). Your vocal tone has nothing to do with either how flat, or how interesting your voice is. It's not about the highs and lows in the sound when you speak (that's called your vocal range). Instead, your tone refers to the resonance of your voice or how smoothly your sound reverberates through the resonating chambers of your face when you speak. Listen to anyone who has been to four years of acting school and notice that they speak with a rich resonant tone. The good news is that you too can warm your tone — and when you do, you'll automatically improve your credibility with it.

If you'd like to warm up your tone, you need to do some big guttural yawns. Forget what your parents told you about yawning with polite manners and be sure you open your mouth very wide. As you do so, make a guttural sound from the back of your throat that sounds a bit like this, 'Ahhhhhh'. Do this five times in a row. You can do this on the way to work each morning (although maybe not on public transport), before an important meeting or whenever you have a spare moment because the results are cumulative. The more you do this, the deeper your tone will be. The benefits last for hours after each set of five yawns.

Add some big yawns into your morning voice warm-up routine upon waking.

Pause for power

The ability to hold the silence and not fill it with meaningless chitchat is the sign of a true Commanding Eagle. Writer Mark Twain wisely said, 'No word was ever as effective as a rightly timed pause'. Pauses help you separate one point from another. They give your stakeholder a moment to reflect on what you said. Pauses in the right places make you more persuasive.

Use vocal flexibility

Ending a sentence on a high note sounds like you're asking a question. When you end your sentence on a down note, it comes across more confidently, and more like a command. Commanding Eagles speak with conviction, which means they generally end their sentences on the low note.

Eliminate annoying linguistic habits

People with personal credibility give you that impressive sense that they are a complete expert, and they express their message in a way that makes their assertions undeniable. They don't say 'Um' and 'Ahh', they don't use words that are overcomplicated, and they are confident you heard them the first time, so they don't repeat themselves unnecessarily. And because of these habits, any reasonable person would not be able to disagree with them!

To appear personally credible, it's important to do three things to eliminate annoying linguistic habits:

1. Speak plain English.

2. Don't repeat yourself.

3. Don't use words that turn people off.

SPEAK PLAIN ENGLISH

Be sure to use the right words in your sentences. Don't try to use complicated words that no-one understands, and don't accidently use the wrong word or the wrong pronunciation of a word in an attempt to sound sophisticated (unless you're doing it on purpose to get a laugh). Using the wrong word, or a mispronounced word, makes you look like you're trying too hard and is a turn-off.

A classic example of using a word you don't really understand to sound clever (and then having the moment backfire) occurs many times in the funny Australian sitcom *Kath and Kim.* In one of the episodes from season 1, for example, Kim (one of the lead characters) talks about aspiring for a better life and a desire to be 'effluent'. (Effluent, of course, means sewage.) What she really means is 'affluent', which means wealthy. Oh dear! When we use big words that we don't understand we generally end up appearing silly.

DON'T REPEAT YOURSELF

Commanding Eagles communicate clearly and succinctly. They are so confident in their knowledge and capability that they expect you heard them the first time, even if you don't give them an active listening signal. For this reason, they rarely repeat themselves unnecessarily. To build this as your habit, say something once and clearly, and don't fall into the trap of thinking people didn't hear you the first time and repeat yourself!

DON'T USE WORDS THAT TURN PEOPLE OFF

Persuasive people choose their words carefully. As I cover in chapter 2, certain actions when you're hoping to persuade can turn people off. Similarly, we should never say particular words when we're aiming to persuade because they disrupt our spoken elegance. Eliminate words that confuse people, turn people off, cause your stakeholder to argue with you or cause conflict.

What are these words you shouldn't say when conveying personal credibility? Here are the most commonly used words that you might want to re-think when you are persuading:

- 'um', 'ahh', 'so' and 'like'
- 'sorry'
- 'for those of you who don't know me'
- 'please don't hesitate'
- 'thanks for coming' or 'thanks for your time today'
- 'cost'.

Why shouldn't you say 'um' 'ahh' 'so' and 'like'

When your aim is to be as persuasive as possible, avoid filler words such as 'um', 'ahh', 'so' and 'like'. These words imply that you are not sure about what to say next, that you haven't organised your thoughts and that you're a bit scattered in your thinking. If you use these filler words, some people will assume you are less intelligent than you are.

Further, some people are 'counters'. These people count how many times you say 'um' or 'ah' in the conversation — and they are ruthless in their endeavour! In my experience, they are more common than you'd realise too. Make life easy for these people by avoiding these filler words so they can just sit back and listen to your argument.

To avoid using filler words, aim to take a big pause and breathe diaphragmatically — right down to the bottom of your tummy. You don't need to fill the quiet space with unnecessary talking. By pausing and breathing, you're giving the other person a moment to reflect on what you said in the silence. They will concentrate better on your overall message if you give them some brief pauses. Remember — the pause is powerful!

Handy tip: *You can't expect to reduce your use of filler words when you persuade if you say them every other time you talk. If you want to be sure that you don't use filler words when you are persuading, aim to eliminate them in your everyday talking.*

TRY THIS

Spend some time focusing on whether you say 'um', 'ah', 'so' or 'like' when you speak. If this is a problem for you, try hard to spend a few weeks eliminating this habit.

Why shouldn't you say 'sorry'

When I'm coaching people on the best way to deliver their business pitch, many can say the word 'sorry' (without even realising it) as many as five or six times in a five-minute pitch. And most of the time, they're apologising for something the audience didn't even notice or care about.

The problem is that we tend to say sorry when we really shouldn't — for example, when our error is very small, or the other person really doesn't care. For example, we put up the wrong slide — we say sorry. We say the wrong word in our sentence, or trip over our articulation — we say sorry. Or we trip a little bit over our own feet — we say sorry. In situations such as these, you don't need to say sorry!

Here's the theory that explains why. A cool part in your brain is the reticular activating system (RAS). In essence, the RAS is like a gatekeeper of information — it tracks for what it knows and cares about, and filters out the rest. Have you ever bought a car and then you see that car everywhere on the road? The same colour, same model. It's everywhere. That's your RAS noticing that. Have you been on a holiday and then found yourself noticing deals for that destination for months after, even though your holiday is over? That's your RAS noticing that too.

When something is important to you, the RAS helps you by highlighting experiences or things that can help you. Let's say you're getting married. Now your RAS helps you by highlighting all the things in your environment that might help you with this significant life moment. You start noticing florists all around you, or wedding venues. You see what I mean? Your RAS highlights these things because your brain knows that this of interest to you.

When you say sorry in a business pitch or meeting, guess what your stakeholders' brains start looking for now? Yes, the word 'sorry' highlights for them that an error has occurred (something that's serious enough to apologise about) and now their brains start tracking for all the other mistakes that you're about to make. In other words, by saying sorry you've effectively asked your stakeholders to look out for future errors or blunders you make.

Handy tip: Don't respond to a question with 'sorry'. Many people mistakenly ask, 'Sorry?' when asked a question in a meeting or pitch and didn't hear what the asker said (as though they should apologise that they didn't hear properly). This is another time when sorry is not necessary and should be replaced with something like, 'Please could you repeat your question?'

The point is if you do something offensive, please do say sorry. Otherwise, don't worry about saying sorry. Just take a breath and keep going. The other person probably didn't even notice you made a little mistake anyway.

Why shouldn't you say 'for those of you who don't know me'

One of the things you don't need to say when you're introducing yourself in a meeting with several attendees is, 'For those of you who don't know me…' It's a common thing to say when you want to pre-empt your introduction of yourself. A Commanding Eagle would never say this. And they don't want to hear you say it either.

This is an exclusive statement. 'For those of you who don't know me' implies that you're only talking to those people who don't know you and that all the other people in the meeting who do know you don't matter.

A better way to impress the Commanding Eagles is to own the room and just say your name confidently. For example:

- 'Good morning, everyone. I'm Michelle.'
- 'How wonderful to see you all. I'm Michelle.'
- 'It's terrific you're all here today. I'm Michelle.'

The people who know that you're Michelle won't mind that you did it that way, and the people who didn't know your name now know it. There you go.

TRY THIS

The next time you introduce yourself at the start of a meeting make sure you don't say 'for those of you who don't know me'. Instead, just say your name.

Why shouldn't you say 'please don't hesitate'

Another thing that you shouldn't say or write is, 'Please don't hesitate to…' For example, 'Please don't hesitate to leave me a message' or

'Please don't hesitate to contact me'. Why is that not a good idea? Well, let me demonstrate: whatever you do right now, don't think of a pink elephant. See, even though I said not to, you're still thinking of a pink elephant, aren't you?

When you say, 'Please don't hesitate to contact me' or 'Please don't hesitate to leave me a message' your audience hears the word 'hesitate', not the word 'don't'. What that's doing unconsciously is sending a message that you don't want them to leave a message, and you don't want to talk to them.

A much more positive way to say this is to use something like the following:

- 'Please leave me a message.'

- 'Please contact me.'

- 'Please reach out to me.'

Be positive, on the front foot, passionate and persuasive in the way that you communicate.

TRY THIS

Look at the 'out of office' message on your email and listen to your message on voicemail. Notice whether you've said, 'Please don't hesitate to leave me a message' and fix it if you need to.

Why shouldn't you say 'thanks for coming' or 'thanks for your time today'

At the start and finish of their meetings, a lot of people say, 'Thanks for coming' and/or 'Thanks for your time'. If you want to build more Commanding Eagle into your persuasive approach, I'm going to suggest to you that you don't say this anymore.

'Why not?' I hear you asking — after all, isn't it just manners to thank someone for coming? And yes, you're right; it is polite and lovely manners to thank people for their time. The problem with thank you in this context is that it enacts the law of reciprocity — and the law of reciprocity states that if you do me some sort of favour, I'm going to owe you in return. If you turn up to my meeting and I'm thankful for that, then I will owe you. When you say to the other person, 'Thanks so much for coming today' or 'Thanks for your time', or you say to your client, 'Thanks for the opportunity to meet with you today', you're implying that this other person has done you some kind of a favour by turning up or giving you their time. Now the law of reciprocity kicks in and you are going to owe them in return. You are going to have to work hard to pay them back for their generous gesture of turning up today!

While it is nice manners to thank people and, yes, on plenty of occasions saying thank you is a great idea, don't say it unless you mean to enact the law of reciprocity. Instead, just be gorgeous. Say something equally generous or joyful. Just don't use the exact words 'Thank you'.

For example, you could say:

- 'It's great to see you.'

- 'This has been an exciting meeting.'

- 'How wonderful that we get to discuss this important initiative for your team.'

- 'This is a great opportunity to go through your needs and see how I might help you.'

You can see that in all these examples the need for reciprocity doesn't arise because the comment implies that both parties are winning, and no-one owes anyone anything.

Handy tip: *Also remove that slide you've got in your standard slide deck at work that says, 'Thank you,' at the end. It's unnecessary and sends the wrong message. (Check out chapter 6 and note that you can say, 'It's been my pleasure to speak with you today' at step 8 of the Persuasion Blueprint instead of 'Thank you'.)*

TRY THIS

Take a look at your company template and get rid of the 'Thank you' slide at the end!

Next time you are running a meeting or having an important conversation, plan in advance that you won't say 'thank you' and make an alternative plan for a better thing to say instead.

Why shouldn't you say 'cost'

We know that words have power. We attribute meaning to words based on our experiences. Can you notice the difference between the following sentences?

- 'The cost is *x*.'

- 'The investment is *x*.'

In the second example, you can see that that 'investment' implies the strong chance you'll get a return; whereas the word 'cost' in the first example implies you're giving or outlaying something with no benefit in return. Cost implies an expense and a sacrifice.

The first principle of persuasion is that you must believe that the thing you're persuading about is worth the investment (in time, effort and money). If you don't believe it's worth it, you certainly won't convince anyone else about it!

My stepfather, Tom, taught me not to say 'cost' at the start of my business journey and I can't tell you how many times I've had to catch myself saying 'cost' when I meant to say 'investment'. It's been a very important little tip that has helped convey a positive vibe in my proposals and pitches over decades. Don't ever talk about the 'cost', whether that be time, effort or their money. Instead, always convey the value your stakeholder will gain. Always choose the word 'investment' over the word 'cost'.

TRY THIS

Look at your company proposal and replace the word 'cost' in the investment table with 'investment'. Where else can you replace the word 'cost' with the word 'investment' in your practice?

Back yourself

It's common to suffer from self-doubt and not put yourself in situations where you might make a mistake or embarrass yourself. After all, no-one wants to be thought of as a fool, especially when persuading someone about their big idea. With their undeniable personal authority, Commanding Eagles naturally exude confidence and conviction in their ability and ideas — they always back themselves.

You backing yourself and having faith in yourself and your ideas is very contagious. As my sassy daughter Holly reminds me, 'Mum, moods are contagious. Is yours worth catching?' Ha! She's so sassy — and so right!

To back yourself is to have faith in yourself. You know you can do it. Commanding Eagles are confident about their strengths, because they know they have the runs on the board and that they are the best person for the job at hand. They are passionate and committed to their causes. They are confident at articulating their perspective and they don't shy away from difficult issues — or back down easily unless the evidence is compelling. Because Commanding Eagles take advantage of opportunities to collaborate with others and contribute to their favourite causes as a way of building their expertise and skills, they generally move through life feeling excellent.

TIP

Michelle says,

'Commanding Eagles are confident about their strengths and don't shy away from difficult issues.'

Ways to back yourself

You can become better at backing yourself by consciously developing actions that remind you why you should be listened to. The following section outlines some of these techniques.

JOURNAL

One way to make sure you back yourself is to use a journal to note down all your strengths. Don't be shy about this. Write them all down and then celebrate this daily. Another way to use your journal while you build your confidence in communication is to write down what you think (and why you think it) about a variety of issues and challenges. Use your writing to clarify your thinking and refine your perspectives. This, in turn, means you'll be better able to express what you mean when the time is right.

FILE COMPLIMENTS

Start a file or folder where you store positive memories, including compliments and praise from others. When you are feeling less than confident, you can read through the file and give yourself a boost.

REMEMBER YOU ARE THE EXPERT

Do everything you can to be an expert in your field and own your lane. Strive to know everything you can about all aspects of your niche and then consciously celebrate your knowledge and experience gains. It's very important to believe you are the best person for the job, your idea is excellent, and your products and services are second to none. You'll be best placed to feel this way about yourself if you've done the work. You likely know that Malcom Gladwell (bestselling author of *Outliers*) says it takes 10 000 hours to become an exceptional person who is superior in their field of expertise. Today is the day to focus on getting those 10 000 hours under your belt so you can feel confident that you are becoming the expert you want to be.

MANAGE CONFLICT

We all move through life dealing with the contrary opinions of others that test our boundaries. When someone tries to railroad you or force you into something you believe is wrong, it's time to stretch your Commanding Eagle wings. Strive to deal with conflict in a functional way where everyone wins.

A fantastic model for managing conflict involves five steps:

1. State the objection.

2. Say 'and' or 'so' or pause.

3. Say 'actually' or 'in fact'.

4. Solve the objection

5. Use the word 'because'.

You can find all the details for using this five-step objection handling technique in chapter 6.

Lydell's story

Lydell is my wonderful client. He's clever, experienced and incredibly innovative in his thinking. He achieves ground-breaking wins for his business. Do you know what? He knows it! Before you groan and say something less than friendly, he doesn't know this in an arrogant way that is a turn-off to the people he works with and for. He just knows that he is the right person for the job. He knows what he is doing. He has years and years of exciting and relevant experience. He's an expert in his field. And he knows this about himself. He backs himself. Lydell exudes confidence when he speaks up in a meeting and, I can tell you, he is very attractive and persuasive to his colleagues, suppliers, team members and leaders. Lydell is undeniable.

TRY THIS

What could you do to start the process of realising your strengths so that you are even better at backing yourself and your ideas?

Try using a journal to note your strengths. Or find someone you trust and respect and have a heart-to-heart conversation with them where you map out your strengths. Enjoy the process!

Tell stories that impress

Stories help to make us memorable. When your main aim is to establish or cement your personal credibility, choosing stories that are about you and how you were involved in some successes in your past is so important. Indeed, Dr Howard Gardner, Research Professor at Harvard University, argues, 'Stories constitute the single most powerful weapon in a leader's arsenal'.

Commanding Eagles use stories to turn the explanation of a seemingly boring project or task into something impressive and relevant to their stakeholder, so they are seen as trustworthy and essential to the client, project or business.

How do you tell stories to establish your personal credibility?

You can use a few models to tell a story. My preferred method for telling a memorable story is to use what is known as the 'magic formula' story. This is a simple technique invented by the bestselling author Dale Carnegie.

The magic formula for storytelling, also known as the 'IPB model', involves three steps:

1. *Incident:* This is where you tell the story. Aim to deliver a short, interesting account of what happened (the incident). Keep up the momentum so you don't lose people. Link any

facts with emotions. Make the story fascinating so that it's easy for the listener to repeat.

2. *Point:* You know how some storytellers tell the story, tell the story, tell the story — and you sit there thinking *Get to the point!* Well, it's important that you deliver the point of your story as soon as you can. Don't assume that the point is obvious to your audience.

3. *Benefit:* This is where you link your story, and the point of your story, to the listener. You explain the relevance of the story to them, so they know why they just listened to your story. The benefit may even be a call to action where you ask the person for something.

Here's an example story that uses the magic formula:

1. *Incident:* 'When I was National Sales Manager at Salesforce, we focused on ensuring that all our people were rewarded for their lag metrics as well as their lead conversions.'

2. *Point:* 'This meant that we improved loyalty and commitment to the business, reduced churn and generally exceeded the budgets.'

3. *Benefit:* 'We should implement that system here too.'

Can you see that this story cements personal credibility? You'd likely now ask this person to either implement a similar system, or advise you how to do it.

TRY THIS

Think of three past experiences that you could tell a story about. If you are a business owner or founder, one of your stories could be your foundation story – why did you start your business? Craft stories based on these experiences, making sure you use the magic formula, or IPB model, to impress your prospect or stakeholder, and help them find you credible and undeniable.

(continued)

Try your stories out on a few people first to see if they resonate. Take their feedback, refine your stories, and be ready to tell them when the perfect moment arises in your life.

Always exceed expectations

Exceptional service or delivery is rarely forgotten. While going the extra mile might feel like hard work to you, you'll be the one people come back to the next time they need your product, service or advice. As management consultant and bestselling author Tom Peters highlights, 'If you under-promise and over-deliver, you will not only keep the customers satisfied; you'll keep the customers'.

Exceeding expectation is where you deliver more than you promised. Commanding Eagles constantly exceed expectations.

Ways to exceed expectations

As the quote from Tom Peters shows, under-promising and over-delivering is a great way to exceed expectations. But this is just one option. The following sections cover this option and some further ideas.

UNDER-PROMISE AND OVER-DELIVER

Under-promising and over-delivering means being realistic about what you can achieve and promising the other person just less than what you deem possible. In this way, when you achieve slightly more than what you offered, it seems wonderful to your stakeholder because you have exceeded their expectations! This is a minimum for the Commanding Eagle. May I suggest it's even better to over-promise and then over-deliver! For example, let's say you've been asked to write a proposal in the next two weeks. If you know you can have it finished and sent by this Wednesday, offer to send it over by Friday. When it arrives two days earlier (but a week and two days earlier than their deadline) you will be impressive to your potential client. You send a message that you may always exceed expectations.

Under-promising and over-delivering (or better still, over-promising and over-delivering) creates trust that when you say you'll deliver, you will. And you won't only achieve what you say, you may even exceed it.

ALWAYS BE COURTEOUS

Courtesy means being polite and having polished manners. When you are courteous, people have a good impression of you and are more likely to trust and respect you. And showing a little courtesy often means you exceed people's expectations. Courtesy creates a respectful work environment and improves everyone's morale so they can be positive — and more productive. Courtesy is often a demonstration of the little things. US attorney and statesman Henry Clay said, 'Courtesies of a small and trivial character are the ones which strike deepest in the grateful and appreciating heart'.

To improve your courtesy skills, be as respectful as possible. Aim to use the words 'please' and 'thank you' sincerely and where appropriate. Be sure to read the room and only use slang, swearing and humour where appropriate.

Handy tip: Let your Commanding Eagle out and allow people to pass through doors ahead of you, open doors for people if you're there first, and don't get involved in workplace gossip.

TRY THIS

Plan to show courtesy to everyone you meet today, even just in small acts such as holding doors open, standing back for someone at the lift, or picking up an item that someone has dropped near you and passing it back to them. Start today!

ONLY MAKE PROMISES YOU CAN KEEP

Have you ever had a colleague who promised they would send you a response to your email by the close of business and then...crickets. Nothing! They disappear. The next time you needed something, did you trust their estimation of the delivery date? Probably not. Our personal credibility is damaged when we make a promise we can't (or choose not to) keep. Promises that are kept reinforce your integrity and solidify your relationships.

A promise is an undertaking or oath; it's a commitment to something. A person who breaks their promise is known as deceptive — or simply a liar. Commanding Eagles keep their promises. They build trust and personal credibility because they are thought of as someone who can always be relied upon.

COMMUNICATE REGULARLY

Isn't it frustrating when you are working with people who don't update you on their progress in a project? Sometimes this causes us to assume they are not going to meet the deadline. We might even go off and finish the task ourselves, only to find out later that the person was working on it all along and now you've doubled up. Groan. A waste of everyone's time.

And what about all those unanswered emails in your inbox? How do they make you feel? Waiting for a reply from someone so you can finish your part of a project is very annoying.

One of the most important things to do if you want to be perceived as credible is communicate regularly.

Felicity's story

Felicity is Regional Head of Bids in a huge corporation that regularly pitches for deals in the hundreds of millions. Felicity is the *master* at regular proactive and responsive communication. When she finds out something relevant to her team or her client, she lets them know immediately. When her clients contact her, she promptly replies. She's unbelievable. Yes, the company she works for is excellent at delivering their technology with value, but if Felicity wasn't so awesome at her part of the bid process, they wouldn't win anywhere near as many deals. Felicity and her personal credibility are a very important part of the persuasive process for her bid team.

Regular communication with people helps them to perceive you as focused, committed and competent. This improves general morale and efficiency in your team and cements your personal credibility with your stakeholders far and wide.

TRY THIS

Make a concerted effort to reply to people as quickly as possible, even if it's to tell them you're not ready to reply properly to them just yet.

FOLLOW UP

Growing up, my mum, Barbara, always insisted my brother and I sent thank-you cards when someone gave us a gift. As a result, I am awesome at thanking people for things and following up after meetings. This is one of the persuasive behaviours that sets me apart from my competitors. And you know what? People often post my cards, my gifts and my follow-ups on their social media because they are so surprised and delighted to have received them! It's a small thing that makes a huge difference to your persuasiveness.

Thanks to my mum I'm also awesome at following up prior to agreed or expected deadlines. Every time I follow up, people know I'm on it, and I care about them. I am consistently exceeding people's expectations and people frequently say, 'Oh, wow! Thanks for your speedy reply!' They are surprised, relieved and impressed at this very simple action.

Following up is a clever way to cement your relationships and demonstrate that you are thinking about your stakeholder and their needs. Without a follow-up message, the person may make the mistake of thinking you have moved on or don't care about your shared goals, project or team. There's no excuse for not following up.

Handy tip: If you are a forgetful person and following up doesn't come naturally, set yourself reminders so you are forced to remember to stay in touch. Always follow up!

TRY THIS

The next time you are asked to do anything, set a deadline with the other person that is realistic and then be sure to exceed their expectations. Deliver earlier than promised with regular communication and courtesy. This will begin the process of everyone knowing they can rely on you and builds your personal credibility.

Remember — most people are not good at exceeding expectations. If you do it, you will stand out for all the right reasons — and you'll also feel very good about yourself! It's worth the effort. Go forth and impress people!

A final word about personal credibility

Remember — no-one is just a Commanding Eagle. We all have a combination of the types in us, just in varying degrees. Regardless of whether personal authority is one of your strengths or not, you can see from this chapter that you can start focusing on so many wonderful things right now, so you build and develop your inner Commanding Eagle! Some of the tips are small things and very easy to adopt. Others are more of a stretch and will take longer to embed as habits. Perhaps pick one or two ideas each day and keep doing those things until they feel easy and like a normal part of your behaviour.

In most persuasive situations, personal authority is something your stakeholder is expecting from you. You want to be able to do all the actions outlined in this chapter all the time, not just in particular persuasive moments, such as an important meeting, conversation or business pitch. Remember also that you cannot *not* influence! You have an exciting opportunity to use personal authority to improve your overall persuasiveness in life.

TOP TIPS
The Commanding Eagle

- Personal authority causes people to trust and respect you.

- You have personal authority because you are an expert in your field, have done this before and are known as someone people can trust.

- You can do 10 things to establish personal authority:

   1. Become an expert in your niche through seeking opportunities for work experience, accessing mentors, studying and reading widely, and gaining relevant certification.

   2. Communicate your credibility — let everyone know! Put your qualifications on your email signature and social media profiles, display achievements and awards, use client testimonials, use examples of successful projects and your role in them, and incorporate credible words.

   3. Raise your profile through various activities, including joining committees, attending company events and contributing to podcasts, vlogs and blogs.

   4. Be trustworthy through cultivating your authenticity, consistency, integrity, kindness and availability.

   5. Refine your elevator pitch so you have a short, snappy response that helps you stand out when someone asks you the inevitable, 'What do you do?'

   6. Calm your farm! Meditate, plan your responses in advance and breathe to help you stay calm under pressure.

   7. Speak with elegance by removing filler words, speaking plain English, not repeating yourself, rehearsing, planning your responses in advance and articulating your words.

(continued)

8. Back yourself! Develop actions that remind you why you are an expert in your field and why you should be listened to.

9. Tell stories that impress to further establish your personal authority in the mind of your stakeholder.

10. Always exceed expectations through under-promising and over-delivering, being courteous, keeping your promises, communicating regularly and following up.

- Remember — no-one is just a Commanding Eagle. We all have a combination of the types in us. In most persuasive situations, conveying personal authority is something your stakeholder is expecting from you if they are to believe you — so use personal authority to improve your overall persuasiveness in life.

CHAPTER 8

Type 3: The Friendly Budgie

So, you'd like to build more of the Friendly Budgie into your persuasive approach? Maybe this is because the Friendly Budgie type isn't your strength. Maybe someone you have to persuade often — such as a manager, team member or even family member — is a Friendly Budgie and you want to demonstrate the behaviours that are most persuasive for them. Or maybe the Friendly Budgie is your strength, but you'd like to be even more proficient in persuading by building goodwill. Maybe you love the Brazilian proverb, 'Goodwill makes the road shorter'.

The Friendly Budgie is one of the charismatic types. They are thought of as friendly because they are warm and caring, and naturally build rapport with others. This chapter will show you how to do this. Firstly, though, let's look at why goodwill is so important.

Why you need goodwill in persuasion

Goodwill is the existence of friendly and cooperative feelings. Creating goodwill with others is important in persuasion because goodwill makes people feel great about you and increases the likelihood that they will be persuaded by you. Goodwill is the foundation of positive, thriving relationships that ensure both your success and the success of your prospect or stakeholder. Goodwill encourages the influence principle of reciprocity, which is where the recipient of a favour unconsciously feels they'd like to do a favour in return.

Building goodwill

You can focus on developing and cementing 10 actions if you're keen to bring out your inner Friendly Budgie and build goodwill. These actions are:

1. Know and accept yourself.

2. Accept others.

3. Be likeable.

4. Show warmth.

5. Build rapport.

6. Make people feel good.

7. Find ways to help people.

8. Connect.

9. Listen actively.

10. Don't use words that damage your goodwill.

The following sections look at each of these in more detail so you can make these your new (or stronger) habits.

Know and accept yourself

The first step to creating goodwill is to know and accept yourself. As far back as the 18th century, economist Adam Smith noted, 'The first thing you have to know is yourself. A man who knows himself can step outside himself and watch his own reactions like an observer'. Gender bias aside, this means you should aim to recognise what it is that makes you uniquely you, and embrace your individuality and perspectives. Understanding who you are and loving yourself gives you inner confidence and helps you be authentic throughout the persuasion process. When you're true to yourself, you are comfortable with the choices and actions you take, and your comfort in yourself is very contagious. Others will trust you too!

As Buddha said, 'You, yourself, as much as anybody in the entire universe, deserve your love and affection'. In addition to knowing yourself, it's very important to accept yourself for who you are. Being comfortable in your own skin is great for your overall health and wellbeing. Self-acceptance results in an inner confidence that is attractive to others. When you accept yourself and you know what makes you happy (and do more of that), your happiness is contagious. When you work out who you are and what you stand for, it's easier to build a meaningful connection with others because you can turn up the traits that work for the other person to cement your likeability and goodwill.

Working on accepting yourself

To get in touch with your true self, try some of the following activities.

JOURNAL DAILY

Journaling helps you define your sense of self and solidifies your identity as you move through the world. Choose an attractive diary that gives you joy and write for between five and 20 minutes daily. Let all the thoughts swimming around in your head out onto the paper. The point is to get it out of your head and into your journal so you can make better sense of what you're thinking and feeling about any of the matters in your life. You don't need to plan it or edit it like an essay; just let your thoughts flow. As the English poet and writer William Wordsworth said, 'Fill your paper with the breathings of your heart'.

PINPOINT YOUR STRENGTHS AND WEAKNESSES

You can also use your journal to pinpoint your strengths and weaknesses. What do you like? What don't you like and why? What are you good at? What are you not so good at? What are your strengths?

What are your weaknesses? Why do the people who like you feel that way? Why do the people who don't like you feel that way? (Try for full honesty here!) What are some of your favourite things? What are some of your least favourite things? What gives you joy? What makes you sad?

The point here is to derive a better sense of what others see and feel when they are around you. From here you are well placed to turn up the qualities that people like and turn down the qualities they don't!

TRY THIS

Why not pinpoint your strengths and weaknesses right now? Create two columns in your journal. In one column, write out all your strengths; in the other, all your weaknesses. Here are some questions to get you started:

- What am I good at?
- What can I do for hours without getting tired? Why is this?
- What are my hobbies, favourite foods, favourite colours, favourite people?
- What have other people complimented me on?
- What makes me happy?
- What am I not good at?
- What have other people had to help me with in the last few months?
- What activities make me very tired or sad? Why is this?

Eddie's story

Eddie is a lovely guy, but he wasn't great at reading the room. His speech was often too loud for the space, his eye contact wasn't great, and he tended to talk at you rather than with you. These traits made him unconvincing and a bit annoying when he was trying to tell a story or connect with others. Eddie also didn't seem to have any awareness about what he did or said to turn people off.

I recommended to him that he might like to pick a few friends that he felt comfortable chatting to and ask them what they thought his likeable characteristics were, and also what was unlikeable about him. This is a confronting exercise and not for everyone, and the good news is it transformed Eddie. Once he knew what to dial up or dial down about his character, he was much better placed to put his best foot forward and build strong connections. He is still himself. Now he's just the best version of himself in each contrasting moment. He hasn't looked back and describes himself as much happier these days.

SIT AND THINK

In this busy life, sitting still can be difficult! It's a wonderful idea to try to find between five and 20 minutes every day to just sit and think. I sit on a chair in my backyard and just look at the nature around me. I listen to the birds. I observe the wind blowing in the trees. I smell the fragrance of the flowers. Sometimes I lie down and look up at the moving clouds in the sky. I try not to determine what my mind will focus on, and instead just let it wander. If doing nothing doesn't sound like something you'd enjoy, you could replace this with a meditation.

Some of my most clever and productive ideas have come during or just after this lovely time simply sitting. Sitting and thinking helps you realise what you think about life and sets you up to better connect with others.

KNOW WHAT MAKES YOU HAPPY — AND THEN DO IT!

Pursue your passions! What is it that makes you happy? Is it going for a run, singing in a choir, working on your car, helping injured animals or all of the above? Work out what makes you feel truly happy and make sure you go and do it more.

Handy tip: *The happier you are, the more people want to spend time with you and the more goodwill you build.*

MAKE DECISIONS THAT ALIGN WITH YOUR VALUES AND BELIEFS

When making decisions, listening to both your inner voice and the needs of others is good practice. Accept what you believe about matters and, after thinking through the consequences, be confident in always finally choosing what you believe is best.

ALLOW YOURSELF TO BE VULNERABLE AND OPEN-HEARTED

Being vulnerable doesn't mean being a pushover. It means being brave and owning your feelings. Vulnerability is a sign of courage. Research Professor Brené Brown is an expert in vulnerability, and argues, 'Courage starts with showing up and letting ourselves be seen'.

Friendly Budgies foster powerful goodwill when they embrace who they truly are and what they are feeling, and can open up to others in their various communication moments.

Handy tip: *Talk frankly and openly about your thoughts and feelings while still caring about the resulting impact of your words and actions on others.*

TRY THIS

Start something that makes you happy. Sign up for a group, take a class, go for a walk — whatever floats your boat. Do things that make you happy and you'll be contagious!

If you struggle with feelings of low self-worth, you'll also struggle to build rapport and goodwill. Low self-worth can cause you to incorrectly conclude that others are better than you, which can lead to you feeling unworthy of spending time with them. If you're feeling freaked out, you can't persuade effectively. Friendly Budgies know they are enough.

Believing you are enough is part of the foundation of goodwill and persuasion. You are worthy. You can persuade and create win–win situations for both you and your prospect or stakeholder. I believe in you! Now you need to believe in you. You can do it!

> **TIP**
>
> **Michelle says,**
>
> 'Believing you are enough is part of the foundation of goodwill and persuasion.'

Accept others

One of the most wonderful feelings you can experience as a human is acceptance from others. The writer George Orwell said, 'Happiness can only exist in acceptance'. Yes, indeed, being seen for who you really are and then being unconditionally accepted by others is a very special experience. Feeling that people accept you gives you joy, peace and calm. Acceptance of others is what unifies us as a species. And, importantly, acceptance is the foundation of rapport. I can't believe that you like me if you don't accept me. When people feel accepted by you, they are more likely to be persuaded by you.

Working on accepting others

If you want to try to accept people more, tolerance is something to master. Tolerance is about broad mindedness, open mindedness and patience — three qualities that Friendly Budgies possess in spades.

The following sections outline some ways to nurture tolerance and acceptance of people.

DON'T JUDGE

Listen without jumping to conclusions. Aim to take everyone as you find them and give everyone the benefit of the doubt. Prejudging is one of the big mistakes people make when they are not naturally strong at building goodwill. Try as hard as you can not to judge a book by its cover. You may well find that if you treat everyone as though they are worthy of your time, they will rise to the occasion. In business, they may even become your most valuable client or ally.

ACT 'AS IF'

Have you ever stopped to realise that even those people you seldom interact with tend to respond favourably when you approach your relationship with them as if they are a long-lost valuable friend? It's a basic fact of influence that if the other person perceives you to be committed to the relationship with them, they will generally respond in kind. Ask yourself if you need to change the way you interact with your team members, manager, or clients.

REMEMBER PEOPLE ARE NOT THEIR BEHAVIOUR

What a great concept this is! It means that although someone's behaviour might be horrible, that doesn't mean the person is a horrible person. It's just their behaviour, not their definition. The actions they are taking are the best they can offer in the situation.

Holly's story

My daughter Holly is strongest in the Friendly Budgie type – she naturally and genuinely likes all people. For many years, Holly worked as a make-up artist on a prestigious cosmetic counter in a large department store. Boy, did she have to deal with a variety of personality types and moods!

One day, a lady (let's call her Flossy) attended Holly's counter for a makeover. Flossy was cranky, rude and snappy with Holly for the first half of the appointment. While Holly found this behaviour hurtful and unnecessary, as a natural Friendly Budgie she has developed an innate drive to show kindness and compassion to everyone she meets. So Holly put up with Flossy's rudeness and snappy replies – for around 30 minutes, and then, understandably, she hit her limit of tolerance!

At this peak of Holly's frustration and hurt, however, instead of returning Flossy's rudeness, Holly made the awesome decision to ask Flossy if she was okay. And guess what happened next? Flossy showed a look of horror on her face and then burst into tears. She said, 'I'm so sorry I have been so rude to you this morning. I am on the way to my father's funeral. That's why I'm having my make-up done. I'm just so sad and I'm very sorry I took it out on you. Please accept my apologies'. Remember — people are not their behaviour.

I know that it's not always possible to be this tolerant. If you can do this, however, it will help you accept people more readily and strengthen your rapport.

TRY THIS

Think of someone you have been judging lately. Embrace your inner Friendly Budgie and reframe them and their behaviour in your mind. Start acting in a more friendly, open-minded way toward them. Start today!

Remember — people won't feel that all-important sense of goodwill toward you if they feel you are intolerant of them and their behaviour. Do what you can to accept people around you, and notice how your relationships improve!

Be likeable

It's a fact that likeable people are the ones who get furthest in life. Even if you're not the smartest or most experienced, if you are the most likeable, you'll often be the most persuasive in the moment. In contrast, unlikeable people are a turn-off. They destroy the joy and can make people feel uncomfortable, judged and fearful.

Building your likeability

In a survey I did with my clients, the most unlikeable behaviours in others highlighted were unsatisfactory grooming, killing the fun, and ignoring or talking over others.

You can do plenty of things to increase your likeability! Let's look at five easy options.

BE ATTRACTIVE

Whether you like this fact or not, attractive people get more breaks in life than their 'plain' counterparts. Did you know that attractive women enjoy a net worth that is 11 times greater than the net worth of average looking women? Attractive people in general earn 12 per cent more money than others. Teachers are more likely to give good grades to attractive children, and children report that they learn better when their teacher is attractive. People who are physically attractive are more likely to be interviewed for jobs and they are also more likely to be hired. They are also more likely to advance more rapidly in their careers through frequent promotions. Business psychologist Tomas Chamorro-Premuzic reported in 2019 that people who don't fit a society's dominant aesthetic criteria simply don't get the same breaks in life as those who do. And psychologist and researcher at Harvard University Nancy L Etcoff and her colleagues published a 2011 study that found that groomed woman who were wearing make-up were seen as more attractive, competent, likeable and trustworthy than women who presented with a bare face. Pretty convincing!

The good news, however, is that 'attractiveness' doesn't really relate to your 'natural' beauty. Whatever you look like, you can certainly make the most of your qualities and features.

You don't have to spend a lot of money making yourself attractive. Ask yourself the following:

- Is your hair styled the best way for your face? Is it well kept and stylish?

- Do you keep yourself clean and tidy?

- Are you wearing clothes that flatter your body type?

- Are your nose and ear hairs trimmed?

- Have you groomed your beard/moustache?

- Do you smell good?

- Are your teeth clean?

- Are your fingernails well kept?

- Do you have clean shoes, and are your clothes laundered and ironed without food stains and mess?

- Did you tuck in your shirt?

You may think this is fussy and no-one else's business, and the bad news is that you think that at your own peril. This stuff counts when it comes to persuasion.

SMILE

Smiling is a winning behaviour recognised internationally as a sign of positivity. Dale Carnegie, bestselling author of *How to Win Friends and Influence People*, knew this well, arguing, 'A smile enriches those who receive, without impoverishing those who give'.

Did you know that babies are born with the ability to smile? People who smile are seen by others as confident, positive and attractive. You appear younger when you smile a lot because of the way smiling affects the muscles in your face. Smiling is even good for you because it releases endorphins and other chemicals that help you relax and feel good. Smiling makes you memorable too! Unsurprisingly, an American Association of Cosmetic Dentistry study found that people were more likely to remember your smile than the first thing you said. A Swedish study published in 2010 found that a smile is contagious and causes what's known as a positivity loop — when you smile at someone, they smile back, and then you smile more! The song 'When You're Smiling', popularised by Louis Armstrong in 1929, includes the lyrics, 'When you smilin' the whole world smiles with you'. It's true, isn't it? So, let's listen to Louis!

Handy tip: *A wonderful strategy for persuasion is to not just smile but 'smize'—or smile with your eyes. This is a term coined by supermodel Tyra Banks. Over 50 different types of smiles are possible, but the one that is deemed the most sincere is the smize—it pushes up into your eyes, your eyes sparkle and you look genuinely happy.*

Andrew's story

I have a gorgeous client named Andrew who is the master of the smize. The smize comes so naturally to this Friendly Budgie! Goodness me, he's just so incredibly likeable. Everyone Andrew meets at home and at work feels great when they are in his company. I've sat back and watched Andrew in the company of his colleagues (even in high-pressure pitching moments) and everyone just smiles a whole lot more when they're around him. Wouldn't you love to be that person who makes others feel good and smile more? And guess what? It makes him more persuasive. In fact, people just like him so much they'd do anything for him. I feel the same. I'm always so pleased to spend time with Andrew!

TIP

Michelle says,

'Smiling is good for you because it releases endorphins and other chemicals that help you relax and feel good. And smiling makes you memorable!'

TRY THIS

Practise your smize in the mirror. Contrast it with a fake, insincere smile that only involves your mouth. Teach yourself to release your smize more often!

LAUGH

Friendly Budgies know that laughing is a wonderful way to build rapport with people because playful communication triggers good feelings and a positive emotional connection. You probably know that a sense of humour is one of the first things people look for in a life partner — because people who can laugh are more likely to let go of defensiveness, act more spontaneously and release inhibitions. Funny people are likeable. People who laugh freely are thought of as joyful, light and fun to be around. Who wouldn't want that?

Humour that's working for both parties can also help you negotiate more effectively, resolve conflict and move people forward. It's true that laughter unites people during difficult times. Indeed, Danish-American comedian Victor Borge argued, 'Laughter is the closest distance between two people'. If you want to laugh more, you need to set the intention to laugh more. Befriend funny people and watch and read funny things daily.

SHOW YOUR HANDS

Showing your hands signals safety — the people around you have nothing to fear. Whether you are standing or sitting down, aligning your shoulders with the other person and keeping your hands open and obvious suggests that you are interested and engaged in the conversation. Turning away, twisting your body or hiding your hands signifies either a lack of interest or disagreement.

You also shouldn't do a whole lot of other things with your hands if you're aiming to be trustworthy. For example, don't cross your arms, put your hands in your pocket, hold your crotch, clasp your hands behind your back, hold your fingers in a steeple position, touch your face or hair, or fidget with your rings or clothes. These distracting hand movements stop your stakeholder from listening properly. They may even start to distrust you. You'll be able to read more about winning presence and poise for persuasive communication in chapter 9 (on the Captivating Peacock).

LISTEN

Bestselling author of *The 7 Habits of Highly Effective People*, Stephen Covey wisely said, 'Most people do not listen with the intent to understand; they listen with the intent to reply'. Isn't it just so irritating when you are talking and someone speaks over the top of you? Doing so implies that the person doesn't value what you're saying. It breaks rapport and prevents the forming of goodwill. Try to do what you can to listen when someone is talking. Take a moment of pause before adding your point. For more rich and helpful information in this area, see the section 'Listen actively', later in this chapter.

TRY THIS

While it's true that being liked by absolutely everyone isn't possible, it is a lofty and wonderful goal to make yourself as likeable as possible to as many people as possible. What can you do today to make yourself more likeable to more people?

Show warmth

Warmth is essential for building goodwill with others. American advice columnist and nationwide media celebrity Esther Lederer, better known by the pen name Ann Landers, highlighted this when she said, 'Warmth, kindness and friendship are the most yearned for commodities in the world'.

Warmth is a component of charisma and is unique to the Friendly Budgie. It is your perceived care and acceptance of the other person, and is the opposite of appearing cold and uncaring. Friendly Budgies are warm people who put others at ease and make everyone feel welcome and relaxed. Friendly Budgies make others feel important and as though they matter. This, of course, can be very alluring and addictive to the people around them.

People want to spend time with someone who they trust and who makes them feel warm, safe and cared about. Warmth builds trust and results in open communication. I've seen that the existence or lack of warmth in the workplace determines how supportive and creative, or how withdrawn and competitive people are.

Showing warmth

Especially while you are trying to boost your charisma, don't use trickery to pretend you care about others. Instead, pay attention to all the micro cues around you — including the environmental cues and the cues of your stakeholder — to build your situational awareness and shift your behaviour so you do what you can to really care about others.

Ensure you convey this genuine care in your eyes and facial expressions to dramatically improve your warmth and goodwill. Care about others, and remember key facts about them. Practise treating people as though you are already close friends and you care for them deeply, and be kind. Kindness is about being friendly, generous, considerate, caring and warm. Kindness engenders safety and comfort in others and builds rapport. You are more likely to trust someone who is kind.

TIP

Michelle says,

'Treat all people as though you are already close friends and you care for them deeply. (Don't be weird about this, though!)'

You'll convey warmth by practising the following Friendly Budgie actions regularly:

* Be welcoming and hospitable.

* Make polite conversation with everyone.

* Be genuinely interested in others.

* Allow yourself to be appropriately affectionate and kind.

- Allow yourself to express your appropriate workplace emotions honestly.

- Allow everyone to feel that you accept them for who they are.

Fun fact: Olivia Fox Cabane, author of The Charisma Myth, *says that imagining a person you feel great warmth and affection for can change your body chemistry so that you exude the same warmth that is linked to charismatic people. If you're not a natural Friendly Budgie, or you're not feeling warm towards others, this fun fact may help you.*

TRY THIS

Prior to your next meeting at work, think about some of the people who are going to be there. Will someone be there with whom you've had a bit of mild conflict or disagreement? Plan to make sure that you show kindness on your face when you deal with them, rather than an uninterested stare or gaze.

Yes, a fine line exists between being warm and coming across as weak. Remember — you are aiming for a win–win situation where you don't feel guilty or regretful after the interaction has happened.

Handy tip: Warm people make others feel good without losing out or compromising their values. They trust their opinions and are decisive while kind-hearted.

TRY THIS

Spend a moment reflecting on the difference between your actions when you are warm and when you are weak. Make a list of the behaviours you'd like to do more, and the things you'd like to do less in the pursuit of warmth towards others.

Build rapport

When you are in rapport with another person, they feel a strong emotional connection with you, they sense you care about them, and they like you. Perhaps you've heard the quote, commonly attributed to US President Theodore Roosevelt, 'People don't care how much you know until they know how much you care'.

Rapport is that feeling of a close and harmonious relationship between you and your stakeholder. You are in rapport when the person feels comfortable and at ease with you. They feel an affinity or connection with you. When a rapport exists between you and your stakeholder, you have a shared understanding and an empathy for one another that results in functional and mutually beneficial communication. Friendly Budgies are the heavy-hitters of the rapport building world.

In my capacity as a presentation skills coach, I've often heard people say things like, 'Leadership is not a popularity contest' or 'I'm not here to be liked' or 'I'm their manager not their friend'. These statements completely underestimate the importance of rapport when communicating and persuading. Imagine the power you would have as a leader if you were awesome at building rapport, where you and your stakeholder trust one another, and you win together.

Rapport is important because it builds connection and likeability. Once people sense you care about them, they are more likely to be persuaded by you. And as motivational speaker and coach Anthony Robbins wisely says,

> Rapport is the ultimate tool for producing results with other people. No matter what you want in your life, if you can develop rapport with the right people, you'll be able to fill their needs, and they will be able to fill yours.

When it comes to persuasion, your ability to build rapport with anyone and everyone is an essential capability. You may have noticed that it is easiest to build rapport with people who are like you. As the saying goes, we like people who are like ourselves. That's why you look like your friends! And, may I suggest, it's also the reason many people look like their pets!

Fun fact: It's been scientifically proven that dogs and their owners look similar. Sahahiko Nakajima, a professor at Japan's Kwansei Gakuin University, says evidence from her experiments in 2009 supports the notion that humans and their pet dogs look alike. It's all to do with our comfort with the familiar. We are attracted to the kind of pet dog that has similar features (whether that be personality, hair colour or style, even eye shape) to our own.

So while we like people (and dogs) who are like us, you may also be painfully aware that it is often difficult to build rapport with people you don't like or people who are not like you.

We are not in rapport with everyone we meet, and this affects our persuasiveness.

TIP

Michelle says,

'When it comes to persuasion, your ability to build rapport with anyone and everyone is an essential capability.'

Is it natural for you to build rapport and connect with people quite easily (even when you don't know them)? Building rapport is not complicated but sometimes it can be hard.

Building rapport

Unfortunately, you don't go through life only having to persuade people who are exactly like you. In fact, you will regularly have to persuade people who are nothing like you, and with whom you have no natural rapport, and no connection at all. So while you will naturally build rapport with the people who are like you, what are you going to do about all the other people? The answer, of course, is that you are going to have to manufacture the rapport. You'll have to consciously attempt as many of the tips in the following sections as possible.

SHOW INTEREST

Showing you are interested in the life and wellbeing of someone makes them feel important and valuable, and you help build their self-esteem. The best way to show interest is to:

1. Ask lots of appropriate questions.

2. Listen when they answer.

3. Most importantly, remember their answers.

For example, if you find out someone has a daughter studying ecology, remember this detail and be sure to ask how the study 'in ecology' is going when the next appropriate moment arises.

Also aim to diversify and don't just stick to one or two subjects when getting to know someone — because we are all whole people with a variety of interests and dimensions. For example, you might find out a bit about the person's personal life, a bit about their hobbies and interests, a bit about their career goals and maybe even a bit about their friends. If the person you're trying to know isn't interested in disclosing, then perhaps they are not the best person to start with! People generally respond very positively when you take an interest in them, which is fantastic for goodwill and persuasion.

BE FRIENDLY

Being friendly makes it easier to build positive relationships. When you are friendly you are approachable, and people are more likely to trust you. If you want to be friendlier with people, you need to show you're pleased to see them, smile, always greet people, be kind, don't judge, and make people feel comfortable.

SHOW EMPATHY

Doctor and psychotherapist Alfred Adler said, 'Empathy is seeing with the eyes of another, listening with the ears of another, and feeling with the heart of another'. Don't we just love it when we feel seen and truly heard? As the quote from Adler reflects, empathy is when you can read a person's emotions and thoughts, and respond accordingly — and it is essential for rapport and goodwill, and expected of you by Friendly Budgies.

The best way to make sure you're being empathetic is to listen actively, and respond to facial expressions, voice changes, body language and any other emotional cues (positive or negative) that the person is displaying. Don't be scared to reflect some of these same cues.

For example, say Nancy grimaces and looks like she's about to cry as she tells you something terrible that happened to her. To show your empathy, you might say something like, 'Oh, that must have been terrible for you, Nancy'. Importantly, empathetic people don't judge others and they don't try to solve the problem, they just listen and respond with care and compassion. And, of course, keep in mind that you don't need to reflect all of the other person's cues. Be sure to hold your composure when someone has just opened up to you. Looking horrified, bored or like you'd love to run away from this difficult conversation is a serious turn-off and breaks rapport.

As another example, say Madi tells you, 'I'm so excited about my road trip with Georgia over the holidays'. In this situation, you could smile, look Madi in the eye and reply with similar excitement, 'Yes, how exciting!'

SHOW GENUINE ENTHUSIASM

You don't have to go over the top with this one. Just be sincerely interested and act it. Friendly Budgies are genuinely thrilled for others when something great happens in their life.

FIND COMMON GROUND

A lot of research suggests we like people who are like ourselves, and that the more similar we are to a person, the more likely they will perceive common ground and be open to persuasion. Psychologist Donn Byrne was one of the first to study how perceived similarity, or common ground, affects our relationships. His 1961 study found that most people need certainty in their life and that, as a result, we tend to prefer values and viewpoints that support and reinforce that certainly.

This means that when people are like us — when they agree with us and validate our attitudes — we are more likely to feel safe in the sameness. On the other hand, when people are unlike us and disagree with our ideas, it tends to create negative feelings such as anxiety and confusion, breaks rapport, and may well repel us from a productive relationship.

To find common ground, get really good at two things:

1. *Self-disclosure:* When you disclose small details about yourself, you open up the relationship and encourage the other person to share something too. This is how you get to know people and find common ground.

2. *Small talk:* Small talk is general, light chitchat about nothing too important. That's why it is called 'small' talk — it's about the little things. And while small talk might not bring about world peace, it does lay the foundation for you to get into more satisfying, deep conversations about more important matters down the track. If you are not naturally a Friendly Budgie, you may struggle with small talk. Many Wise Owls (in particular) hate small talk and throughout life they will do what they can to avoid it!

Here are a few tips for mastering the art of small talk:

- *Tell yourself you love it:* Yes, going into a communication situation thinking you hate small talk and can't wait for it to end is pointless. Your voice, your facial expressions and your body language will give you away! Remind yourself that relationships make the world go around. Small talk is a common start to long-term friendships and an important element of nearly all relationships.

- *Be genuinely interested:* Nothing is worse than talking to someone who obviously isn't listening to what you're saying, would rather be somewhere else, and is only talking to you until someone better comes along. Make sure you genuinely care about getting to know people. Master the Friendly Budgie art of learning about people in a way that makes them feel good.

- *Give hooks:* The other person needs something fascinating or memorable to hook onto if they are going to continue the conversation. For example, say the person says something like, 'It's been such lovely weather lately'. (You know someone is going to mention the weather, right?) Instead of just saying, 'Yes it has', you could say something like, 'Yes, I have a beautiful rose garden in my front yard and the sun is bringing out all these beautiful blooms'. Can you see that doing this gives them the opportunity to tell you about their gardening, ask you more about roses or just chat about flowers — or even what they did on the weekend. One-word or short responses shut down the conversation.

- *Combine closed questions with open ones:* The research suggests that you are best to start small talk with a simple question such as, 'What work do you do?' Then follow up with something more open-ended such as, 'What led you into that kind of work?'

We can all do so many wonderful things to get better and better at building rapport. Friendly Budgies expect you to do what you can to build and maintain rapport.

> **TRY THIS**
>
> Reflect on your current skills and ability in this area and make improvements where you deem necessary. Without rapport, you're going to find it very difficult to persuade anyone about anything.

Make people feel good

Going through life making other people feel good is such a wonderful skill. As poet, writer and civil rights activist Maya Angelou highlighted,

'When we give cheerfully and accept gratefully, everyone is blessed'. People will do almost anything for someone who makes them feel good. This is linked to the law of reciprocity, which states that when you do me a favour, I feel compelled to do a favour for you in return.

People feel good when they are safe, comfortable, happy and positive about themselves and their life.

Gus's story

Gus Arianto is a CEO and world-renowned podcast host – and one of my favourite clients. Gus reminds me a lot of the persona of Richard Branson. If you know anything about the entrepreneur Richard Branson, you'll know that he is excellent at making his staff feel good. In fact, Richard makes people feel so good that they will outperform simply to make him happy. And Gus is the same!

Gus is a great guy. If you met him, you'd like him instantly. I recall hearing about a time when one of Gus's factories had to move to two shifts to avoid infections during a COVID-19 lockdown. It meant that one of the shifts had to begin at 4.30 pm and operate until 12.30 am. Gus said to himself, 'Oh no, I can't do that to my staff!' However, when they put the option to the team, they all unanimously agreed that they would *do it for Gus*. People will put themselves out for someone who makes them feel good.

Gus makes a point of intermittently calling the shift workers during their late shift. Yes, the CEO personally calls the factory workers at around 9 pm in his leisure time! As you might imagine, they are often very surprised to hear from him and say something along the lines of, 'Gus, why are you calling us this late? You should be resting'.

He replies, 'Why should I be resting when you are working hard for our business? It is my pleasure to thank you for working today and to let you know how important you are to me'. Imagine how good you'd feel if that was you receiving that call from your CEO when you are a factory employee. Being around Gus gives everyone a boost.

Similarly, making people feel good gives both you and them a wonderful boost that's hard to get any other way!

How to make people feel good

The following sections outline a few more ideas for how to make people feel good.

PRAISE PEOPLE

We all know that sincere praise makes us feel good. When someone gives us a genuine compliment, we feel pride in our performance or actions, and pleasure at being noticed. Our self-esteem automatically improves — and our brain chemistry changes. Positive feedback causes dopamine to be released in your brain. Dopamine is a neurotransmitter that helps control the reward and pleasure centres of our brain — and helps us strive, focus and find things interesting.

And praise isn't just a one-way street. Praise causes a two-way benefit, because when you praise someone, you feel good too. And you may also be on the receiving end of a return compliment! Praise enacts the law of reciprocity. In other words, when you praise someone, they are often more willing to return that generosity by also recognising your efforts — and may even help you out or share useful information. This is a wonderful basis for positive long-term persuasive relationships.

A lot of research has been conducted on the role of praise in the workforce, and we now know that, sadly, even when it's genuine, the effects of praise don't last. In fact, 2004 research from Gallup shows that employees who feel they are not amply recognised at work are three times more likely to leave their job within the following 12 months. So, yes, as a leader or aspiring leader in your business, you do need to keep the praise coming. Mary Kay Ash, founder of Mary Kay Cosmetics, famously said, 'There are two things people want more than sex and money...recognition and praise'.

Here are a few quick tips for giving sincere praise:

- *Catch people doing things right:* We reward the behaviour that we want to see repeated. Aim to reward the positive rather than punish the negative. Catch people doing things right and make them feel good. For example, 'Lily, I noticed that you followed that new procedure perfectly today. Thanks so much for your efforts with this process change'.

- *Notice the quiet achievers and the unsung heroes:* These are the people who often fly under the radar and are rarely complimented for their efforts. In exit interviews, these people often recount how they felt undervalued and ignored. To rectify this, you might give feedback to an unsung hero with something like, 'Ben, I realise that we don't say this often enough. You are so wonderful in the way you manage customer complaints. It's important that you know I regularly notice your efforts and commitment to our service standards. Thank you!'

- *Praise people publicly:* Let everyone know the person has excelled in some way. Make it everyone's business. Public praise creates a culture of recognition and achievement, and it makes people feel good. For example, you could put a note in the company monthly ezine or email everyone in the team with a message that says, 'Three cheers for Jo who won us the Google account this week. Jo is responsible for bringing in over $50 000 in work over the next three months!'

You can praise people at home as well as at work. I have three children and often their friends and/or partners join us for our evening meal. A regular feature of our family meals is that we go around the table and I ask everyone to talk about something they did that day that made them feel proud. We have a rule that it can be a little thing like, 'I did well in my exam at university' or, 'I cleaned out the fridge for the family today' through to a bigger achievement such as, 'I helped my friend transition to university in America'. Once explained, we all give the person a clap and 'snaps' (clicks of the fingers). We smile and compliment them, and we sit in the positive moment with them.

This process is also a great way for my husband and me to find out what's happening in our children's lives, and to share what we're doing. Ultimately, it gives us all an opportunity to congratulate and celebrate the family member for their achievement. And, as an extra benefit, it also causes my kids to be hyper-aware of their daily actions, so they find themselves unconsciously evaluating whether their actions are for the good of others or not. I am sure they feel recognised for these positive acts in their lives.

TOUCH WHEN WELCOME

Some forms of touch make people feel good. Physician Kerstin Uvnäs Moberg is recognised as a world authority on oxytocin (known as the 'love hormone'). Uvnäs Moberg and colleagues in 2015 reported that 'welcome touch' lowers stress and activates the release of oxytocin, which helps promote attachment and connection and is actually good for your health. Examples of welcome touch are a handshake or fist pump. An example of unwelcome touch in business, at least in many western cultures, is a kiss. It's too familiar and is fraught with the possibility of misunderstanding. (I can't tell you how often I've been on the receiving end of a weird slobber on my ear or a near miss for my lips by a well-meaning male colleague or client. And then I feel rude trying to discretely wipe the slobber off my face!) In western society, whether you are a male or female, don't kiss.

USE PEOPLE'S NAMES

Most people love it when you remember their name. Remembering someone's name creates an instant connection, makes them feel good and builds rapport. Remembering someone's name says, 'I care enough about you to remember what to call you!'

Here are my top eight tips for remembering names:

1. *You must care!* That might sound a bit blunt, but the truth is that when someone tells you their name you really must put every other thought out of your mind and fully focus on what they are saying. Look them in the eye. Be present. Make it important to yourself that you listen and remember their name.

2. *Repeat the name:* Saying the name again imprints it in your brain.

3. *Rhyming:* 'That's Nancy and she's fancy.' 'That's Sophia, mamma mia.' 'That's Gurmit, cousin of Kermit!' 'I'm Michelle, it rhymes with smell.' Okay, you get the point!

4. *Face recognition:* As you look at the person, try to find something outstanding about their face. Do they have bushy eyebrows or sparkly eyes? And connect that feature with the person's name to reinforce it to yourself — for example, 'That's Indira with the sparkly eyes'.

5. *Association:* Link the name of the person with something you already know. For example, 'That's Rosemary; I like rosemary on my roast chicken; roast chicken — Rosemary'. Or, 'He's Matt; the guy from downstairs is also Matt'. When you look at Matt whose name you are trying to remember, you'll think of Matt downstairs and the name will come to you. Or Ruby is wearing red. 'The person in red is Ruby'. As another fun example, did you watch the hilarious episode from *Modern Family* where the Phil Dunphy character (the father in the show) explains how he remembers people's names? He says, 'You can't be in sales and not remember people's names…that's why I use mnemonics — little tricks to help you remember'. Then the scene cuts to a moment when Phil is talking to his young son Luke and the phone rings. The person's name does not appear on Phil's phone, but Phil looks into Luke's eyes and says, 'He looks like the drummer from Foreigner. A foreigner is from France. France rhymes with Ants. Ants ruin a picnic. What's up Nick?!' According to the research, the more vivid or unusual the mnemonic, the easier it is to remember.

6. *Break it up:* Split up complicated or longer names. For example, 'Prasanna is Anna with a Pras = Prasanna'.

7. *Write it down:* As soon as possible, write the name down. If it's a tricky name, write it phonetically so you remember what you mean. I have a client whose name is Saniya, for example. I wrote her name down the first time she said it to me as 'San-knee-ah'. I must admit, I keep a document in

my notes app on my iPhone with people's names, the names of the parents of my kids' friends, the names of my friends' kids, the names of the girls in my favourite nail salon — the list goes on. I expect they think I'm amazing because I always know their name. Spoiler alert: it's because I can look it up before I bump into them.

8. *Use your phone:* Add someone's number to your phone so you can add their name at the same time. If it's not weird to ask the person for their number, then do so and add their name and other details in a way that you'll remember. For example, 'Lachie — from the pub in Manly' or 'Sendy — Bianka's mum from school'.

Emma's story

Emma goes to lots of sales meetings where she meets new and interesting people. When a lot of people are in the meetings, she struggles to remember everyone's name. In the days of business cards, Emma would place her clients' business cards in front of her on the table in the order they were sitting. These days, she jots down their names in the order of seating on her consultant's notebook. They can't see what she's written, and it means when she needs to address someone, she can always call them by their name. Simple and clever.

REMEMBER KEY FACTS ABOUT OTHERS

How good do you feel when people remember things about you? Just as important as remembering names is the ability to recall important information about people. The other day I ran into someone who remembered that I have three children, my husband is an ocean swimmer and I teach public speaking for a living. And I must admit that in that moment I felt important and special. I felt as though I was worthy enough for the person to remember key details about me. It most definitely strengthens my relationship with them. I felt an instant connection and rapport with this person because they remembered some facts about me. Would you feel the same? Even just a bit?

And what about when someone doesn't remember your name? Or forgets that you are allergic to shellfish and books a seafood restaurant for your outing? Does it hurt your feelings? The other day my daughter was given some peanut chocolate for her birthday by a close friend. My daughter is allergic to peanuts — and has known this friend for 10 years. How would you feel if your good friend gave you a birthday gift that you were allergic to? Friendly Budgies know that it's important to remember things about people, because it helps them feel seen and builds goodwill.

Many of the techniques for remembering facts about others are the same as remembering their name. You do need to care. You need to listen carefully to what they are saying. Be present and inject yourself into the experience so you embed it in your memory rather than half listening — which will cause you to forget what you hear. Writing important details down also helps.

How do you make people feel good?

In his awesome book *The 7 habits of highly effective people*, Stephen Covey describes something that he calls the 'emotional bank account'. The emotional bank account works just like a financial bank account. You make deposits and withdrawals, and your balance goes up and down accordingly. You are making a deposit into someone's emotional bank account when you do them a favour or you are nice to them in some way. And, conversely, when you forget their name, can't remember they are newly divorced, or don't turn up for that power walk that you had arranged last week, you're making a withdrawal from their emotional bank account.

Your ultimate 'balance' with people depends on how many deposits and withdrawals you make into their emotional bank account. Of course, if you want to make people feel good, you must put effort into constantly depositing, rather than withdrawing. Friendly Budgies set the goal of always making people feel good, so they are in constant credit.

Colin's story

I have a Friendly Budgie friend called Colin. Our children were friends many years ago. I don't see Colin very often these days because he lives around four hours' drive away, but every now and then I bump into him when he's visiting his parents. Every time I see Colin, it's an outstandingly positive experience for me. Despite the fact we may not have seen each other for 10 years, Colin always appears so pleased to see me! And he asks me obscure things about my kids that no-one would ever remember, even me! He seems to genuinely care enough to remember stuff about my life. It's like he is a witness to my life. This quality makes Colin someone I am so pleased to see. I can guarantee that if Colin ever needed a favour I'd oblige immediately. People who care about you build powerful goodwill.

Find ways to help people

When you do a favour or good deed for someone, you affect their life in a positive way and create a lasting bond. A simple good deed for someone builds trust. And the good news is that this trust brings the other person closer to you, and you closer to them. When you help people, you give positive vibes. You're very contagious and uplifting to be around, and people want to be your friend.

When people want to be your friend, they are more likely to be persuaded by you. Australian basketball legend Patty Mills wisely said, 'Pour in more than you pour out and find joy in bringing value to others'. What a great life hack!

Fun fact: A very cool phenomenon known as 'helpers high' is where you feel a boost in your happiness from helping someone. You'll feel good because you made them feel good. If that's not a win–win, I don't know what is!

Helping people more often

The best and simplest way to help people more often is to get into the other person's shoes and ask yourself, 'What would I need right now if I was in this situation?' And then make sure you offer that thing (or just do it) for the other person.

Alex's story

I was recently away from my young adult children on a mountain bike adventure with my husband. We were six hours from home, and we received a call to let us know that they were all close contacts of a friend who had been diagnosed with the COVID-19 virus. At that distance, we couldn't do anything more than offer our sympathies and reinforce that the girls should stay put in our home until their (hopefully) negative result.

After getting their COVID-19 test, they went about cancelling all their appointments for the coming week while they isolated. One appointment that they had to cancel was a personal training session with our superstar legend personal trainer, Alex. Instead of being angry and rude to my daughter and threatening to charge her for the last-minute cancellation, Alex exclaimed, 'Oh, I'm so sorry you might have COVID! Can I pick up some groceries for you and leave them at your front door for your meals this week?' This amazing offer only made us more loyal to Alex as our personal trainer. Find ways to help people.

By helping other people, you also set the law of reciprocity in motion. This results in a cycle of goodwill between you and the other person. When you are generous and often find ways to help people, you'll be the first person others think of when they feel the need to be generous.

Warwick's story

Warwick Merry is Australia's leading online event host, online meetings specialist and 'master MC' — and Warwick says he's also his wife's favourite husband. Yes, as you can see, he's funny too! Warwick is one of the most generous Friendly Budgies I know, and

(continued)

that's saying something because I value generosity above most other traits in a human.

One day I asked Warwick why he continued to offer so many unsolicited favours to people. He told me,

> It would be easy to say it is because I am kind, it gives me a good feeling, or it fits in with my 'gentle giant' persona. And while they are all true, they're not the main reasons. The main reason I continue to give (to the point that I question whether I am giving too much) is that a kind and giving world is the kind of world I want. While the evidence sometimes points to the contrary, I choose to believe that the world is a great place and people are morally good, supportive and generous to each other. And if that is the kind of world I want to live in, then I need to take what action I can to create that world. For me, giving or contributing to others is a simple way to make the world a better place for me to live.

Wow! What a great approach, right? Yes, Warwick receives lots of benefits from finding ways to help people, including that he does genuinely feel like the world is a better place, and he gets to celebrate the success of people he has helped. (I am one of them!) He also feels great.

Knowing Warwick, I can tell you these things are not the only benefits he derives from finding ways to help people. Warwick would tell you quite plainly if you asked him that he also gets a very positive financial return from finding ways to help people. For example, at the start of the COVID-19 pandemic when our events industry shut down almost overnight and speakers were in a state of shock, panic and fear, Warwick asked himself, 'What can I do to help people?' His answer was to start a weekly group called What's Up Wednesday, where people in events could catch up and learn things online. He invited anyone and everyone to attend and, whatever you need, you can talk about it in Warwick's group. More recently, he has created a social media group called Making Events Awesome and is helping people via this medium too.

Warwick does this because he knows people want to stay connected. He realises that everyone in our speaking and events industry needs support. I was one of the first to attend his weekly group, and many more followed. One of Warwick's colleagues in the United States who regularly joins in the sessions referred him to one of her clients and her client became his client. The initial four-event booking from this new client turned into over 30 events over an 18-month period with a view to ongoing work. In November 2021, Warwick was a recipient of the Global Outstanding Intrapreneur Award for his service to the speaking industry. In 2022 he was awarded the Professional Speakers Australia (PSA) Breakthrough Speaker of the Year award for his massive shift to online event hosting and production. He also won the highest honour of PSA, the Nevin Award, for his continued service to the people in the speaking and events industry. I have heard on the unofficial grapevine that this Nevin Award was one of the most nominated awards in the history of PSA. Everyone is grateful for Warwick's unflinching support and guidance. As you can see, if you make people feel good, you might reap amazing benefits too!

TRY THIS

How might you bring out your inner Friendly Budgie and help someone in a way that makes a difference? Could you share a free tip, do someone a favour, send someone a copy of a business book you enjoyed reading or maybe even introduce a small business owner you know to someone who needs what they sell? Helping someone will make you feel great and builds genuine goodwill.

Connect

Positive relationships with other people contribute greatly to our overall psychological wellbeing. As humans we are social beings, and when we connect in a meaningful way with others, we feel good, we have a sense of belonging and we have a greater purpose in the world. Indeed, psychiatrist and founder of analytical psychology Carl Jung noted, 'The meeting of two personalities is like the contact of two chemical substances: if there is any reaction, both are transformed'.

Positive connections with others cause us to feel happy, supported and valued. Developing social connections is very important if you want to be persuasive.

Research Professor Brené Brown sums up the definition of connection perfectly with the following:

> I define connection as the energy that exists between people when they feel seen, heard, and valued; when they can give and receive without judgment; and when they derive sustenance and strength from the relationship.

In other words, to connect is to really see the other person, care about them and display warmth and kindness.

Connecting with more people more deeply

The following sections outline some methods to really build your connections — with more people, and more deeply.

ACTIVELY TRY TO GET TO KNOW PEOPLE

Make it your mission to know people. Bestselling author of *How to Win Friends and Influence People*, Dale Carnegie, said if you are actually interested in the other person, they'll like you faster than if you spend all day trying to get them to be interested in you!

Ask genuine questions that help you better understand the person — just be careful you don't come on too strong! One way to make sure you ask the right questions is to think about whether the question has a purpose. For example, 'What's your favourite colour?' is unimportant in the scheme of things and may seem an unusual thing to ask someone you don't know every well. On the other hand, asking a question such as, 'How long have you worked here?' might be a more relevant question that leads to a more meaningful conversation. Influence guru Kurt Mortensen also suggests you ask direct questions to draw your audience out and pull them into a conversation with you — such as, 'What do you think about...?'

Another way to get to know someone is to find an activity that you can share — and a great story from my own life illustrates the benefits of this perfectly. I have a wonderful friend called Monica who I met through my work. The minute I saw Monica, I just knew we would get on like a house on fire! I wanted to be friends with her but wasn't sure how I could start this process without being weird. I thought I'd seem very strange just asking her to be my friend — I mean, 50-year-old women don't normally offer to be friends with other women in a business-type relationship without it being very odd indeed!

So, I began by just embracing the idea that I'd support her in her business where possible because I respected what she was doing. If she posted on social media, I liked the post if it resonated with me. After realising that Monica's posts were valuable to others, I invited her to join a work-related social media group that I'm a part of. Through this group, she received a lot of career benefits. Then, over time, we chatted. After some time, I offered to help her with a video she was filming, knowing I had some presentation skills advice that could make her even better on camera. We got to chatting and, sure enough, found we do have a lot in common. Eventually, I invited her to go walking with me along Manly beach — we walked and talked and stopped for a coffee. We have now become great lifelong friends and I value her tremendously.

Now at the time, I didn't premeditate any of this activity. To me, these kinds of Friendly Budgie actions come naturally. I'm a relationship builder and I love people. I am very 'others focused' in my personality and style. Only in retrospect did I realise there was a process that I followed to connect with Monica to build that strong rapport and emotional connection in a way that worked for us both. This is what persuasive people do naturally. They are good at getting to know people. If you want to build mastery in this area you may have to plan your actions until they become 'natural' for you.

TIP

Michelle says,

'Persuasive people are naturally good at getting to know people. If you want to build your own mastery in this area, you may have to plan your actions until they become 'natural' for you.'

BE SOCIALLY ACTIVE

Get out and about. The busier we are at work or at home, the more stressed we are, and the less likely we are to make the effort to be socially active. We are social beings. To 'get out more' perhaps you could join a gym, pick up a social hobby, or volunteer somewhere where you'll meet like-minded people. Make a conscious effort to catch up with people, have a shared meal, a walk, a coffee or whatever social activity works for you both. Is it time to plan a social outing or event of some kind with someone you haven't seen in a while?

MAINTAIN DIRECT, CONNECTED EYE CONTACT

In most western cultures, we think of eye contact as an essential component of effective communication and, out of respect, people tend to pay more attention to those who look them in the eye. The key is to connect with the other person through the eyes. Just be careful when giving eye contact — don't over-focus with crazy eyes!

The distinction here is to look right at the person and really see them. Aim to look into the white part of their eye — in this way, you won't stare in a crazy way and make everyone uncomfortable. And be sure to look away every now and then to give you and them a break. Letting your eyes wander, looking from left to right and back again over and over, or not really letting your gaze settle on the other person is called 'shifty eyes' — and no-one is persuaded by someone who has shifty eyes. So find a good balance between looking people in the eye and breaking eye contact once in a while.

When you master the art of direct, connected eye contact, you'll build stronger rapport and improve your persuasiveness. If you don't connect in this way with others, creating goodwill and being persuasive is going to be very difficult.

TIP

Michelle says,

'When you master the art of direct, connected eye contact, you'll build stronger rapport and improve your persuasiveness. If you don't connect in this way with others, creating goodwill and being persuasive is going to be very difficult.'

TRY THIS

Do what you can today to make some meaningful connections with the people in your life.

Listen actively

Active listening is one of the most important skills you can master, and is a skill that creates so many wonderful benefits in your relationships — for example:

- You'll better understand the other person's feelings, attitudes and opinions.

- You'll be better placed to respond empathetically.

- You'll be better set up to ask the best questions to ensure a deep understanding and an enhanced connection.

When others feel you've listened, it creates a strong sense of goodwill and opens them up to your ideas.

Note also a big difference exists between simple listening and listening actively. Active listening is where you pay attention to the other person very carefully. It's where you are so focused that you can't be distracted by anything going on around you. As psychiatrist and bestselling author of *The Road Less Travelled* M Scott Peck highlighted, 'You cannot truly listen to anyone and do anything else at the same time'. Friendly Budgies expect you will listen actively when they are speaking with you.

Learning to listen actively

I'm yet to meet anyone who can truly listen actively all the time. It's not easy to do! The following quote by Epictetus the Greek Stoic philosopher helps: 'We have two ears and one mouth so that we can listen twice as much as we speak'. What a great first step for active listening!

The following sections outline some specific steps to improve your ability to listen actively.

PAY ATTENTION

Be present and don't lose focus on what the person is saying. Tune out anything else that is happening around you.

Don't plan what you're going to say next as you're listening. For example, don't plan your rebuttal or form your counterargument while the other person is still speaking.

NOD YOUR HEAD

Nodding your head in agreement while the other person is talking shows that you are listening to what they are saying and agreeing with them. You don't want to overdo this because being too vigorous with your nod might cause your stakeholder to feel you're trying too hard and not really listening.

Handy tip: Nod while listening, and *while talking! Nodding while speaking is called the 'nodding head convincer strategy'. A convincer strategy is a set of behaviours that you demonstrate to make yourself more persuasive. So, of course, the nodding head convincer strategy is where you nod your head and then find your stakeholder nodding back at you! It's a wonderful sign that you are in rapport with your stakeholder/s.*

USE VERBAL AFFIRMATIONS

In 2013, phonetics researcher from Stockholm University Mattias Heldner reported that making affirmative sounds while talking with someone is a very good idea. These sounds tell the other person that you are with them, and they can keep talking. Heldner reported,

> We use the sounds to show that we are listening and that the message from the person we are talking to is getting across. It creates a common ground within the conversation.

The suggested sounds are, 'mmm', 'mhm' or 'uh-huh'. May I suggest that you can also use full words such as, 'yes', 'I agree' and 'Oh no!' You get the picture! Heldner did warn that you want to be careful you don't overuse this technique. If you make these sounds too often you can come across as sarcastic or as if you are pretending to listen.

Handy tip: A technique exposed is a technique lost. In other words, be careful. If the person realises you're using a technique on purpose to influence them, and that it's not your natural behaviour, it could be a turn-off and break rapport. Always remember you're making these sounds to help you listen better, not to fake attention.

TIP

Michelle says,

'A technique exposed is a technique lost. If the person realises you're using a technique on purpose to influence them, and that it's not your natural behaviour, it could be a turn-off and break rapport'

EXPRESS YOURSELF

Let your face do the talking! This means that your face should show the appropriate emotions from one moment to the next in the conversation. Are they sad? Be sorry. Are they happy? Join them.

BE OPEN

Make sure your posture is open and facing towards your stakeholder. Your open posture suggests you have an interest in what they're saying. Turning away or holding your arms in front of your body in a protective manner suggests you're uninterested, uncomfortable or bored.

REPEAT THE KEY MESSAGES

Use expressions like, 'Yes, I agree that [insert what they said]'. Or 'What I'm hearing you say is [insert a summary of what they said]'. If you can do this, you are definitely listening.

DON'T INTERRUPT

Yes, you know this! It's rude to interrupt. Interrupting says you think your point is more important that theirs. It can also suggest that you want them to hurry up and you are not interested in giving them your time. To stop yourself interrupting, try to form a picture or a graphic in your mind that summarises what the person means while they are talking. Another tip to stop you interrupting is to imagine the emotion that the person is feeling as they talk.

PAUSE

Wait for people to pause for a millisecond before you add what you think. If you do this, you won't appear to be jumping in with your thoughts too soon. It shows respect for what they just said and is wonderful for building goodwill.

TRY THIS

Active listening takes some effort. I highly encourage you to do what you can to listen better. Pick one of the tips listed in this section and aim to master it over the coming week.

Don't use words that damage your goodwill

Sometimes, even when we have the very best intentions, the words that we say can negatively affect our persuasiveness. Political ethicist

Mahatma Gandhi advised, 'Always aim at complete harmony of thought and word and deed. Always aim at purifying your thoughts and everything will be well'. This kind of harmony is not always easy!

Misunderstandings can occur and, before we know it, our friend, our colleague (or our partner who we love) is furious with us. We find ourselves wondering, 'What did I say?' It's very important to be careful with the words you choose.

Words to avoid

Plenty of words should be used mindfully when you are communicating in life. Some of these are:

- 'but' and 'however'

- 'okay?', 'obviously', 'basically', 'you know?' 'right?' and 'alright?'

- absolutes such as 'all', 'everyone', 'can't', 'mustn't', 'shouldn't'.

You also need to consider your use of 'you', 'we', and 'I' language and aim to use it correctly.

WHY YOU SHOULDN'T SAY 'BUT' OR 'HOWEVER'

When you say 'but' or 'however' in your sentence (spoken or written), you are likely to be perceived by your stakeholder to be negating what they just said. Let me show you an example. Imagine you have just bought yourself a stylish black suit. You look terrific in it. You ask me for some feedback. I say, 'Wow! You look terrific in that black suit. The colour really works, it's very flattering and the fabric is gorgeous. You look great. But I'd really love to see you in navy'. Ouch! Doesn't it sound like I just said you look terrible in black, and navy would look better?

You can see that no matter how positive you are before the 'but', that little word is a big rapport breaker. The word 'but' negates whatever you just said. 'But' also activates the limbic system in your stakeholder's brain and pushes them into a 'fight–flight' response. This means your stakeholder feels a surge of adrenaline and endorphins that causes them to either fight you (become aggressive and gnarly with you), or flee (switch off their ears and not even listen to what you're saying).

As an example of this, have you ever been in a performance appraisal where your manager gave you a whole heap of lovely compliments? Your mood soars until they suddenly say the infamous 'but' followed by one small area for improvement. For example:

> Your attention to detail is amazing, you have worked brilliantly with our clients and your commitment is something I'm really pleased about, but you know you missed the deadline on that report last week.

You instantly forget about all those lovely compliments and become focused completely on the thing you need to improve. All you hear is that you're not good enough because you missed the report deadline. Your posture slumps, you feel awful.

At all times, and especially when you are giving feedback to people, be careful of 'but' and 'however' because they can rob the joy and value from compliments you've given and damage your goodwill.

What can you say instead? Especially when we're managing conflict, we want to use inoffensive, unemotive words such as 'and' or 'so' (or you could just pause and say nothing). Another option is to pause and add, 'and the good news is...' or 'and the bad news is...'

The following examples show some ways to replace 'but' in your conversations:

- 'Our sales are down but...' becomes 'Our sales are down (pause), and the good news is that we have secured three new clients today!' Or, 'Our sales are down *and* unfortunately that's why we have to team up and redo our business plans for the next quarter'.

- 'I know you don't want to work overtime but...' becomes 'I know you don't want to work overtime *and* unfortunately we are expecting 20 per cent increase in calls, and you are our expert technician, so we really need you here'.

You won't believe how much more effective you'll be at managing conflict and objections in your work and home conversations when you do this.

Handy tip: *Try to avoid 'but' or 'however' in your emails as well as in your face-to-face communication, and even over the phone. Don't say these words and see how much more persuasive you become.*

Ben's story

Ben is a client of mine. When a person attends my Persuasive Presentation Skills Masterclass, I always offer them the opportunity to send me their scripts in the Persuasion Blueprint any time. I will check them for free and send them back with my tips. Lots of people sensibly take up this offer!

Ben sent me a Persuasion Blueprint script about six months after attending my masterclass. In the attached email he wrote,

Hi Michelle, it's Ben here. I attended your masterclass back in May. At the time, you offered to check our scripts for us. I've attached my script here for you to review if that's still okay.

PS By the way, I took out all the buts, ha ha ha!

He thought he was making a funny joke — and the joke was on him. Guess how many 'buts' I found in his script? 17. Yes, 17 'buts' even when he thought he had checked it and removed them. Do you realise that it's such a common and over-used word that you don't even read it in your own writing? You might have to read your emails and proposals through a few times to find them all.

Use 'but' or 'however' when you mean to negate what you've just said — otherwise, replace it with a better choice when persuading. Good luck!

TRY THIS

Go back to the last email you wrote. Have a close read of your writing and ask yourself if the 'buts' could be removed to reduce perceived conflict for your reader.

WHY YOU SHOULDN'T SAY 'OKAY?', 'OBVIOUSLY', 'BASICALLY', 'YOU KNOW?', 'RIGHT?' AND 'ALRIGHT?'

You want your audience to be in rapport with you as much as possible. And you may not realise that certain words can cause your stakeholder to disagree with you and break rapport. These words are 'okay?', 'obviously' 'basically', 'you know?', 'right?' and 'alright?'

A personality filter in each of us determines how readily another person agrees with us when we assert an opinion. This personality filter is known as the 'matcher/mismatcher' filter. Research from scholars such as Richard Bandler, Michael Hall and Bob Bodenhamer suggests that you will either prefer matching or mismatching when in conversation.

Matchers look for sameness. When you speak with them, they try to find something in what you are saying that they can agree with. For example, you say, 'I love working on this project!' and the person who is a matcher might say, 'Yes, I love it too' or, 'I love the analysis component of our work' or 'It's great working together'. You see what I mean?

Matchers tend to be very good at roles in customer service where 'the customer is always right'.

Mismatchers, on the other hand, are driven to find an alternative perspective to your point of view. They easily find fault in your argument and naturally disagree with your point. They are looking for difference. For example, you say, 'I love working on this project!' and the person who is a mismatcher might say, 'Yes, but the project last month was better' or, 'I'm so busy I haven't had a moment to work out if I love this or not!' or 'It would be even better if we had more help'.

Mismatchers tend to be very good at roles where they need to forecast risks, notice when something doesn't match, or notice when what someone's saying isn't quite right. They are very good at auditing, analysis and problem solving, and make great accountants, doctors, lawyers, engineers, analysts and scientists — in fact, lots of people need to be good at mismatching to do their jobs well.

Let's look at how a matcher and mismatcher would respond to the same scenarios.

Say you're in a clothes store and a customer says, 'Do you have this in blue?' A matcher would reply, 'The blue ones are right here' or 'Oh, you'd look lovely in blue, let me find one for you'.

A mismatcher would say, 'I'm not sure blue will suit you. Would you like to try black?'

And don't misunderstand the positive and negative aspect of matchers and mismatchers. Here's another example.

You're standing in the tearoom and Sally says to you, 'I hate working with Flossy. Flossy is lazy and slow and she's holding me back from achieving my deadlines'. A matcher would reply, 'Yes, Flossy is slow and lazy, and I hate working with her too' — or at least find some aspect of Sally's complaint to agree with.

A mismatcher, on the other hand, would say, 'It's not her fault. Flossy is always here early and she's working on that huge project that's made her slow to respond to the daily requests'.

You can see how it's not negative or positive to be a matcher or mismatcher. It just is!

Sometimes, of course, you will prefer one over the other — and I have an example of this. My dishwasher doesn't dry my dishes. It's frustrating. My family is currently made up of five people, two dogs plus a huge boyfriend and lots of friends and visitors who eat a lot. We put the dishes into the dishwasher in good faith that they will come out clean and dry — and what do you know? Even after an overnight wash, they are still soaking wet! Then one (or more) of us has to get Grandma's tea towel out and dry everything before we put it in the cupboard. Frustrating! To fix the problem, I rang the company who manufactured my dishwasher and I said, 'My dishwasher doesn't dry my dishes'. Guess what the customer service representative said to me? He paused, and then said, 'Lady...(another pause) it's called a dish-washer not a dish-dryer!' Seriously?! That's all he had for me. He is a classic example of someone with a mismatching preference who would be better suited to dishwasher repairs than dealing with irate customers on the phone!

You will come up against people with both matching and mismatching preferences in situations where you're hoping to persuade — at work and in your social life. The point to keep in mind is that when we say words like 'okay?', 'obviously', 'basically', 'you know?', and 'right?' and 'alright?' they are easy to mismatch. Let's take a look:

- You ask or say 'okay?' — in response a mismatcher will think or say, 'no, it isn't okay!'

- You say 'obviously' — in response a mismatcher will think or say, 'no, it's not obvious'.

- You say 'basically' — in response a mismatcher will think or say, 'no, it's not basic'.

- You ask or say, 'you know?' — in response a mismatcher will think or say, 'no, I don't know'.

- You ask or say 'right?' or 'alright?' — in response a mismatcher will think or say, 'no, it's not right' or 'no, it's not alright'.

These words cause mismatchers to start looking for other parts of your message that might be inconsistent or inaccurate. Once they start disagreeing, a mismatcher will be on a roll and you'll find your persuasion becomes hard work.

Instead, try to avoid saying these words altogether. Replace them with a pause and a diaphragmatic breath. If you are asking 'alright?' because you are genuinely checking with your stakeholder that they agree with you, ask a more specific question such as, 'What is your feedback about what we've discussed so far?' Eventually, you will find you eliminate these words when you speak.

TRY THIS

The next time you write an email or speak up in a meeting, aim not to say 'okay?', 'obviously', 'basically', 'you know?', 'right?' and 'alright?' Try to have other words and questions ready to use instead.

WHY YOU SHOULDN'T SAY ABSOLUTES

Absolutes such as 'all', 'everyone', 'can't', 'mustn't', 'shouldn't', 'won't', 'isn't' and 'never' (as well as many more similar words) are more words that are easy to disagree with. In the previous section, I talked about the fact that you'll have people with both matching and mismatching preferences in your persuasive situations at work and in your social life. When you use absolutes, you may cause the mismatchers in the conversation to start disagreeing with your point of view. Further, using absolutes can imply that the situation is black and white when it rarely is. Also, you may seem biased and lacking in thought about your point of view.

What should you do instead? If you are sure that the absolute is the best choice in the conversation or writing, then use the absolute. Most of the time, though, you can change the absolute to make the sentence more palatable for your stakeholder.

Table 8.1 (overleaf) shows some words to avoid and the substitutes you might choose to use instead.

Table 8.1 Alternative words so you avoid using absolutes

Absolute to avoid	Alternative words to use
Never	Uncommonly, occasionally, intermittently, irregularly, seldom, rarely, infrequently
None	Few, little, rare, a small number, occasional, scarce, uncommon
Everyone	Most, mainstream, many, the majority, the greater part
No-one	Few, a limited number
Always	Usually, often, frequently, consistently, regularly, repeatedly

TRY THIS

Use a sticky page marker to mark this page for future reference or write the words and their alternatives from table 8.1 on a post-it note and stick it near your desk so you can fix your business emails and writing. Remember – the more you practise fixing absolutes in your writing, the more likely you'll use the alternatives when you speak.

Remember also that you want to be persuasive all the time, not just in the soapbox moments. Have a read of your most recent email and note whether you have inadvertently used absolutes that will be easy for your stakeholder to disagree with. Fix the email so it's more palatable to the other person.

USING 'YOU', 'WE', AND 'I' LANGUAGE CORRECTLY

One of the simple tricks to managing your communication outcomes in a persuasive situation is to be careful about which word you choose from 'I', 'we' and 'you'. At times, 'I' is a good choice; at other times, 'you' or 'we' is a better one.

How do you work out which word to use? When we communicate in life, we do so from three main positions (or perspectives or points of view) — known as first, second and third position.

First position is when you are standing in your own shoes, and you are completely self-indulgent in your thinking. All you care about is yourself and your needs. Needless to say, persuading from first position is very difficult, because you're more likely to take a passive or aggressive approach.

Second position is when you are standing completely and utterly in the other person's shoes. All you care about from this position is their wants and needs.

Third position is both. Third position is often referred to as the helicopter view or the fly on the wall. From up in third position, you can look down and better understand your needs (first position) and also better understand the other person's needs (second position). From third position, you can make some very good decisions about what is best for you and also what is best for your stakeholder.

When it comes to deciding which word is best in the persuasive moment, it's important to spend some time in third position and ask yourself, 'What is best for both parties?'

For example, if you are in an argument with another person, saying 'you' can make the person feel you are attacking them or accusing them of something, and may result in them becoming defensive. In these moments, 'I' is a better choice because it's demonstrating that you are taking charge of your feelings. For example, instead of saying, 'You made me feel x', you could say, 'I feel x'. This approach removes the blame and maintains rapport with the other person.

Alternatively, let's say you're in a leadership role and you want your team to adopt a certain approach, If you said, 'I want you to go away and do x', you can see that the use of the word 'I' places you in first position. While they might do what you've asked, they may well also grumble about it behind your back! Instead, you could say, 'You can see it's important that we all do x'. In this example, saying 'you' and 'we' makes your communication about the benefits for the other person and the team (not you) and, for this reason, they will be more likely to do what you are asking. Choosing to use the words 'you' and 'we' maintains your rapport with your team member.

Aim to choose your words wisely when you are persuading to enhance your rapport and build that all-important goodwill!

Michelle says,

'Aim to choose your words wisely when you are persuading to enhance your rapport and build that all-important goodwill!'

A final word about building goodwill

Remember — no-one is just a Friendly Budgie. We all have a combination of the types in us, just in varying degrees. Regardless of whether building goodwill is one of your strengths or not, you can see from this chapter that you can start focusing on so many wonderful things right now, so you build and develop your inner Friendly Budgie! Some of the tips are small things and easy to adopt. Others are more of a stretch and will take longer to embed as habits.

Plan to tackle one or more of these actions each week and over the coming months you'll see people's connection to you grows as your goodwill improves. You want to be able to do all these things all the time, not just in particular 'soapbox' persuasive moments such as an important meeting, conversation or business pitch. Remember — you are always influencing!

Without goodwill, being persuasive will be very difficult for you because cooperative feelings and attitudes are an essential part of persuasion. You have an exciting opportunity to use goodwill to improve your overall persuasiveness in life.

TOP TIPS
The Friendly Budgie

- Goodwill is the existence of friendly and cooperative feelings that build connection and likeability — and your persuasiveness.

- You can do 10 things to improve your ability to build and cement your goodwill with others:

  1. Know and accept yourself to build your inner confidence and help you be authentic throughout the persuasion process.

  2. Accept others and build strong feelings of goodwill through not judging, acting 'as if' you are already close, and remembering that people are not their behaviour.

  3. Be likeable through being attractive and well presented, smiling, laughing, showing your hands and listening actively.

  4. Show warmth through making polite conversation with everyone, being genuinely interested in others and allowing everyone to feel that you accept them for who they are.

  5. Build rapport so others feel comfortable and at ease with you by showing interest, being friendly, showing empathy and genuine enthusiasm, finding common ground and learning the art of self-disclosure and small talk.

  6. Make people feel good — praise them, give welcome touch, use their names and remember key facts about them.

  7. Find ways to help people — ask, 'If I were this person in this situation what would I need?', and then when you can, give it to them.

(continued)

8. Connect with people through actively trying to get to know them, being socially active and maintaining direct eye contact.

9. Listen actively by such actions as paying attention, not planning what you're going to say next, giving physical and verbal affirmations, expressing with your face, and using open posture.

10. Don't use words that damage your goodwill, including emotive words or words that can be mismatched.

- Remember — no-one is just a Friendly Budgie. We all have a combination of the types in us. In most persuasive situations, goodwill is something your stakeholder is expecting from you — so use goodwill to improve your overall persuasiveness in life.

CHAPTER 9

Type 4: The Captivating Peacock

So, you'd like to build more of the Captivating Peacock into your persuasive approach. Maybe this is because the Captivating Peacock type isn't your strength. Maybe someone you have to persuade often — such as a manager, team member or even family member — is a Captivating Peacock and you want to demonstrate the behaviours that are most persuasive for them. Or maybe the Captivating Peacock is your strength, but you'd like to be even better at persuading by arousing enthusiasm and passion. (And you believe the best line in William Shakespeare's *As You Like It* is 'All the world's a stage'.)

The Captivating Peacock is one of the charismatic types and is thought of as captivating because they command attention, exude charm and excite. This chapter is all about exploring how to do this.

Why develop your inner Captivating Peacock?

An engineer in one of my presentation skills training programs said to me, 'But I'm an engineer, Michelle. I don't have to be interesting!'

Ahhh! Are you serious? This is a classic misconception! This engineer is not the first person who thinks that when they speak up in meetings, their superior intelligence, technically robust subject matter, and overloaded slides are enough to persuade people. Surely the people who need to convince others about technical or dry subject matter need to try the hardest to be interesting?

People (mostly Wise Owl types) often think that their data will sell itself. This is simply not true. Data is generally inanimate. In a room full of clients or stakeholders, each person will process the data differently based on their own experiences and values in life. The stories and the remarkable delivery techniques are what will take all those different people in your meeting on the journey through the data. The person who can capture the attention of people and arouse enthusiasm for the argument will persuade. The truth is that we all need a little bit of Captivating Peacock in us to ensure we persuade!

We've all been in that dreadfully boring meeting, social engagement or conversation where the person who was talking droned on and on. Their message was well structured, their knowledge and expertise were beyond evident, and they seemed like a genuinely nice person. But oh no! It was just so boring you wanted to poke out your eyeballs! You know it doesn't matter how smart you are, how robust your research is or how conclusive your opinion is if no-one is listening! You can be the smartest, most experienced person in the room, with the most undeniable argument, but if you bore the pants off everyone listening to you, you'll never be able to persuade them to your point of view. People will sit up and listen when you talk with a passionate and infectious enthusiasm that makes even the most technical conversation interesting!

TIP

Michelle says,

'It doesn't matter how good your message is if no-one is listening!'

Captivating Peacocks use their presence, stance, gesture, voice, eye contact, personality, interaction, humour, storytelling and engagement to hook their stakeholders' attention and keep it! Captivating Peacocks engage the senses of their prospect or stakeholder and are described as enthusiastic, charismatic and passionate.

Building your ability to arouse enthusiasm and passion

You can do several things to arouse enthusiasm and passion and bring out your inner Captivating Peacock! They are:

- Turn up your charisma.

- Be confident.

- Be passionate.

- Be expressive.

- Speed up your speech and be accurate.

- Use repetition.

- Engage the senses.

- Make a good first impression.

- Dress for success.

- Use clever delivery techniques.

The following sections look at these actions in more detail so you can make these your new (or stronger) habits.

Turn up your charisma

Charisma makes you more persuasive. Charismatic people possess a compelling attractiveness that inspires commitment and agreement in others. They convey a contagious enthusiasm for their point of view and can win people over with their magnetic personality and charm. When someone is charismatic, people want to be like them, and they also want to spend time with them. Every successful person I know is somewhat charismatic, and they are incredibly good at persuading people — because when someone is charismatic, they are more believable, no matter their point of view.

Charisma is a special quality, appeal or charm that attracts attention and admiration. Some theorists describe charisma as a 'presence'. Author and activist Marianne Williamson said, 'Charisma is a sparkle in people that money can't buy. It's an invisible energy with visible effects'. Others call charisma the 'X factor'. Charisma is a synonym for appeal, attractiveness, allure, captivation, personality and magnetism. Who wouldn't want to be described like that?

Becoming charismatic

You can work on three areas if you want to build your perceived charisma with others. They are:

1. warmth

2. presence

3. power.

Warmth is covered in the previous chapter because it is particularly a characteristic of the Friendly Budgie. The following sections cover how to make having presence and power your habits.

CHARISMATIC PRESENCE

Captivating Peacocks who are characterised by their charismatic presence have a *wow* factor everywhere they go. They draw people to them and charm others as they move through life.

Presence is about your poise, confidence and attitude, and is characterised by a smoothness of activity. Imagine a swan gliding along the water. They seem calm, serene and controlled. Under the water, the legs are padding furiously, but you don't see all that commotion. All you see is the grace and poise on the top of the water. People with charismatic presence are smooth on the surface just like that swan!

You can demonstrate charismatic presence by paying attention to the following:

- *Poise:* Your poise relates to your posture and the way you carry yourself through the world. People with charismatic poise appear focused, balanced and in a state of equilibrium, like the swan just mentioned, or like a ballerina *en pointe*. To improve your poise, limit stressful behaviour such as jerky movements or closed body language. Be sure to brace your core so you hold your shoulders back with strength and move your hands smoothly and with elegance.

- *Confidence:* Believing in your skills and abilities is very important. Be positive about your strengths. Communicate with conviction so you inspire trust and admiration. (See the section 'Be confident', later in this chapter, for more information in this area.)

- *Calmness:* People with charismatic presence are calm under pressure. They are aware and focused and have a clarity of mind that allows them to think on their feet no matter the situation. They are unlikely to become flustered in arguments or heated discussions because they take the time to think before responding. (Refer to chapter 7 for a lot more information on calmness.)

- *Grace:* Grace is behaving with elegance, courtesy and generosity. Always act in service of others, be bounteous. Reduce impulsive comments or actions so you always appear dignified rather than awkward.

- *Attention:* To ensure you seem 'smooth on the surface' like a swan, make sure you are present, focused and 'in the moment'. Block out distractions and be generous with your focus on the other person, who should feel like they are important to you and you are pleased to be with them.

Janine's story

My friend Janine is a leadership coach with an excellent under-standing of business issues and human resource management strategies at both the strategic and operational level. Janine has charismatic presence in spades. While she is consistently described as 'joyful', she is also characterised by an outstanding level of calm and reflection. She does not speak without thinking or say anything unless she believes it. She holds the silence in a respectful way that indicates she's listening when you talk and reflecting on your points, and she only replies when her response is undeniable. Her grace, calm and conviction are very persuasive.

Janine has developed these qualities over time. She attributes much of her ability to say what she means to writing a work-related blog. Her blog helps her formulate and refine her thoughts on matters that are topical in her work life.

TRY THIS

Build more poise, confidence, calm, grace and attention into your daily activities.

CHARISMATIC POWER

Charismatic people have powerful personalities that captivate and mesmerise others. They sweep others up in their passion for the matter and people get hooked! Just look at the way leaders such as Martin Luther King Jr, Mahatma Gandhi and Nelson Mandela captivated their followers and influenced their actions.

What is charismatic power? Charismatic power is about your self-belief and inner confidence that radiates from you and implies success to everyone you meet.

How do you build more charismatic power into your approach? If you're not sure that you are radiating power, the good news is that you can 'fake it until you make it'! You can demonstrate charismatic power by paying attention to:

- self-confidence

- stance

- eye contact

- storytelling.

Self-confidence

Have you ever seen a peacock fan open their fabulous feathers? They do not do that in way that makes them look self-conscious. They fan those fabulous feathers as though everyone is looking at them and is surely admiring them! They exude incredible levels of self-confidence because the most persuasive peacock gets the prize — they get to reproduce when the peahen chooses them. Captivating Peacocks in the workplace do the same. They portray a deep-down assuredness that belies any inner shyness. When they shake your hand, it's firm. When they introduce themselves, they say their name, company name and purpose with confidence and clarity. They walk with longer strides than others, and their shoulders are back. They speak up in meetings when they have something helpful and inspiring to say, and they do so with confidence and charismatic power.

Handy tip: If you want to have perceived charismatic power, pay attention to your introduction. Instead of just saying your name in a forgettable way, try something similar to this (using your own name): 'Hello, I'm Michelle. Michelle Bowden'. (Similar to the famous, 'Bond, James Bond'.) I repeat my first name so that the person hears it twice. When I'm at work, I nod my head confidently and enthusiastically and say, 'Hello. I'm Michelle. Michelle Bowden. Persuasive Presentation Skills trainer'. When I call someone back, I say impressively and confidently, 'Hello [name]. This is Michelle Bowden [pause], Persuasive Presentation Skills trainer calling you back.'

Practise introducing yourself in a confident and powerful way that impresses.

Stance

A confident stance implies you have a higher status than most and that you are of high value to others. It helps you to breathe diaphragmatically and project your voice with certainly and belief. It both helps you feel calm and assured on the inside, and appear awesome on the outside!

If you want to portray charismatic power, the stance to adopt is the natural stance. This is an upright, commanding posture — even when you are sitting down. To do this (whether sitting or standing), place your feet under your hips, brace your core and hold your shoulders back. If you're sitting, place your hands in front of you on the table (rather than hiding your hands on your lap, under the table).

Felix's story

Felix attended an important meeting when he was feeling sick. If you're tired or weak, you'll find your core collapses so that you appear concave in your posture. And this is exactly what happened to Felix. Because he was feeling unwell, he had a slumped (concave) posture that caused his colleagues to decide that he was drained and inadequate in some way. On this occasion, Felix reflected that he didn't persuade.

I'm sure you can relate to feeling and looking fragile when your core is weak. It's not good for persuasion! Either do what you can to brace your core and hold your shoulders back, or postpone your meeting until you are strong and confident inside and out!

TRY THIS

Do what you can to safely strengthen your core — perhaps with sit ups, yoga or Pilates. A strong core gives you inner strength that affects your mental and emotional confidence and is obvious to others.

Eye contact

Captivating Peacocks know that maintaining eye contact during a conversation sends a message that you are friendly, interested and confident enough in yourself to be able to hold someone else's gaze. As far back as 1978, researchers Richard Tessler and Lisa Sushelsky reported that we judge others by whether they really look at us when we speak. (For more information on eye contact, refer to chapter 8.)

Fun fact: In a 2016 research article, Nicola Binetti and colleagues released their findings that people prefer a duration of three to nine seconds of eye contact. After that, they need you to look away—anything longer is a bit creepy!

Storytelling

Charismatic people are great storytellers. They know how to link a story to almost any situation that arises. And when they tell the story, they communicate with confidence, passion and enthusiasm. They sweep people up in the fascination of it all.

An important part of being able to tell attention-grabbing and memorable stories is being 'in the know' about what's happening in the world. Being able to link the conversation that you're having with a thought-provoking story makes you appealing. This helps you improve your charismatic power as you participate confidently in the conversations around you. Be careful, though, that you are not talking too much and that you are listening carefully. Try to inject a short story, an example or a metaphor into relevant conversations so you are interesting and memorable. (See the section 'Use clever delivery techniques', later in this chapter, for more on storytelling.)

Developing your charisma is easier if you know someone else who is charismatic and can adopt some of their traits. You don't need to take on all their behaviours, just the ones that suit your personality and work for you and your stakeholder. If you don't have family, friends or colleagues who you'd describe as charismatic, perhaps you could watch footage of a charismatic leader such as former US President Barack Obama or the founder and former CEO of Apple, Steve Jobs. The point is that we can all cultivate charisma. It's about mastering one step at a time.

Be confident

Confidence is both obvious and attractive to others and an essential part of persuasion. In my role as a presentation skills coach and trainer, I talk to thousands of people each year who tell me they'd like to be more confident. We know that for a variety of reasons, confidence doesn't come that easily to most people. Marcus Tullius Cicero, the Roman statesman and philosopher, wisely said, 'If you have no confidence in self, you are twice defeated in the race of life. With confidence, you have won even before you have started'. Captivating Peacocks have an inner confidence that they convey easily to others.

Confidence is believing that you're worth it. You can do it. And while you may feel self-doubt from time to time, if you're a confident person you are comfortable with yourself.

TIP

Michelle says,

'Confidence is believing that you're worth it. You can do it.'

Becoming more confident

The following sections outline a few ideas for you on how to improve your overall confidence in business and in life. If you try to do these things every day of your life, you'll find your confidence will grow steadily and you'll start seeing changes in your success when you're persuading.

BE DEFINITE

Confident people don't waffle when they talk. They express themselves clearly, succinctly and with conviction. They don't use wishy-washy words such as 'sort of', 'it might', 'I guess' or 'like'. They use definite expressions such as 'it is', 'it will' and 'I know'. They also don't use non-specific words such as 'thingy', 'what's it' or 'yada yada'. When you say those words no-one knows what you mean!

TRY THIS

Do what you can today to use definite language to show your confidence.

BODY LANGUAGE

We stand and walk a certain way when we're confident, and another way when we're nervous. Most people can tell in seconds if we're apprehensive, relaxed, outgoing or aggressive. To project a confident image with your body language, avoid placing your hands in your pockets or across your crotch, don't cross your arms, stand tall, lift your head up, walk in long strides, breathe from your diaphragm, and shake people's hand firmly. You'll love the way you feel when you do all this in combination.

GOOD GROOMING

You want your hair, face and even your smell to work for you, not against you. Pay attention to the details. Always shower and use fragrance that works for your body chemistry. Style your hair to flatter your face and dress for your shape. And remember — nothing makes you look unkempt and unprofessional more than dirty fingernails and/or a forest of hair in your nose and ears.

Being well-groomed says you've got self-respect, you are disciplined and you pay attention to detail. These are all qualities that are admired by others. When you don't take charge of your grooming, it can be very distracting to others. For more information in this area, see the section 'Dress for success', later in this chapter.

Norman's story

Norman Swan is a Scottish Australian physician and ABC journalist who captivated Australians with his commentary and insights on the COVID-19 virus. When people in Australia wanted to know what was happening in the world, and what to do next to stay safe, they turned to Norman. Norman is immaculately groomed, shaves his beard precisely and looks perfectly into the camera when speaking. Norman generally wears dark coloured suits with well-coordinated shirts and ties. He appears exceptionally professional and intelligent, and people feel they can trust what he says. When Norman speaks, you are not distracted by his appearance, and you listen to what he's saying.

Contrast Norman's impact with Marcy (not her real name), who is an infectious diseases expert in Australia. When COVID-19 came to Australia, she was frequently in the media giving pandemic-related insights on current affairs programs. During these appearances, Marcy had dishevelled hair, unironed and crinkled clothing, and she didn't hide her tired, overworked bags under her eyes from the viewer. These aspects distracted viewers from what she was saying.

Sadly for Marcy in this superficial world in which we live, Norman will always be thought of as more persuasive and believable than she.

What can you do to improve your grooming by 1 per cent today?

SMILE

Have you ever tried to think negatively or act sad while smiling? You can't. It is impossible! Smiling affects our emotions because of a brain–body connection. What this means is that the bodily act of smiling triggers scientifically measurable activity in the left prefrontal cortex — the area of the brain where happiness is registered. Comedian and actress Phyllis Diller said, 'A smile is a curve that sets everything straight'. So, smile often. You will feel more confident, and you will increase your ability to persuade others.

DIRECT, CONNECTED EYE CONTACT

Earlier in this chapter, I noted that good eye contact builds your charismatic power. It has a similar effect on how confident you appear. Confident people make eye contact and engage with others. Your eye contact reflects your level of interest in the person or audience. As they say, the 'eye is the window to the soul', and when you make eye contact you connect to others deeply. Don't dart your eyes around — instead, hold your gaze just long enough to connect with the other person.

BE GRATEFUL

Heartfelt gratitude is a deep feeling. Unlike forced gratitude (where you make yourself think of the positive even though you feel dreadful), heartfelt gratitude is a feeling of appreciation and connection with life that makes you feel fantastic — and more confident.

Handy tip: Volunteering is one activity that can improve your feelings of heartfelt gratitude because it connects you to something bigger than yourself.

TRY THIS

Aim to contribute in some way to a cause greater than you. As well as contributing to the cause, your heartfelt gratitude will increase as you see the bigger picture.

(continued)

You can also begin a gratitude journal — where you write down all the things you feel grateful for each day. Every day I write seven things I'm grateful for, and I've done this for years. It keeps me feeling positive and confident on the inside. I look confident on the outside too!

USE AN ICON

Many excellent business speakers use what's known as a 'presenter icon' to help them get 'in the zone'. I often imagine the warm rays of the sun shining through me to the audience. A client of mine always wears bright red lipstick to board meetings. A past manager used to play a certain song to pump himself up before delivering a training course. I have many friends who wear certain undergarments to improve their confidence. Lou Heckler, the amazing American speaker and coach, once admitted to me that he imagines he's talking with his wife when he presents. You should see the love in his eyes when he's on stage — it's powerful stuff. Before you leave for the day, or go into a sales meeting, give a presentation, speak to your board or find yourself in a challenging conversation, find your icon — and use it.

TRY THIS

Plan to do one thing from each of the sections on building your confidence every single day. For example,

> I will breathe diaphragmatically (especially under stress), use definite language, groom myself neatly, smile more, and look at people and really see them in conversations. I will also write down the five things I'm grateful for every day in a journal, and use a particular lipstick or pair of socks to anchor my confidence.

Make sure you write what you are going to do on paper and, even better, put the action in your online calendar so an alert pops up about it and reminds you about your plan. Remember — you're only aiming for 1 per cent each day!

Be passionate

Commanding Peacocks exude passion. Passion makes you more positive, which gives you more energy and more contagious confidence. Passion brings vitality to just about everything you do. As far back at the 18th century, German philosopher Georg Wilhelm Friedrich Hegel noted, 'Nothing great in the world has ever been accomplished without passion'. And US TV personality Oprah Winfrey agrees, saying, 'Passion is energy. Feel the power that comes from focusing on what excites you'. When you are passionate, you feel great, your argument is undeniable, your stakeholder feels great (because passion, optimism and excitability are also very contagious) and everyone wins!

Fun fact: Research has also found that passionate people have higher levels of the neurotransmitters oxytocin and dopamine in their brains. The more you release these two neurotransmitters, the more open to passion you become. Yes, your passion changes your brain chemistry and makes you more likely to feel passionate more often.

You'll naturally put more commitment and energy into something you feel passionate about. Greek philosopher Aristotle said, 'Pleasure in the job puts perfection in the work'. Finding your own passion and enthusiasm is essential if you want to persuade others.

Passion is a strong feeling of emotion or desire. You can have passion for an idea, a product, a service, a job, a hobby, a company, a team of people or a person.

Becoming more passionate

You can do many things to increase your passion! They are:

- Eliminate energy suckers.
- Express yourself.
- Just do it.

- Stick with it.

- Get excited.

The following sections look at each of these actions in more detail.

ELIMINATE ENERGY SUCKERS

My friend and motivational speaker Rowdy McLean calls energy suckers 'dream stealers'. You know who he means — they're the people who make you feel like everything you're excited about is ridiculous and never going to happen. Energy suckers can be people or activities. Here are some ways to start eliminating them:

- *People:* Identify the people in your life who impact your mood and have you feeling flat or lacking in vitality. They could be a family member, a colleague or even certain customers. Either reduce the time you spend with them completely, or spend selective time with them. As an example of this, Megan was part of a mother's group that sucked the life out of her. The mothers were all lovely people, but the group was tiresome. She always felt sad and apathetic after attending. Megan realised that attending wasn't helping either her or her son. She made the difficult decision to break contact with the group. Her confidence and dynamism returned in no time, and she's never looked back.

- *Activity:* Sometimes the energy sucker is an activity — for example, your job, your hobby or a group you're part of. For example, let's imagine James. James is a great guy. He's highly intelligent and interesting — and, poor James, his job is so boring it nearly drives him to tears. Take it from me — it's time for James to find another job!

In some circumstances, you may need to stick with a dissatisfying role — for example, because it's a stepping stone to something else, you need the money right now, or you need the experience to get where you want to go. If that's the case, find the best in the role and put your head down and become an expert. No point complaining! If you can leave the boring job, though, please do. Don't sit around waiting for a miracle!

EXPRESS YOURSELF

Captivating Peacocks express themselves through their personal brand and their opinions. For example:

- *Brand:* Some people dye their hair blue, others wear cartoon socks. I wear a hot pink lipstick. You don't have to change everything about yourself, just pick something that gives you joy and expresses 'you'.

- *Opinions:* Be confident and bold as you express your ideas. Be expressive, captivating and undeniable in the way you speak and act while conveying your thoughts.

JUST DO IT

Don't just talk about it, do it. Passionate people back up their exuberance with action. They commit and then take the necessary risks to see the project through.

STICK WITH IT

Not everything that makes you passionate is easy. Don't give up. Stick with your passions until you can get into a state of 'flow' — where you will enjoy the passion even more!

GET EXCITED

Sometimes we feel excited, but we worry that we may be judged as 'over the top' if we show how excited we really are. Be confident in your passion and let your excitement out. Don't worry about the judgement!

TRY THIS

Think about what makes you feel passionate and do it some more. For example, do you like art or animals, or do you have a hobby such as bushwalking, cooking, sport or gardening?

Plan to add more of these things into your week.

(continued)

Slowly increase the amount of time you spend doing fun things and being with people you love.

Over time, you'll find that this passion for your hobby or pursuit translates into other parts of your life and others will find this very attractive in you.

Be expressive

Expressive people are interesting people. When you are expressive, you are communicating on an emotional level that sweeps people up. You're also more free — as political ethicist Mahatma Gandhi highlighted, 'I want freedom for the full expression of my personality'.

Have you ever had someone completely misunderstand the meaning of an email or text message you've sent them because they couldn't see your face or hear your voice? In face-to-face communication, if you only listen to the words your stakeholder says, without also watching and deciphering what their face is telling you and what their gestures are indicating, and without listening to the words they are accentuating, you might miss their true reaction to your persuasive moment.

You can focus on three areas when aiming to increase your expressiveness and your communication skills:

1. gestures

2. facial expressions

3. vocal emphasis.

Gestures

A gesture is a movement of the hands to express meaning. You can bring your message to life with informal and formal gestures:

- *Informal gestures:* Informal gesturing is when you talk with your hands. Yes, that's right — you just wave them around while you are speaking with no set aim. If you're keen to arouse enthusiasm and passion, you need to be comfortable moving your hands when you speak. Just be sure to take a break from your hand movements every now and then. Place your hands down and make sure they are still for a moment. Placing your hands down after gesturing is called 'cleaning the slate', and this is important in persuasion because it gives the other person a break from your movement so they can focus on something else you are doing or saying.

- *Formal gestures:* A formal gesture is a definite movement and is generally rehearsed in front of a mirror. Formal gestures aim to reinforce a particular point. For example, you say, 'This is a holistic approach to *x*' and you make a circular movement with both hands when you say the word 'holistic'. Rehearsed gestures are an essential part of the Captivating Peacock's toolkit, and a crucial way to arouse enthusiasm and passion.

When you use formal gestures consider three things:

1. The gesture should reinforce your point. Take a minute to work out the best thing to do with your hands for each part of your message.

2. Give yourself enough time to practise in front of the mirror to refine the gesture.

3. Ensure you have lots of 'air under your armpits' when you do it! People need to see what you're doing, and you need to look like you meant to do it.

Facial expressions

It's very important to let your face do the talking. Facial expressions help your listener understand your point. A still, bland face is a dull, disconnected face! As lecturer, poet and essayist Ralph Waldo Emerson said, 'Beauty without expression is boring'. A face that moves with emotion is a face that we want to keep looking at. And a face that moves with a variety of emotion (from worry and fear through to excitement and enjoyment) is a face we are watching intently.

Be careful of two things when adding facial expressions to your persuasive moment: authenticity and connection. Make sure you are always connected to the right emotion in your heart and make sure you let your face indicate that emotion while you're speaking. Additionally, make sure that you are also very present with your stakeholder so that you are deeply connected while you are expressing your point. This way you won't find that your expressions are 'over the top' or break rapport.

Fun fact: The facial expressions for fear, happiness, anger and sadness are universal. No matter where you're from, your natural facial expression when experiencing these emotions will be readable by everyone.

Vocal emphasis

Aim to try to say the important words in your sentences a bit louder than the other words so they stand out and are reinforced. Improving your ability to accentuate the right words in sentences helps the person feel interested and derive the actual point you are making.

When you are persuading someone, expressiveness is essential. When executed well, expressiveness will help you sell your point.

> **TIP**
>
> **Michelle says,**
>
> 'When you are persuading someone, expressiveness is essential. When executed well, expressiveness will help you sell your point.'

Speed up your speech and be accurate

I'm sure you can recall a conversation you had with a person who spoke quickly and swept you along in their enthusiasm. Former US

President John F Kennedy is one of the most charismatic figures in history for many reasons. One reason for his obvious charisma was that he spoke quite quickly and with a smooth, articulate rhythm. He is said to have often spoken seamless English (without glitches) at 180 words per minute. That's fast! (Conversational talking speed is about 120 to 150 words per minute.) And people found Kennedy — and his fury of words — captivating.

Interestingly, Kennedy also knew when to slow down — he slowed his speaking rate for his inauguration speech down to about 96 words per minute, for example. He did this for a reason: to carefully emphasise the meaning of his message. Conversely, you may have had a conversation with someone who was a slow talker with no clear message. You likely got bored while they were speaking and zoned out, as you started thinking about something else and not listening.

As Kennedy knew, if your aim is to build enthusiasm and passion for your product, service or idea, a fast pace is best. And if you can articulate your point quickly *and* accurately, you're seen as more intelligent and competent. In 1969, Albert Mehrabian (an expert in the relative importance of verbal and nonverbal messages) and Martin Williams reported that people who spoke louder, faster and more fluently were perceived as more persuasive than people who spoke slowly and with glitches in their flow.

This means both speaking speed and accuracy are essential in persuasion. Your speaking speed is the number of words you can say in a minute. Your accuracy is the clarity and exactness of the words as they hit your listeners' ears.

Mastering faster and more accurate speech

You can do three things to gradually increase your speed and accuracy of speech. They are:

1. *Plan properly:* Think through what you want to say. In chapter 6, I outline the best method for structuring your persuasive message using my Persuasion Blueprint.

2. *Practise:* If you know you need to talk about certain things, practise saying them. The more you practise, the quicker and more accurate you'll become.

3. *Articulate:* Articulation is the clarity of your words. This happens with a thorough warm-up of your teeth, lips, cheeks and tongue.

When we are tired, overworked and time-poor, making a commitment to warming up before we speak can be difficult. Or perhaps you just don't know the best way to do it. So let's delve into this important part of articulation a bit more deeply.

Working out how to warm up

One way to warm up your articulation so you improve the clarity of your words is to blow raspberries and to make the shape of an orange (the fruit) and a pea (the little green vegetable) with your lips. Additionally, it's a good idea to practise some tongue twisters daily. As a rule, I suggest you find a variety of tongue twisters that have a mix of different consonants and vowel combinations, so you are warming up a mix of different sound combinations.

Here is a sample of some of my favourite tongue twisters:

- The sixth sick sheik's sixth sheep's sick. (This one's featured by Guinness World Records as the most difficult tongue twister in the English language!)

- Black background, brown background.

- How much wood would a woodchuck chuck if a woodchuck could chuck wood?

- Which witch switched the Swiss wristwatches?

- She sells seashells by the seashore.

- Can you can a can as a canner can can a can?

If you do these warmups every day, you'll make faster speech a habit and you'll always sound credible and authoritative. As an example of this, I have a favourite client called Andrew who does his vocal warm-up exercises every single day of his life. He has found that his ability to speak quickly and accurately and convey intelligence and trust has grown impressively.

Are you a fast talker often told to 'slow down'?

If you are a fast talker and regularly receive feedback that you should 'slow down' — don't! If I had a dollar from every person who has come to me for presentation skills coaching because they have been told by their manager that they speak too fast, I'd be very, very wealthy indeed!

People who are fast talkers are commonly told to slow down, and this is not good advice. I have found over my decades of presentation skills coaching, those fast talkers are generally fast thinkers. If you're a fast talker and you slow down your speech, you also slow down your thinking. Sometimes slowing down even prevents you thinking or speaking at all! Instead of slowing down, aim to pause longer between bursts of fast talking. This is doable for a fast thinker and talker — and much more useful advice!

If you are a fast talker, practise pausing longer between bursts of talking so that your stakeholder can use the break to think about what you just said.

Vijay's story

Vijay is a client of mine who's a middle manager in a large corporation. He came to me for help because he said he hated his speaking style. He had been told (to the point of aggravation) by a senior manager to 'slow down' when he spoke. Vijay had been trying for months to slow down his speech, but to no avail. Despite his concerted efforts at reducing the speed of his speech, he still spoke as quickly as ever!

(continued)

He explained to me that when he got excited, he sped up and, when he tried to slow down, he lost his ability to think or speak at all. And he also lost interest in the subject himself and became boring to his colleagues.

I explained to Vijay that it was not his fast speed that was the problem. Fast speech is an indicator of high intelligence. What he needed to do was to pause longer in the breaks between his bursts of fast speech. Vijay practised this for many months and eventually received very positive feedback from his manager that the problem was fixed and that he found Vijay's ability to express himself had greatly improved.

You can see here that Vijay didn't actually slow down his speech. What he did was speak quickly, with slightly longer pauses in between. This gave him time to breathe properly, and gave his manager a moment to reflect on Vijay had just said. Everyone wins!

Use repetition

Most people talk in long boring sentences with little punctuation and emphasis. This makes it very difficult to keep listening, let alone agree with their ideas! Repetition is the action of repeating something that has already been said or written, and it's a powerful tool that will help you emphasise your key numbers, information and ideas so that they stick in the other person's mind. As former British Prime Minister Winston Churchill counselled, 'If you have an important point to make, don't try to be subtle or clever. Use a pile driver. Hit the point once. Then come back and hit it again. Then hit it a third time'.

Zenna's story

Zenna is a high-performing legend and a client of mine who works in a bank. In a meeting she held recently, she used repetition to reinforce that what she was advocating was not the 'same old, same old' strategy. This was something new and exciting for people to embrace.

Zenna said, 'Welcome to today's session on the FY22 strategy, which will introduce new — yes, *new* — tools and ways of working that will improve and strengthen our relationship with stakeholders'.

The simple repetition of a word reinforced the key point — it's new!

Using repetition

You can use repetition to bring out your inner Captivating Peacock in two ways: literally and through repackaging.

The following sections look at both of these actions in more detail.

LITERALLY

This means you say the point, sentence, tip or number in exactly the same way twice and within seconds of the first mention — just like Zenna in the preceding case study. My client Dennis Fox, the former CEO of Asteron, repeated his key phrase, 'Exceptional people create' throughout a company-wide update presentation. When I asked people afterwards what they remembered from Dennis's presentation they all said instantly, 'Exceptional people create'! That was his whole point and the reason he held a conference. They got it! Mission accomplished!

If you are stating key numbers in a meeting or conversation, repeating them is a good idea. Let's look at two examples.

My daughter Madi is very good at public speaking. At the age of 10, Madi went right through to the finals in the Bear Pit Public Speaking Competition (for primary school–aged students) at NSW Parliament House — and won! Here's the beginning of her speech, where she used clever repetition:

Recently up in Cairns a whale beached itself. Sadly, the whale died. The environmental scientists called to the scene were distraught. What is it that causes these beautiful creatures to beach themselves? They thought they'd better conduct an autopsy. When they opened the whale, they found six square metres of plastic bags inside the whale's digestive system (pause). Six square metres!

You can see in this example that, through the use of repetition and emphasis, you will remember the six square metres. How could Madi not win?!

As another example, Ruchika is a clever client of mine who works in data analysis. Here's Ruchika's icebreaker from an important presentation designed to persuade her management team to change a reporting practice:

> Did you know tableau data extracts can take up to two hours to refresh! This delays 40 per cent of our tableau reporting dashboards every week! Yes (pause) 40 per cent! I am Ruchika and let's see how we can refresh the tableau extracts in minutes!

Again, you can see that repeating the key (and alarming) number reinforces it and makes Ruchika captivating. When you also do this, you will be more persuasive.

REPACKAGING

Repackaging is where you say the point again but not in the exact words. For example, the first time you say the point you might just use your words. Then the second time you might show a graph that illustrates the same point. Or you might tell a story that reinforces the point.

Handy tip: *Regardless of which repetition technique you use, keep the repetition to a maximum of three times for each idea.*

TRY THIS

When you are next talking with someone, plan to use repetition to reinforce your key point.

Engage the senses

When persuading others, it's important to realise that people learn and take in information differently from one another. Some people have a predominantly visual preference, others are more auditory in their preference, and others prefer the kinesthetic (or touch, movement and emotions) channel. Then other people again have a strong gustatory sense — the sense of taste. Others have a strong olfactory sense — that's your sense of smell. Engaging the senses in different ways adds up to making people feel more — and, as Carl W Buehner highlighted, 'They may forget what you said, but they will never forget how you made them feel'.

People use a variety of these modalities but will commonly have one or two as their preference. Interestingly, a person's preference during one activity might then switch for a different task. For example, you may be kinesthetic–visual when you are relaxed at home. And when you are at work you are auditory–kinesthetic. Depending on the activity, your preferences change.

Engaging the senses when persuading

Picking the sense preference in others is often difficult when you are moving through the world. My advice is just do as much as you can to incorporate as many different sensory channels as possible when persuading others.

The following sections look at all the things you can do to stimulate the visual, auditory and kinesthetic channels when you communicate.

STIMULATING SOMEONE WITH A VISUAL PREFERENCE

People who favour their visual modality take a lot of pride in their appearance, often have an organised desk and demonstrate attention to detail. They often have trouble remembering verbal conversations.

If your stakeholder is visual, use slides, gestures, movement, charts, posters, props, handouts, videos and eye contact when persuading. Also pay attention to the 'detail' in your personal appearance (shine your shoes, brush your hair and iron your clothes, for example). You should also get to the point quickly, because people with a visual preference tend to process information quickly and will be frustrated by time wasting. You could also use visual language, such as 'look', 'reveal', 'vivid'.

STIMULATING SOMEONE WITH AN AUDITORY PREFERENCE

People who favour their auditory modality often move their eyes from side to side when accessing information. They don't always look at the communicator when listening. They may turn their head and use their ears as their primary information–gathering channel. They are easily distracted by noise and often breathe from the middle of the chest. People who prefer auditory processing often have the 'gift of the gab', articulate their words beautifully, and with different pitch, volume and speed.

If your stakeholder is auditory, you can use music, and vary your speaking speed, pitch and volume. You can also ask questions and get the person talking. Work on your vocal range, tone, power and articulation. Pause. Use repetition and *alliteration* (where successive words start with the same sound). You can also use *anaphora* (where successive sentences start with the same word or phrase) to sound very impressive and presidential! *Epistrophe* is the opposite of anaphora and is where you end successive sentences with the same words. For example, in his 2008 election campaign, former President Barak Obama said, '… yes we can' at the end of many of his sentences. And, finally, you can use auditory language such as 'hear', 'discuss', 'resonate'.

Handy tip: People who are more auditory need to focus on their ears and listening when you communicate with them. Don't be put off if they turn their eyes away and their ear towards you.

STIMULATING SOMEONE WITH A KINESTHETIC PREFERENCE

People who favour their kinesthetic modality respond to touch, movement and emotions. These people breathe from the bottom of their lungs. They move and talk slowly and dress for comfort. Often referred to as 'touchy–feely', they respond to touching and physical sensations. Many kinesthetics stand very close and often touch you when they talk.

If your stakeholder is kinesthetic, you could smile, use the person's name, shake hands, use samples or pass around a prop, and get them to take notes. Ask them to participate in an activity, such as a role-play or group discussion. Give them a handout or brochures. Tell stories. And, finally, you can also use 'kinesthetic' language such as 'feel', 'ecstatic', 'hot'.

Handy tip: *Don't expect an immediate response from someone with a kinesthetic preference. They need time to focus, think about and process your information. Coming to a decision on the spot is difficult for them because they often need to 'mull it over'.*

TRY THIS

The next time you have to run a meeting or have an important conversation with someone, think about one visual, one auditory and one kinesthetic action you can take so that you engage your stakeholder, regardless of their personal sensory preference.

Make a good first impression

As humans, we can't help judging someone when we meet them. Social psychologist and researcher Nalini Ambady called this quick first impression 'thin-slicing'. This is where, based on very minimal information — such as a person's looks or facial expression — we form very quick ideas about them, including their general characteristics and expected behaviour.

To explore this idea further, behavioural investigator Vanessa Van Edwards from Science of People researched what makes certain TED Talks outrank others. She found that 'participants made their decisions about the speaker and the entire talk in the first seven seconds of the video'.

And don't think this only happens for TED Talks, either. In other words, people form their first impression of you the moment they see you. The latest research suggests that in the first seven to nine seconds of meeting you, people conclude what they think of you. And this is based completely on your appearance — are you tall, short, big, thin, pretty, handsome, well dressed, shabby? Do you wear glasses or not? What is your hair colour, skin colour, smell, and your overall 'vibe'? While they say you shouldn't judge a book by its cover, the fact is that most people do!

TIP

Michelle says,

'While they say you shouldn't judge a book by its cover, the fact is that most people do!'

Once your stakeholder or prospect has noticed all the superficial things about you in the first seven to nine seconds, they then use a further 25 seconds to pay attention to three extra things:

1. *How comfortable you appear in your skin:* In other words, do you move well? Or do you seem self-conscious?

2. *How direct and connected your eye contact is:* We've already talked about the power of excellent eye contact, and the same ideas also apply to your first impression.

3. *How deep, rich and resonant your voice is:* It's a fact that people with a rich, resonant vocal tone are seen as more authoritative, attractive and believable than people with a high pitch or a blocked nose. (Refer to chapter 7 for more information on how to use your voice well.)

For these reasons, it's important to 'turn on' before you step out into the world — because every time you meet someone new you are creating another lasting first impression.

Knowing how to make a great first impression

You can do many things to ensure you create a great first impression. These include:

- *Believe in yourself:* If you don't believe in yourself, who will? Everyone has something to offer. Do what you can to deeply believe that you are enough.

- *Take long, confident strides when you walk towards someone:* People who have good control of their muscles seem more confident and impressive than those who are 'sloppier' in their movements. Regardless of your actual physical height and weight, aim to be as tall and powerful as possible.

- *Hold your shoulders back and your chest up:* Power posing — where you stand in a posture that makes you feel and behave with confidence — helps you feel powerful (otherwise known as faking it until you make it!) and also suggests to your prospect that you back yourself. I've always said to my clients, 'Boobs to the heavens!' Ha ha!

- *Smile:* Yes, of course, smiling is an important part of a first impression! As author Anthony J D'Angelo says, 'Smile, it is the key that fits the lock of everybody's heart'. Smile often.

- *Remember the other person:* Your brain needs to be switched on the minute you arrive at any event where you'll be meeting people so that you can remember their names. Remember things about them. (Refer to chapter 8 for some clever tips for doing this.) Showing you care through remembering someone's name and some important things about them is a wonderful quality — and it does wonders for the impression you make.

- *Shake hands or greet the person:* Positively greeting someone says, 'I'm pleased to meet you', 'I care about you even though I may not know you yet' and 'I'm keen to know you'. If you're going to shake hands, do so with a firm grip. Don't engage in power plays where you turn the person's hand over to show you're stronger. Keep it equal and respectful. You only need to pump twice — any longer gets weird! Look at the person as you shake their hand and say their name at the same time. It all goes together!

Handy tip: *It's etiquette to stand before you shake someone's hand.*

- *Warm up your voice:* People with a rich, resonant tone are perceived as more authoritative and impressive than those with high-pitched vocal quality. Do some big open mouth yawns to warm up your vocal tone before you speak. (I provide more information on this in chapter 7 and a whole section on the voice in my book *How to Present: The ultimate guide to presenting your ideas and influencing people using techniques that actually work*, also published by Wiley.)

- *Speak clearly and confidently when you say your name:* Most people mumble their name, their product name and/or their company name. The ability to articulate your key details confidently is impressive to others. Practise this in front of a mirror or record yourself so you can hear what you sound like to be sure you are clear and impressive.

- *Look right at the person when you speak to them:* Direct, connected eye contact says, 'I'm present and, in this moment, there's just you and me, and that matters to me'. (Refer to chapter 8 for more information on eye contact.)

- *Gratefully give and receive compliments:* When someone praises you, try to say something like, 'Why, thank you. Yes [add something interesting]'. For example, 'Oh, thank you. I was given this by an old friend I've known since I was four'. 'Why, thank you. I've been working on that for a while now'. Sometimes you can even return a compliment as you receive one — for example, 'Why, thank you. Well, I love your commitment to our project'. 'Oh, that's so nice of you. I was thinking about how nice it's been to work together on the project'. 'Awesome, thank you. You are a legend at problem-solving!'

- *Find something in common:* We are more likely to remember meeting someone who we thought was 'similar' to us. Ask some questions to show you are genuinely interested in getting to know the person. See if you can find something in common. (Refer to chapter 8 for more information about this and how it helps build rapport.)

- *Get good at networking:* Networking is the art of getting to know people for mutual long-term benefit. We network all the time (often without realising it) with friends, family, and colleagues and associates. When you stand out for all the right reasons in a networking situation, you're the one who will be remembered. This can lead to persuasive moments and opportunities that move you forward in life.

Most of the points in the preceding list are discussed in other sections of this book or are relatively self-explanatory. Networking can sometimes be a little trickier, so let's talk a bit more about it.

Getting good at networking

Effective networking has many subtleties. Some of the main areas to focus on are as follows:

- *Plan:* Do your research! Acquire the list of delegates and find out who is going to be at the event. Work out who will be the best person to meet so that you maximise your return on attending. What do they need in their businesses? Are you the right person to help them? The more time you put into planning before the event, the more value you will gain from attending.

Handy tip: *Look people up on social media and read through their profiles before attending so you know who you can most help.*

- *Believe in yourself:* You need to believe to your core that you have what this person needs. Do what you can to build your knowledge and expertise in your field. Be so fascinating when you talk about your industry, products and services that people can't walk away!

- *Connect:* Give direct connected eye contact when meeting people. Smile warmly. Find humour where you can. Listen carefully. Let them talk about themselves and their business needs. If you don't have what the person needs, be quick and responsive with recommending someone else of high quality who does.

- *Don't become a 'crazy card person':* My friend, and speaker and TV host, Kirsty Spraggon introduced me to this concept. You know that person who runs around the networking event thrusting their business card at people who don't want one? She calls them the 'crazy card person'! Instead, take your time, work the room, build meaningful relationships and only swap details if it's in everyone's interest.

- *Perfect your elevator pitch:* You'll be asked, 'what do you do?' by many people. See chapter 7 for more information on how to craft an impressive and memorable elevator pitch.

- *Be careful not to sound rehearsed:* The key to sounding natural is to rehearse your key messages about your life, your products and your services until you don't sound rehearsed anymore! Practise repeatedly until you sound natural and authentic.

- *Don't brag:* No-one likes a show-off. Refer to chapter 7 for more information on how to sell your personal credibility without boasting.

- *Follow up:* You don't go to a networking event to stay static. You attend so you can meet people who can promote you and/or your product or who could buy your product or service. So, remember this and use the event wisely. Contact every single person you spoke to at the event and be sure to tell them how much you enjoyed meeting them. And then urge them to go to the next stage (whatever that might be). For example, 'Hi Sally, it was so great to meet you at x event. Here's the article I mentioned'. Or 'Hi Shaun, I was wondering if you could share the details of your sister, the one you mentioned is the graphic artist. I may have some work for her'.

Jess' story

Jess is a connector. She works for herself, and she needs all the clients she can find. To her credit, Jess is also very good at knowing when the person she's talking to at a networking event needs someone else (other than her) right now. And when she works that out, she is so on top of 'who is who' in her profession that she's quick to make really warm connections happen immediately. A warm connection is where both parties find it incredibly easy to connect and get straight into doing business together. Jess is an invaluable part of her industry and the go-to person regardless of your needs.

Of course, the upside for Jess is that while she may not get any business initially (when she refers the person to a colleague), she is the first person everyone turns to when they need her products and services. Be a connector. Serve others and you'll end up serving yourself!

Networking is an essential ability if you want to be good at creating positive first impressions.

TIP

Michelle says,

'Networking is an essential ability if you want to be good at creating positive first impressions.'

Can you think of a networking event you can attend? Make sure it's somewhere you want to go. Make sure people will be there you want to meet. Apply some of the tips from this networking section to your experience.

Dress for success

Captivating Peacocks know that when you dress for success, you are attractive and memorable, and you feel confident in yourself. In return, you'll encourage respect from others, and you'll be very persuasive! And dressing for success isn't about how much you spend — designer Christian Dior put it best when he said 'Simplicity, good taste and grooming are the three fundamentals of good dressing, and these do not cost money'.

A side benefit to dressing for success is your productivity. Have you ever chosen to wear your track pants or gym tights while working from home, and found yourself less productive than usual because your brain thinks you're off to the gym (or about to have a nap on the couch)? Quite a lot of research suggests you need to dress in line with the achievements you want to reach that day.

Anita's story

Anita works in a role where the people around her choose to wear jeans and T-shirts—a very casual look for the workplace. Anita, on the other hand, always wears a well-tailored suit to her office. Anita is regularly complimented on how great she looks. Why am I mentioning Anita to you? Well, she has been promoted way faster than her colleagues. She has been given a great deal more respect in meetings. She has been given way more opportunities for exciting stretch projects than anyone else with the same experience and intelligence in her office. Yes, Anita has to be diligent in her approach to her work but she does put this special treatment down to her attention to her personal presentation.

Kubi Springer, the founder of female brand marketing agency SheBuildsBrands, further demonstrates the importance of dressing for success. She says,

> We know that 80 per cent of communication is non-verbal, so people see before they hear. My style says that I'm professional, I know my business and I'm to be taken seriously, but it also allows me to be free-flowing and comfortable, yet go-getting.

Dressing for success means you are clothing yourself to send the right, professional, successful vibe to everyone you meet.

Working out how you can dress for success

The main tip for dressing for success is to remember that sloppy dressing implies sloppy thinking. The most important thing about your clothing is that you need to feel confident. Take the time to think about your personal presentation and the impact your choices will have on your stakeholders. Ask yourself, 'What message is this outfit and look sending?' and 'Is this the correct style for this persuasive moment?'

Captivating Peacocks know how to put their 'look' together in a way that impresses people and encourages persuasion rather than distracting or turning people off.

Here are some tips to help you dress for success:

- Choose well-tailored clothing that is the right length for your frame.

- Select items that fit well, rather than being too tight or too loose.

- Ensure your items are not too revealing or see-through.

- Select fabrics that don't crease and look good all day, or iron your clothes before wearing them.

- Make sure the colours flatter you.

- Opt for longer rather than shorter dress and skirt lengths.

- Consider the impact of tattoos and piercings. In certain environments, these elements convey success; in others, they don't.

- Choose jewellery and accessories such as cuff links or scarves that work with your outfit.

- Polish your shoes.

- Style your hair so it suits your face and brings out the best in you.

- Choose an appropriate fragrance for the moment: charm and charisma or beach and party?

- Manicure your nails.

- Manage any forests in your nose or ears and trim long eyebrows so they don't distract.

- Apply make-up to suit your authentic style and remember less is generally more.

Michelle says,

'Captivating Peacocks know how to put their "look" together in a way that impresses people and encourages persuasion rather than distracting or turning people off.'

Fun fact: *Make-up (or lack thereof) can affect how you're perceived. In 2006 Rebecca Nash and colleagues studied the impact of the same group of women wearing basic cosmetics and then not wearing any make-up at all. They found that when the women wore basic cosmetics, they were evaluated as wealthier, healthier and more confident than when they wore no make-up at all.*

Laura's story

Political journalist Laura Tingle is an Australian role model. Among other roles, she has been the chief political correspondent of the Australian Broadcasting Corporation's *7.30* current affairs television program and the political editor of the *Australian Financial Review*. When speaking with almost anyone in Australia, you'll likely hear them describe Laura as 'impressive'. Her personal presentation is incredibly smart. She chooses block colours such as blue and black (sometimes a bolder colour) and beautifully tailored clothing that suits her personality, vibe and physical form. She then accents her outfits with statement jewellery pieces. Of course, Laura must also be excellent at her job to work in this area of journalism. She certainly looks the part. Laura is an excellent role model when it comes to professional image.

The way you choose to dress is a very important element of persuasion and Captivating Peacocks know this and work it!

TRY THIS

Go through the list outlining how to dress for success in this section and then sort through your wardrobe, deciding which items help and which ones hinder your image.

If you have items that you love but that don't help you send the right vibe, save those items for when you are chilling at home.

Hang the items that you know work for you in the same section of your wardrobe so they are easy to access, and you can choose them often.

If you're keen to develop more Captivating Peacock in your approach, dressing for success is essential. You'll feel more confident and exude more charm and power. You might even get in the zone of the moment more often if you're wearing the right outfit, helping you perform better. The people around you will judge you as more attractive and competent when you dress for success.

Use clever delivery techniques

In the context of a persuasive moment in business, such as a conversation, presentation or meeting, we know that 100 slides with eight-point font and diagrams that we couldn't read in an hour (if we had a spare hour) aren't going to make any message worth listening too. Unfortunately, most business meetings are still mind-numbingly dull and boring. I've personally seen thousands of technical presentations and you'd be lucky to stay awake in most of them even with a strong coffee. This is such a shame because, in most cases, the person was a true subject matter expert — they just didn't know how to showcase their professional expertise in a way that was exciting for their stakeholders. If only these people could develop their inner Captivating Peacock!

Plenty of people in your life need to feel something, not just have their logical brain convinced if they are to be persuaded by you.

If you let your inner Wise Owl (in other words, your focus on the facts, research and raw information) overwhelm your message with little focus on your emotional objectives, your stakeholders will not understand, remember or be persuaded by what you've told them.

Remember — you have a responsibility to your stakeholders and to yourself to persuade by using clever delivery techniques that sell your key points selectively and strategically. You want to bring your information alive and stimulate enthusiasm.

Your delivery techniques should include:

- storytelling
- metaphor
- response potential.

Let's look at how to develop your skills in these three areas.

Stories

Captivating Peacocks know how important a good story is when they are persuading someone. As personal branding and media expert Monica Rosenfeld argues, 'I believe stories give us the opportunity to break down barriers, stir conversation and inspire positive change'. Stories suck people in, and are an excellent way to connect and have others wonder what they would have done in the same situation.

When persuading in business, it's important to note that you shouldn't be using either facts or stories. You should be using both facts *and* stories. You should be telling stories that bring your information to life.

Stories are a light in the darkness of dry, technical meetings. If told well, they wake up your stakeholders and bring your content to life. If you're good at storytelling, you will enrol people as advocates for your idea. People will leave your meeting keen to spread the word on your behalf.

Fun fact: When you're processing data in a meeting or conversation, only two small parts of your brain light up. Whereas when you listen to a story, your entire brain lights up. You engage with your whole brain.

The social commentator Seth Godin says the job of a speaker is to be 'worthy of remark — remarkable'. In other words, when you're speaking up in a meeting or addressing a crowd, something you say should be so memorable and fascinating that your colleagues or audience members feel compelled to leave your meeting or presentation and repeat what you said to people who weren't at the presentation. That's the role — and importance — of stories. And according to a Native American proverb, 'Those who tell the stories rule the world'.

Captivating Peacocks tell stories to command attention, exude charm and excite. You may have a friend or colleague who has the gift of the gab — someone who can tell a great story and have people sitting on the edge of their chairs waiting to hear what happened next. It's a terrific skill to have. And the good news is that anyone can tell a great story. You've just got to know what to do and then do it.

Fun fact: Neuroscientists have found that as you listen to stories, you gain empathy for the persuader. The more empathy you experience, the more you release the feel-good hormone oxytocin. The more oxytocin your listeners have, the more trusted you become and, therefore, the more persuasive you will be.

TIP

Michelle says,

'When persuading in business, you shouldn't be using either facts or stories. You should be using both facts *and* stories. You should be telling stories that bring your information to life.'

HOW TO TELL A STORY

My favourite model for storytelling is called the 'magic formula' story, which I cover in detail in chapter 7.

To remind you, the magic formula story follows a simple three-part formula called the IPB model (incident, point, benefit). It's simply where you tell the story (keeping it short and interesting), then you explain the point of the story (that is, what did you learn? What was the positive result? What is a summary of the outcomes?), followed finally by the reason you told the story in the first place, or the link to the subject of your conversation.

Here's an example from my own life:

- *Incident:* When my daughter Madi was five years old and in kindergarten, she attended her first ever athletics carnival. I was unable to attend because I was busy delivering a training course for a client, and I felt so bad that I couldn't watch her. I love attending events where my kids are performing in some way to support them. After the carnival was over, I phoned Madi in my afternoon tea break at work. I said, 'How'd you go in your races today, Madi?' She replied, 'Oh Mum, you won't believe it, I was winning and then I fell down on the track'. She paused and I gasped. And then she said, 'But don't you worry. I got straight up and got cracking, Mum. And guess what? I won my race!'

- *Point:* My kids have always been very motivated to take charge of their destiny and move forward from adversity.

- *Benefit:* There's a lesson in this for all of us. What happens to you doesn't matter; it's how you deal with what happens to you that counts.

How else can you tell stories like a Captivating Peacock? Keep the following in mind:

1. *Love your story:* Tell the story like you own it! Your mood will be contagious.

2. *Talk with not at your audience:* The best stories involve the audience (even when it's only one person). Be sure to give the person (or people) you're talking with eye contact, seek verbal affirmations, ask questions if you can, use their name, and make them feel something through your choice of language.

3. *Keep the story short:* No-one ever said, 'I wish that story in that meeting went for longer!'

4. *Make sure the story is relevant:* Don't be that person who tells stories that are boring and/or irrelevant to the group. Make sure you articulate why the story is relevant because they may not make the connection by themselves.

5. *Keep it to the essential details:* Don't disclose information within your story that's unnecessary from the point of view of the listener. In other words, don't be like Great Aunty Maude — 'I think it was a Tuesday, or was it a Wednesday? No, I think it was a Tuesday because that's when the bins go out'. Oh dear, Aunty Maude, get to the point!

6. *Use your gestures, emotive language and vocal emphasis:* Telling a story is like painting a picture with your words. Adding your body, face and voice into the painting brings the whole experience to life for your listener. These elements give a physical element to the narrative, make your story exciting for your audience and ensure you pull them along with you.

7. *Aim to create a referential index shift:* This is a fancy name that means the storyteller's reference becomes the reference of the audience member. Also known as 'neural coupling' in the scientific world, it's where your listener's brain lights up in the same way as your brain does when you are telling the story. In other words — your story becomes their story, and they feel like they were in it with you. Cool, right?

8. *Be careful not to share inappropriate personal information in a story:* I've always taught, 'Don't do your therapy on stage'! In other words, if the story you are telling does not serve the audience, and it's more about you processing your feelings about something, save it for your therapist!

9. *Practise with your friends before delivering your message to a business audience:* Your friends love you and will be more forgiving!

10. *Listen to other storytellers as much as possible:* You'll learn heaps about what to do and what not to do.

WHEN CAN YOU TELL STORIES?

Anytime! For example, you can tell stories in the following situations:

- *Job interviews:* If you're asked to share some information about your work experience, you could add an interesting story about a specific challenge — what it was and how you solved it.

- *Board presentations:* Stories are the cure to boring boardroom pitches. Just make sure they are short, relevant and memorable.

- *Meetings:* Stories about the foundation of your business, competitors or past experiences can bring your ideas to life.

- *In life:* Tell stories that fit in with whatever is happening in the moment. Let's look at Barbara's story as an example.

Barbara's story

Barbara had a group of friends who were planning a night out for dinner together. Some of the people were keen to try a certain restaurant.

Barbara was in a job where she was responsible for typing up all the health inspector's reports after they had completed their annual restaurant inspections. As it happened, Barbara had just been asked to type two reports for immediate action about each of two restaurants that were situated one on top of the other. The top restaurant had large insects breeding in their floor, walls and food storage. Shockingly, the bugs were falling through the floor of the top restaurant into the dishes in the restaurant below — and being served to customers in their food. Yuck! You can imagine that Barbara was very persuasive when explaining to her friends that neither of these restaurants was a good choice. Very persuasive indeed! No, they will *never* visit either of those restaurants!

How powerful are stories, especially when they are brief, relevant, told in a captivating way?

WHEN A STORY GOES WRONG!

Many of us have been in meetings, just wishing the person talking would hurry up and get on with it. We want this meeting to be over so we can get back to our desk and get on with our real work. The last thing we want is for the person to tell too many stories that waste our time. And when we're busy and someone says to us in a meeting, 'Let me share a little story with you...' Oh, we're all groaning on the inside and thinking, *Please don't share your story. I'm busy and I just need the facts so I can get out of here and get on with things.* The audience for the story has already been put off. The lesson here is don't announce that you're about to tell the story, just launch straight in and tell it well!

TRY THIS

Think of three situations from the last few days. Turn these incidents into a story that can be shared. Ensure you get an emotional reaction when you tell the story. For example, maybe the person laughs, maybe they gasp — you get the point!

Plan your story out and then practise it.

Tell it to a variety of people before you tell it to the person you want to persuade (as further practise). Take their feedback and refine your story so it's an even better, more targeted story that works!

Metaphor

Sometimes a story is not the best way to bring your message to life. On these occasions, a metaphor might be a better option for your stakeholder.

Metaphors create images in your stakeholder's mind that are generally easier to understand and way more imaginative and memorable than a boring description. In fact, the Greek philosopher Aristotle argued, 'The greatest thing by far is to be a master of metaphor. It is the one thing that cannot be learnt from others; and it is also a sign of genius'. High praise indeed!

A metaphor states that one thing is another thing for the sake of comparison, symbolism or description. For example, 'her voice was music to his ears'. American novelist, screenwriter, playwright and actor Truman Capote reportedly said, 'Life is a moderately good play with a badly written third act'. Meaning that life is only moderately satisfying, and the end of life is even more disappointing!

HOW TO COME UP WITH THE RIGHT METAPHOR

Captivating Peacocks naturally speak in metaphor when necessary to paint a picture, to be memorable and bring their ideas to life. To find good metaphors for your persuasive moments, I recommend you think about the qualities of the idea you have, and then see if you can think of something unrelated that also has those qualities. For example, our family playroom is a big mess. What else is a big mess? A disaster zone. The metaphor becomes, 'Our playroom is a disaster zone'.

Sam's story

Sam was the head of sales in an IT company. After learning about the power of metaphor from me, he used to tell this story using metaphor:

> Company X's solution is a magnificent jigsaw puzzle. All the pieces are just the right size and the right shape, fitting together perfectly. It may be tempting to remove one of those pieces and maybe even replace it with another piece. This will create a hole in the jigsaw puzzle. If you decide to replace the existing piece with a new one, it just won't fit into the jigsaw puzzle. You can try to force it in, but it just won't fit in, so it just sits on the side of the jigsaw puzzle. As colourful as that new piece is, it's not the correct piece and the jigsaw puzzle is not the same. Our tools at Company X fit perfectly together to give you the complete picture and solution.

He used the jigsaw analogy for decades and it was very effective!

TRY THIS

Think of a metaphor for your next big idea. Try it out on a few people to see if it resonates and makes your idea more memorable. Take their feedback and refine your metaphor, if necessary, before using it in the actual persuasive moment.

Response potential

You've probably heard a newsreader say something like, 'After the break, we will see the brand-new addition at the Taronga Zoo'. You hear them say this and you think, *I'll rush to get my coffee, so I don't miss finding out about the addition!* This technique is called 'response potential'.

Response potential is a clever engagement strategy that makes people sit up and listen to you because it stimulates their brain and causes intrigue.

Response potential is the technique where you create interest, suspense and even mystique by introducing only a part of your idea, pausing for long enough for the other person to become intrigued, and then revealing the rest. It's called response *potential* because many different reactions from the listener are possible at the point of the pause. For example, you say, 'Guess what?' Your listener would probably reply, 'What?' As they answer, though, they are thinking about many and various possibilities that you might reveal once you have finished pausing.

CREATING RESPONSE POTENTIAL IN A CONVERSATION OR MEETING

Captivating Peacocks are wonderful at creating interest for their ideas by using a pause powerfully between the reveal of two points. The following sections outline a few ways to use response potential.

Words

You can use your words in so many clever ways to create response potential. Just like in the preceding example, you can say, 'Guess what?' Pause and then reveal. Here are some other clever options:

- 'And the good news is' (pause) then reveal.

- 'And the bad news is' (pause) then reveal.

- 'Unfortunately' (pause) then reveal.

- 'And you'll never guess what happened then' (pause) then reveal.

Slides

You can also build response potential with your slides. Reveal the slide first with just the axis for a graph and no data. Then piece by piece, build the data as you choose to reveal it. Or tell your stakeholder that the process has four steps, and build each step one by one on your slides. They must keep listening to get all the four steps. You can see why I'm saying it's a clever engagement technique!

Handouts

Give your handout to the group with only some of the model, results or graphs drawn in, with the rest missing. Only when you get to the perfect moment do you reveal the rest. A handout is wonderful for kinesthetic learners to fill in as you go. It keeps them fascinated!

Flip charts and whiteboards

To build response potential, draw a large number on the flipchart or whiteboard — let's say, 79 per cent — and only reveal what it's for when you're ready. Or, draw half a diagram or picture on your flip chart or whiteboard. Only fill in the rest after a pause and when you think it's the best time to reveal.

I do this! When I am teaching the 4MAT System (from chapter 6) to people in my Persuasive Presentation Skills Masterclass, I draw the 4MAT System axis on the flip chart. I take around seven to 10 minutes to introduce the subject to the group. The whole time, I am standing in front of the axis on the flip chart. I know that they are wondering what the axis is for, and this makes people sit up and listen. Once everyone is captivated, I turn and write the heading of the model on the flip chart above the axis and then I go about filling in the quadrants of *Why?*, *What?*, *How?* and *What if?* People are fascinated as each area is revealed. That's the power of response potential.

Props

Place the prop on the table and don't reveal what it's for until you get to that moment in your pitch or meeting.

Maeve's story

Maeve is a sales director who tells a funny story in her induction training that involves something she was doing while wearing ugg boots. (Ugg boots are sheepskin boots with the fleece on the inside that many Australians wear in the winter.) Maeve always places the ugg boots on a table at the front where everyone can see them. The minute people walk into the training, they start wondering what the ugg boots are for. Finally, she pauses and does the reveal. And everyone realises why the boots are sitting on the table. I bet people who have heard Maeve's story about the ugg boots still remember it years later because of her clever prop placement and her ability to create powerful response potential.

You can do this too. Spend a moment thinking about the best way.

TRY THIS

Try to include one of the examples of response potential from this section in your next email.

Does a particular expression resonate with you? I personally love, 'And the good news is ...' If, like me, you have a favourite, plan to use it a little bit more often in your daily conversations, so you make saying it your new habit.

A final word about arousing enthusiasm and passion

Remember — no-one is just a Captivating Peacock. We all have a combination of the types in us, just in varying degrees. Regardless of whether you naturally arouse enthusiasm and passion or not, you can see from this chapter that you can start focusing on so many wonderful things right now, so you build and develop your inner Captivating Peacock! Some of the tips are small things and very easy to adopt. Others are more of a stretch and will take longer to embed as habits. Perhaps pick one or two ideas each day and keep doing those things until they feel easy and like a normal part of your behaviour. You want to be able to do all these things all the time, not just in particular persuasive moments such as an important meeting, conversation or business pitch. Remember — you cannot *not* influence!

Without the ability to arouse enthusiasm and passion, being persuasive will be very difficult for you. In most persuasive situations, your stakeholder needs you to be enthusiastic and captivating if they are to be persuaded by you. You have an exciting opportunity to use your Captivating Peacock skills to improve your overall persuasiveness in life. Come on! Shake your tail feather!

TOP TIPS
The Captivating Peacock

- Without the ability to arouse enthusiasm and passion, being persuasive will be very difficult for you.

- Captivating Peacocks are thought of as captivating because they command attention, exude charm and excite.

- You can do 10 things to arouse enthusiasm and passion:

    1. Turn up your charisma and be remarkable through working on your presence and power.

2. Be confident through your use of your body language, good grooming, your smile, direct eye contact, gratitude and an icon.

3. Be passionate — finding your own passion for your subject is essential if you are to persuade another.

4. Be expressive in your gestures, facial expressions and vocal emphasis.

5. Speed up and be accurate — aim to speak faster, slightly louder and more fluently to captivate others.

6. Use repetition to embed your point, either through literal repetition or repackaging.

7. Engage the senses and work to stimulate the visual, auditory and kinesthetic in others.

8. Make a good first impression through knowing the best aspects to focus on in your appearance, voice and actions, and getting good at networking.

9. Dress for success and send the right — professional and successful — vibe.

10. Use clever delivery techniques such as stories, metaphor and response potential to help people remember your point.

- Remember — no-one is just a Captivating Peacock. We all have a combination of the types in us. In most persuasive situations, enthusiasm and passion is something your stakeholder is expecting from you — so improve your ability to arouse enthusiasm and passion in others and increase your overall persuasiveness in life.

PART III

Perfecting your pitch process and bringing it all together

CHAPTER 10

Perfecting your next bid or pitch

This chapter is specifically aimed at bid and pitch teams and is a reflection of my learnings as a pitch coach for multimillion-dollar pitches over the past few decades. So if you're on a team about to prepare for a new bid or pitch, you need to pay attention to this!

Increasing your chances of success

You've completed your tender response and now you're on the short list. You've been asked to present the key themes from your proposal over the coming weeks or months (sometimes even years) to the panel who will ultimately choose the successful bid. And, yes, you want to win! You now need to do plenty of things:

1. Pick the right people for the pitch team — considering diversity every time.

2. Prepare thoroughly.

3. Work out what your win themes or unique selling propositions are.

4. Design your message so that it appeals to all kinds of audience types.

5. Improve your persuasive strengths (using chapters 6 to 9 of this book).

All of this is likely pretty obvious. You definitely need to do these things. Pitch coaches like me have been teaching this for decades.

You might not be as conscious of a whole lot of other, seemingly little, things that greatly affect your pitching success. They are the often-unspoken cultural elements that slip under the radar and can indiscriminately undermine your success. These elements are often simple things that should not be left unsaid or unmanaged. In fact, when you take charge of these considerations, you'll ensure everyone brings their best to your pitch presentations and you'll increase your chances of winning.

Over the years I've seen some winning teams who thrive in each other's company and, yes, frequently win big deals. And I've also been involved in some truly toxic cultures that leave their people feeling sad and worthless regardless of whether they win. To take your bid or pitch team's performance to the next level, always keep the following in mind.

Resourcing

When I work with pitch teams, I can have up to 20 meetings with each person who is pitching (depending on the size and duration of the pitch). It's my nature to ask people, 'How are you?' throughout this process. And I'm sure you can guess the answer — almost always, people reply, 'Busy!' Pretty much everyone in business is busy, whether you're pitching for a deal or not. If you are managing a bid team, asking yourself the following question is worthwhile: 'If people are busy in their "real" job, how on earth are they going to find any extra time to help us win this pitch?' And don't just ask the question, answer it! Find yourself a solution before the pitch process begins.

In my experience, when resourcing isn't managed well, you end up with people who are trying to do two full-time jobs: their real job and your pitch. They are too exhausted to think properly, they are distracted, their contribution is limited, and their performance is often (and understandably) flat and unimpressive in meetings and rehearsals. Their inability to focus, meet project deadlines, and perform with rigour and vitality is also very demotivating to others in the team who have found a way to prioritise your pitch.

What's the solution? If you're going to pull team members into your pitch, it's important you work out how to give them the time to focus on the deal. In some industries, when pitching for really big, multimillion-dollar deals, the people in the pitch team are taken off their usual duties so they can focus solely on winning. Doesn't that sound like a good idea? If this is not possible because you're understaffed, you need to find another way to make sure that competing priorities don't stop your team members from contributing in a meaningful way. They need a backup person, or they need a senior leader to re-organise their priorities from the start, so they can move your pitch to the forefront of their daily activities.

Boundary and role setting

Just like you would in any important project at work, setting the rules of the pitch upfront is essential. When we all know the rules and stick to them, it reduces re-work and time wasting, and increases our collaborative spirit. It's my experience that companies who are regularly involved in pitches and bids forget to set these rules because they think that everyone is so experienced, they already know the rules. Not setting clear boundaries for each new bid or pitch can lead to misunderstandings and ill feelings among project team members.

TIP

Michelle says,

'Not setting clear boundaries for each new bid or pitch can lead to misunderstandings and ill feelings among project team members.'

The sorts of boundaries or rules you need to set relate to the areas covered in the following sections.

Roles

Who is the actual client? Who will ultimately make the decision to award the job? What are the roles of the various people in your pitch team? Who is the project sponsor? Who is the bid manager or pitch champion? Who are the subject matter experts? What are the roles and responsibilities of all these people? Who liaises with the client? Who answers technical questions?

Importantly, I've seen many a pitch process go south when it's not clear who is in charge. Ensure you let everyone know who is ultimately in charge — that is, tell everyone in the team (including your executives) who has been nominated to make the final call on a matter in the case of a difference of opinion, and then empower them to do so. Who will communicate the rules of this pitch to the various team members? Who has the role of enforcing your project rules and behaviours when they are flouted throughout the process? State all of this upfront to avoid misunderstandings.

Process

Process is about dates, activities and actions. What is the timeline for all pitch activities? I recommend you send out the proposed dates for all the activities early in the process, so people know what is going to be expected of them and by when. When will you do pitch training? Who is involved in that? Who will explain the reason for pitch training and justify the agreed pitch approach, so all team members are on board with your process? What preparations need to be made prior to any pitch training? Will you have accompanying scripts for your slide deck? Who writes the presentations? Will individual pitch coaching or script checking occur and, if so, when will that happen? When will you rehearse your presentations and who will be there during the rehearsals? Do you have rehearsal Q&A sessions? And, again, who will attend those sessions?

One of the most critical parts of the process that must be determined (and then fixed in cement) early in the process is the date by which all presentations will be finished, slides designed, and no more changes made.

Communication

You need to ask — and answer — some key questions regarding communication during the pitch process. What is your communication process? Does everything go through the bid manager? Can people contact various team members about elements of the pitch? For example, can anyone contact your slide deck designer with changes whenever they like? Or do all slide variations go through the bid manager? Who is allowed to contact or speak with your prospect? Can people reach out to your external pitch coach for assistance without approval, or is a process in place that they need to follow? When you communicate with one another, does everything need to be in writing?

Behaviour

It's very important to set clear boundaries about the way the team talks about their involvement in the pitch with their colleagues. Are you okay with people whinging about how busy they are? Do you find it acceptable for people to use their busy schedule as an excuse to not put in the time and effort that's required to win? When you give feedback to your colleagues during rehearsals, does a process exist to do that? Who must attend which meetings and what's the protocol if you can't make it? What's the best way to raise an objection to someone's content or delivery style in a rehearsal? What feedback is helpful and what feedback is best kept unspoken?

In a recent pitch preparation, one of the more arrogant members of the pitch team told a colleague that they looked 'nervous and unprepared'. Is this helpful feedback early in a pitch rehearsal process? No! Guidelines about acceptable behaviour should be agreed with the pitch team at the start of your process to ensure team members are empowered to be both empathetic and supportive.

Consistency

I hate last-minute stress in a pitch! While last-minute slide changes will almost always happen, what you don't want is silly mistakes that take hours of formatting the night before your pitch. Please spare a thought for your slide designer who is probably not a 'last-minute-Nelly' either! You have enough to worry about when you're making a life-or-death pitch without stressing over slide changes at the last minute — and, to be honest, you should be rehearsing with your slides at least a week out from the big day. Starting rehearsals a week out should mean any errors in the slides are picked up earlier than the day before — and reduce everyone's stress while boosting your overall performance.

One way to combat last-minute stress is to ensure that everyone has the template for the slides from the outset and an instruction to make sure they use it. This means you can't pull slides in from other presentations (that often have different formatting applied) because you think it's quicker! Instead, project members should redesign all slides (including pre-existing slides from old slide decks) in the agreed template from the start. In this way you'll ensure less work is required to standardise the slides close to your presentation date.

Another important consideration with regard to consistency is backup presenters. What will you do if someone is sick on the big day? Will you have a backup person involved from the outset (including attending rehearsals) just in case they are required on the day?

Managing fear

It's my experience that fear is a common emotion at some stage in the pitch process when people are passionate about winning. After all, we know that presenting in public is one of many people's top fears. I have often found that people (who are usually fully functioning, confident experts) experience a sense of overwhelm at some point in the pitch process. This overwhelm causes them to start asking themselves a whole lot of unhelpful questions such as, 'Will I be good enough?', 'Will I let the team down?', 'How will I make sure I don't go blank?', 'What if I don't know the answer to the questions?', 'How am I going to be ready in time when I'm so overwhelmed by my workload?' and 'Why am I being asked to go the extra mile here when no-one else is?'

What's the solution? My recommendation is to understand that what's often referred to as 'victim behaviour' is an inevitable part of the pitch process and needs to be managed by your pitch champion or bid manager — who is empowered to do so by the executive team. This means that the senior manager states clearly and up-front at the formation of the bid team that the bid manager is in control of the overall process. The senior manager also asks everyone to respect the bid manager's requests and deadlines upfront.

Victim behaviour is when people:

- *Deny:* 'I wasn't at that meeting.' 'I didn't know.' 'I haven't seen it.'

- *Blame:* 'How much of this process did *you* say we *have* to use?' 'Fred isn't prepared yet so I couldn't finish my part.' 'I don't have the template.' 'I'm just so busy so I haven't prepared as asked.' 'You didn't send me that.'

- *Justify:* 'I didn't have time to fix my slides yet.' 'That's not how we usually do it.' 'I never talk like this.' 'I'd rather be unprepared, so I sound authentic.' 'I don't like being scripted.' 'I don't have time to rehearse.' 'I haven't had time to incorporate the feedback.' 'I haven't used the model because it doesn't suit me.'

- *Quit:* 'I am just going to make this up.' 'I am not doing that.' 'I won't say that.' 'I can't do that.' 'I am not interested in rehearsing.'

You'll better manage the fear paradigm in your team if you know in advance that victim behaviour is going to set in with some of your team members at some stage. It is going to happen, and you need to set out clear boundaries at the outset of your pitch process that clearly state the behaviours that are expected from team members and the consequences if they are not followed. In this way, your bid manager or project sponsor has the authority and permission to call out the behaviour when it happens to nip it in the bud!

If you don't manage this kind of behaviour, you'll find that your other team members are deeply affected by the bad behaviour and so the cycle continues. In my experience, not managing the less than acceptable behaviour in your pitch process is one of the main reasons people quit companies after working on a bid — they just didn't respect the behaviour of their colleagues throughout the pitch process.

TIP

Michelle says,

'In my experience, not managing the less than acceptable behaviour in your pitch process is one of the main reasons people quit companies after working on a bid — they just didn't respect the behaviour of their colleagues throughout the pitch process.'

Role modelling

You know that if the more senior members of your pitch team behave in a certain way, the rest of the team will follow in their footsteps. Many a senior executive or project lead has behaved in ways I personally find inappropriate throughout a pitch process. I sometimes even find myself celebrating that as an external consultant I don't have to work with those people on a regular basis!

Role modelling can be negative or positive. If your leaders are seen by the whole team to empower the younger, less-experienced members of the team, you'll often find that other team members follow suit. This sort of role modelling is amazing for the confidence of those junior team members, and awesome for team cohesiveness. Similarly, if your leaders struggle to give positive feedback to team members in rehearsals, others will copy and then people may end up feeling threatened and disillusioned. If your project leaders imply that they don't support a particular approach or process that has been predetermined, it sends a message to the whole team that they don't rate it and are only doing it reluctantly — which, of course, is terrible for productivity and morale.

When everyone role models functional, supportive, purpose-driven collaboration, then wow — it's the best thing ever. And you know what? The client can feel it. They can sense whether your team is truly cohesive or not. They can tell when you respect and rate each other's expertise, and it's exciting and contagious — a winning formula!

TIP

Michelle says,

'Your client can sense whether your team is truly cohesive or not. They can tell when you respect and rate each other's expertise, and it's exciting and contagious – a winning formula!'

What's the solution? My recommendation is that you develop a set of behaviours or a code of conduct in collaboration with the senior leaders who run your bid teams. Alternatively, I've seen some companies create a suite of behaviours that are set in stone and that comply with their company values, ethics and culture. These behaviours are used in all pitches — it's just 'how we do things around here'. The code of conduct clearly states the behaviour that is and is not acceptable. Please don't take for granted that your senior leaders know this stuff — they definitely don't! And, in some cases, they don't care (yet) either! So you need to show them why setting behaviour expectations is so important.

There you have it — some food for thought. When you take charge of these considerations, you'll ensure everyone brings their best to your pitch presentations and you'll increase your chances of winning. If you'd like to develop the presentation skills of your pitch team, you may like to read my bestselling internationally published book *How to*

Present: The ultimate guide to presenting your ideas and influencing people using techniques that actually work (Wiley). And, of course, if you'd like some help with your next big deal, please reach out. It would be my pleasure to help you.

TOP TIPS
Protecting your next bid or pitch

- To take your bid or pitch team's performance to the next level, always keep the following areas in mind:

  1. *Resourcing:* If you're going to pull team members into your pitch, you need to work out how to give them the time to focus on the deal.

  2. *Boundaries:* Not clearly setting the rules for each new bid or pitch can lead to misunderstandings and ill feelings among project team members. Set boundaries around people's roles, the processes they must follow, communication expectations and how you'll ensure consistency to reduce re-work and time wasting, and increase collaborative spirit.

  3. *Managing fear:* Understand that the victim behaviours of denying, blaming, justifying and quitting are common under stress. Plan to avoid them and/or deal with them promptly when they arise.

  4. *Role modelling:* Develop a code of conduct that outlines what sort of behaviour is acceptable and which is not, and ensure your leaders follow it.

- Your client can sense whether your team is truly cohesive or not. They can tell when you respect and rate each other's expertise, and it's exciting and contagious — a winning formula!

- When you take charge of these considerations, you'll ensure everyone brings their best to your pitch presentations and increase your chances of winning. Good luck!

CHAPTER 11

And now it's up to you

Congratulations! The end of this book marks the rest of your journey to becoming your most persuasive self — how exciting!

By reading this book, you have demonstrated your commitment, desire and motivation to improve your ability to persuade. Now it's time to seize as many opportunities to communicate as persuasively as possible. You can use what you've learnt here to increase your chances of success in every moment of your life. Please let go of your old habits — even though, yes, they do die hard! In fact, the latest research suggests that very ingrained behaviours tend to take on average 63 days to rewire (rather than the 21 to 28 days most people think). This means if you're serious about making best practice your 'normal', in some cases you'll need to really put your mind to some of the actions in this book for many months at a time.

When it comes to those 'soap box' persuasion moments, I encourage you to make a serious decision to take your communication seriously. This means every time you have to persuade someone, you need to think through the best approach and give something in this book a red hot try.

Here are some suggestions for continuing your learning:

- *Assess yourself:* If you haven't yet completed your Persuasion Smart Profile, please do so. It will give you an insight into your persuasive strengths and weaknesses. Once you better know yourself, you'll be able to make more-informed decisions about what to strengthen, develop and change about your persuasive approach. Just go to shop.michellebowden .com.au/products/persuasion-smart-profile.

- *Make a plan:* I suggest making a plan for what you will do differently, starting today. Write down and commit to three key steps in your overall development — and then be sure to re-read this commitment regularly and take action.

- *Implement your plans:* Find as many opportunities as possible to implement daily what you've learnt in this book. How will you approach your informal conversations, phone calls, virtual meetings, team meetings, tender submissions, business cases and workplace presentations now that you know what you know?

- *Re-read this book:* Keep this book handy and refer to it where necessary. Dip in and out when the mood takes you.

- *Teach others what you now know:* Colleagues, friends and family need these skills too! And if you have children, teaching them is a great place to start. Imagine the power of knowing everything in this book from childhood!

And if you're keen to access some more knowledge from me, you can do so via the following:

- *Read my other book:* Grab a copy of my bestselling, internationally published book *How to Present: The ultimate guide to presenting your ideas and influencing people using techniques that actually work* (Wiley).

- *Attend my Masterclass:* Come and join me at one of my live or virtual Persuasion Smart programs or Persuasive Presentation Skills Masterclasses. For more information on these simply visit my website at michellebowden.com.au.

- *Read my free ezine:* Visit me at michellebowden.com.au and subscribe to my monthly ezine. This essential resource is packed full of techniques and tips for results-focused persuasive presenting in business.

- *Connect on LinkedIn:* Just go to linkedin.com/in/ michellebowdenenterprises.

- *Visit my blog:* Visit my comprehensive blog filled with free tips for presenting and persuading in business at michellebowden .com.au/blog.

Most importantly, please do contact me via my website (michellebowden.com.au) with your stories of success and tell me all about how you have achieved exciting results using the lessons contained in the pages of this book. I would really love to hear from (and celebrate with) you.

When you implement any or all the suggestions throughout this book, you will become more and more persuasive — and that means getting more of what you want in life. I'm so excited for you!

Happy persuading!

Michelle Bowden

OTHER TITLES AND RESOURCES BY MICHELLE BOWDEN

How to Present

- Do you get nervous when presenting at work?

- Do you want to showcase your knowledge, influence people and accelerate your career?

- Would you like to learn the secrets of successful speaking, communicating and presenting?

How to Present: The ultimate guide to presenting your ideas and influencing people using techniques that actually work (Wiley) reveals how you can be a confident, clear and influential presenter every time. Presentation skills expert Michelle Bowden shares her internationally proven formula for presenting, starting with analysis (plan what you would like to achieve), and then focusing on design (put your presentation together) and delivery (communicate your message for results).

Whether you're presenting or speaking to one person or thousands, this is the essential guide to becoming an outstanding presenter.

How to Present will help you to:

- maximise your impact in meetings, conferences and conversations

- manage your nerves so you feel calm and confident

- engage your audience and master the art of persuasion

- deliver your message clearly and with authority

- command attention and achieve your goals

- transform both your virtual and online presenting.

There is no other book on the market like this that will take you step by step through the process of successful presenting.

Steve Weston, Founder and CEO, Volt Bank

Free resources

You will also find other resources on Michelle's website:

- *How to Present* is a free monthly ezine jam-packed full of tips and techniques to maintain your focus and commitment to results-focused, persuasive presenting in business. To ensure your very own copy of this ezine is delivered straight to your inbox each month simply go to michellebowden.com.au and subscribe today.

- Michelle's blog is full of articles and suggestions for developing your persuasiveness — simply visit michellebowden.com.au.

SUMMARY OF THE FOUR PERSUASIVE TYPES

Persuasion type	Key persuasion qualifiers (KPIs)	Persuades by	Descriptors	Actions
Wise Owl	• Is there wisdom in this argument? • Does this argument seem logical and rational? • Does this perspective make good sense to me? • Is this message irrefutable?	Message credibility	• *Analytical:* Involving the careful, systematic study of something. • *Articulate:* Able to express thoughts easily and clearly. • *Critical:* Exercising careful judgement or evaluation. • *Discerning:* Showing good judgement and understanding. • *Dispassionate:* Unaffected by personal feeling or bias. • *Intelligent:* Having high mental capacity. • *Judgemental:* Skilled in offering an opinion or giving advice based on careful thought. • *Logical:* Based on sound judgement, reasonable. • *Methodical:* Using a systematic approach. • *Prepared:* Organised and ready. • *Rational:* Exercising reason, sound judgement or good sense. • *Researched:* Has studied a subject in detail. • *Scholarly:* Good at learning by studying. • *Thoughtful:* Contemplative, reflective, mindful.	• Structure your message so it resonates and sticks • Use external proof • Use rhetorical questions to guide people • Don't use fluffy language that is ambiguous and distracting • Add power words to liven up your argument • Limit your options • Use numbered lists • Use visual aids to captivate and convince • Package your numbers • Rehearse until you can't get it wrong
Commanding Eagle	• Is this person an authority in their field? • Are they believable and trustworthy? • Do I respect them?	Personal authority	• *Articulate:* Expressing beliefs and feelings easily and clearly. • *Assertive:* Speaking up for beliefs or wants. • *Authoritative:* Confident and deserving of respect as a source of information, advice and expertise. • *Believable:* Perceived as real or true. • *Commanding:* Has authority and demands attention. • *Competent:* Able to do something well.	• Become an expert in your niche • Communicate your competence — let everyone know! • Raise your profile • Be trustworthy • Refine your elevator pitch • Calm your farm

Persuasion type	Key persuasion qualifiers (KPIs)	Persuades by	Descriptors	Actions
			• *Composed:* Calm and in control of emotions.	• Speak with elegance
			• *Confident:* Being sure of oneself.	• Back yourself
			• *Credible:* Believed and trusted.	• Tell stories that impress
			• *Experienced:* Having knowledge and skill through having done something many times.	• Always exceed expectations
			• *Expert:* A high level of knowledge and skill in a discipline.	
			• *Forceful:* Expressing opinions strongly and demanding attention or action.	
			• *Honourable:* Having high principles and doing what's right; deserving of respect.	
			• *Imposing:* Appearing important, stately or grandiose.	
			• *Powerful:* Having great authority and influence.	
			• *Proud:* Feeling satisfaction and pleasure from achievement.	
			• *Respected:* Being admired for one's qualities or achievements.	
			• *Trustworthy:* Seen as reliable, honest, believable and credible.	
			• *Visionary:* Having unusually keen foresight and imagination.	
Friendly Budgie	• Is this person kind and accepting?	Building goodwill	• *Candid:* Expressing opinions and feelings in an open and honest way.	• Know and accept yourself
	• Do they care about me and my needs?		• *Caring:* Showing compassion and giving emotional support.	• Accept others
				• Be likeable
	• Do I feel an emotional connection with this person?		• *Committed:* Loyal and willing to give time and energy.	• Show warmth
			• *Compassionate:* Feeling sympathy and sorrow for someone with misfortune or grief.	• Build rapport
				• Make people feel good
	• Do I feel goodwill towards them?		• *Conciliatory:* Attempting to gain goodwill, reduce hostility or end a disagreement.	• Find ways to help people
				• Connect
			• *Connected:* In a close relationship with someone.	• Listen actively

(continued)

Persuasion type	Key persuasion qualifiers (KPIs)	Persuades by	Descriptors	Actions
			• *Diplomatic:* Using tact to respect others' position and not cause offence.	• Don't use words that damage your goodwill
			• *Disarming:* Naturally and convincingly building rapport with someone who does not expect it.	
			• *Empathetic:* Being able to imagine how someone else feels.	
			• *Generous:* Liberal in giving or sharing; associated with a kindly or noble spirit.	
			• *Genuine:* Sincere and honest, free from pretence.	
			• *Goodwill:* A kind, friendly and helpful feeling or attitude; approval and support.	
			• *Interested:* Being engaged by someone or something and wanting to give special attention.	
			• *Likeable:* Pleasant, agreeable and pleasing.	
			• *Open:* Not decided, certain or closed-minded.	
			• *Respectful:* Showing admiration, politeness and deference.	
			• *Warm:* Feeling of affection, gratitude and empathy.	
Captivating Peacock	• Is this person captivating? • Is their presence magnetic? • Am I inspired by their confidence? • Is their enthusiasm and passion contagious?	Capturing attention and arousing enthusiasm	• *Attractive:* Providing pleasure or delight in appearance and manner. • *Captivating:* Holding attention by being extremely interesting, exciting, pleasant or attractive. • *Charismatic:* A special quality, appeal or charm that attracts attention and admiration. • *Charming:* Delights and fascinates others. • *Confident:* Being sure of oneself.	• Turn on your charm and charisma • Be confident • Be passionate • Be expressive • Speed up your speech and be accurate • Use repetition • Engage the senses

Persuasion type	Key persuasion qualifiers (KPIs)	Persuades by	Descriptors	Actions
			• *Emphatic:* Communicating in a strong, clear way.	• Make a good first impression
			• *Enthusiastic:* Having an energetic interest in something.	• Dress for success
			• *Expressive:* Full of expression in a way that conveys meaning or feeling.	• Use clever delivery techniques
			• *Infectious:* Having the effect of causing others to take on one's positive emotion and join in.	
			• *Inspiring:* To arouse positive thoughts and feelings.	
			• *Interesting:* Holding attention by being unusual, exciting or informative.	
			• *Magnetic:* Extraordinary power or ability to attract	
			• *Optimistic:* Taking a favourable or hopeful view.	
			• *Outgoing:* Openly friendly, energetic and responsive to others.	

INDEX

Printed and bound by CPI Group (UK) Ltd, Croydon, CR0 4YY
09/08/2022
03140628-0001